Multi-resolution Image Fusion in Remote Sensing

The text offers discussion on tools and techniques of multi-resolution image fusion with necessary mathematical background. It covers important multi-resolution fusion concepts along with state-of-the-art methods including super-resolution and multistage guided filters. It includes in-depth analysis on degradation estimation, Gabor prior and Markov Random Field (MRF) prior. The use of edge-preserving filters in multi-resolution fusion is highlighted. The techniques of compressive sensing and super-resolution are explained for the benefit of readers. Fusion methods are presented using spatial and transform domains in addition to model based fusion approaches. Real life applications and plenty of multi-resolution images are provided in the text for enhanced learning.

Manjunath V. Joshi is a Professor at Dhirubhai Ambani Institute of Information and Communication Technology (DA-IICT), Gandhinagar, India. He has been involved in active research in the areas of computer vision, machine learning, and cognitive radio. He has co-authored two books entitled *Motion-Free Super-Resolution* and *Digital Heritage Reconstruction using Super-Resolution and Inpainting.*

Kishor P. Upla is an Assistant Professor at S. V. National Institute of Technology (SVNIT), Surat, India. He has 14 years of teaching experience. His areas of interest include signal and image processing, machine learning, multi-spectral and hyper-spectral image analysis.

Multi-resolution Image Fusion in Remote Sensing

Manjunath V. Joshi
Kishor P. Upla

CAMBRIDGE
UNIVERSITY PRESS

CAMBRIDGE
UNIVERSITY PRESS

University Printing House, Cambridge CB2 8BS, United Kingdom

One Liberty Plaza, 20th Floor, New York, NY 10006, USA

477 Williamstown Road, Port Melbourne, VIC 3207, Australia

314 to 321, 3rd Floor, Plot No.3, Splendor Forum, Jasola District Centre, New Delhi 110025, India

79 Anson Road, #06–04/06, Singapore 079906

Cambridge University Press is part of the University of Cambridge.

It furthers the University's mission by disseminating knowledge in the pursuit of education, learning and research at the highest international levels of excellence.

www.cambridge.org
Information on this title: www.cambridge.org/9781108475129

© Cambridge University Press 2019

First published 2019

Printed in India by Rajkamal Electric Press

A catalogue record for this publication is available from the British Library

ISBN 978-1-108-47512-9 Hardback

To

Smita, Nidhi and Ninad
— MVJ

Dipika, Taksh and Tithi
— KPU

Contents

Figures

Tables

Preface

It is always interesting to visualize the content of a scene with high spatial and spectral resolutions. However, constraints such as the trade-off between high spatial and spectral resolutions of the sensor, channel bandwidth, and on-board storage capability of a satellite system place limitations on capturing images having high spectral and spatial resolutions. Due to this, many commercial remote sensing satellites such as Quickbird, Ikonos, and Worldview-2 capture the earth's information with two types of images: a single panchromatic (Pan) and a number of multispectral (MS) images. Pan has high spatial resolution with lower spectral resolution, while MS image has higher spectral resolving capability with low spatial resolution. An image with high spatial and spectral resolutions, i.e., a fused image of MS and Pan data can lead to better land classification, map updating, soil analysis, feature extraction, etc. Also, since fused image increases the spatial resolution of the MS image, it results in sharpening the image content which makes it easy to obtain greater details of the classified maps. The *multi-resolution image fusion or pan-sharpening* is an algorithmic approach to increase the spatial resolution of the MS image, while preserving spectral contents by making use of the high spatial resolution Pan image. This book is an attempt to present the state-of-the-art in current research on this topic.

The book covers the recent advances in research in the area of multi-resolution image fusion. Different fusion methods are presented using spatial and transform domains, in addition to model based fusion approaches. We extend our model based fusion work to super-resolution of the natural images, which is one of the important areas of research in the field of computer vision. The book also includes comprehensive literature review on multi-resolution image fusion techniques.

The book is addressed to an audience including, but not limited to, academicians, practitioners, and industrial researchers, working on various fusion applications, and project managers requiring an overview of the on-going research in the field of multi-resolution image fusion. The topics discussed in this book have been covered with sufficient detail and we have also illustrated them with a large number of figures for better understanding. Finally, much of the material would be of value for post-graduate and doctorate level students who attend related courses or are engaged in research in multi-resolution image fusion and related fields.

We look forward to comments or suggestions from the readers.

Acknowledgments

This book would not have been possible without the support of many wonderful people. It gives us great pleasure in expressing our gratitude to all those people who have supported us and contributed to making it possible.

We have immensely benefited from the comments and suggestions from the following people: Professors K. S. Dasgupta, Sahasrabudhe, R. Nagaraj, Suman Mitra, Asim Banerjee, and Manish Narwaria. We are also thankful to other faculty members: Professor Mehul Raval at Ahmedabad University and Professor Prakash Gajjar at Government Polytechnic for Girls, Surat, for the many helpful discussions that contributed to developing the content for Chapters 4 and 6.

We thank the reviewers for their constructive suggestions. Thanks to Manish Chaudhary from Cambridge University Press for accepting the proposal. We are also thankful to Gauravjeet, Aniruddha De and other team members of Cambridge University Press for their cooperation and strong support during the review and proofreading stages.

We would like to thank Dr Milind Padalkar, Dr Jignesh Bhatt, Dr Rakesh Patel, Dr Shrishail Gajbhar, Dr Sonam Nahar, Vishal Chudasama, and Heena Patel for their kind help during the writing of this book. The first author wishes to express his deep sense of gratitude to his family members Smita,

Nidhi, and Ninad, and his sisters and brothers, for their constant love and encouragement during the preparation of this book. He is grateful to his mentors Professors K. V. V. Murthy, S. Chaudhuri, and P. G. Poonanacha for their inspiration and support.

The second author would like to thank all his colleagues at SVNIT, Surat, for their constant support and encouragement. He is also deeply thankful to his family for their love, support, and sacrifices. Without the support of the family, the writing of this book would never have been complete. Special thanks to Dipika, who has been with him for all these years and has given him constant support. Lastly, he would like to thank his son, Taksh, and his little doll, Tithi, for their unforgettable and enjoyable times during the preparation of this book.

Finally, we wish to thank all who helped us directly or indirectly for their support during the entire process of publishing this book.

Chapter 1

Introduction

One of the major achievements of human beings is the ability to record observational data in the form of photographs, a science which dates back to 1826. Humans have always tried to reach greater heights (treetops, mountains, platforms, and so on) to observe phenomenon of interest, to decide on habitable places, farming and such other activities. Curiosity motivates human beings to take photographs of the earth from elevated platforms. In the initial days of photography, balloons, pigeons, and kites were used to capture such photographs. With the invention of the aircraft in 1903, the first aerial photograph on a stable platform was made possible in 1909 [120]. In the 1960s and 1970s, the primary platform that was used to carry remote sensing instruments shifted from aircraft to satellites [120]. It was during this period that the word 'remote sensing' replaced the frequently used word 'aerial photograph'. Satellites can cover wider land space than planes and can monitor areas on a regular basis.

The new era in remote sensing began when the United States launched the first earth observation satellite called earth resources technology satellite (ERTS-1) dedicated primarily for land observation [120]. This was followed by many other satellites like Landsat 1-5, satellite pour l' observation de la terre (SPOT), Indian remote sensing (IRS), Quickbird, Ikonos, etc. Change in image format from analog to digital was another major step towards the processing and interpretation of remotely sensed data [120]. The digital format made it possible to display and analyze imagery using computers, a technology that was also undergoing rapid change during this period. Due to the advancement of technology and development of new sensors, the capture of the earth's surface through different portions of the electromagnetic spectrum is possible these days. One can now view the same area by acquiring the data as several images in different portions of the spectrum, beyond what the human eye can view. Remote sensing technology has made it possible to see things occurring on the earth's surface which may not be detected by the human eye.

The formal definition of *remote sensing* can be given as follows [120]: *it refers to the sensing of the earth's surface from space by making use of the properties of electromagnetic waves emitted, reflected or diffracted by the sensed objects, for the purpose of improving natural resource management, land use and the protection of the environment.* Remote sensing has enabled the mapping, studying, monitoring, and management of various activities and resources like agriculture, forestry, geology, water, oceans, etc. It has further enabled the monitoring of the environment, thereby helping in conservation. One of the major advantages of the satellite is its ability to provide repetitive observations of the same area, in intervals of a few minutes to few weeks depending on the sensor and orbit. This capability is very useful for monitoring dynamic phenomena such as cloud evolution, vegetation cover, snow cover, forest fires, etc.

In geology, for instance, remote sensing can be applied to study and analyze large geographical areas. Remote sensing interpretation makes it easy for geologists to identify the types of rocks and changes that occur in an area due to natural events such as floods or landslides. Remote sensing is also helpful in studying vegetation types. A farmer may use thematic maps to monitor the health of his crops without actually going out to the field. Interpretation of remote sensing images allows physical- and bio-geographers, ecologists, those studying agriculture, and foresters to easily detect which kind of vegetation is present in which areas and its growth potential. Those studying urban and other areas of land use also find remote sensing helpful because it allows them to easily pick out inhabited land in an area. This can then be used as data in city planning applications and in the study of species habitat. Because of its varied applications and ability to allow users to collect, interpret, and manipulate data over large, often not easily accessible, and sometimes dangerous areas, remote sensing has become a useful tool for all kinds of geographers. Similarly, a biologist can study the variety of plants in a certain location. In the last four decades, satellite imaging has evolved into a major tool for collecting information on almost every aspect related to the earth.

On-board imaging sensors can acquire information in different spectral bands, on the basis of exploited frequency, or at different resolutions. Therefore, a wide spectrum of data can be available for the same observed site. For many applications, the information provided by individual sensors is incomplete, inconsistent, or imprecise and additional processing may provide complementary data. Fusion of different pieces of information, results in a better understanding of the observed site, thus, decreasing the uncertainty related to information from single sources. In the interpretation of a scene, contextual information is important. For example, in an image labelling problem, a pixel considered in isolation may provide incomplete information about the desired characteristics. Context can be defined in the frequency, space and time domains. Images in different bands may be acquired by using either a single multi-spectral sensor or by using a number of sensors operating at different frequencies. The multi-spectral images improve the separation between various ground cover classes compared to a single-band image.

1.1 Characteristics of Remotely Sensed Imagery

Resolution is an important characteristic feature of aerial images. In a general sense, the term 'resolution' is defined as the smallest physical quantity that is discernable by an instrument. In other words, resolution is the power of the instrument to record fine details. High resolution of an instrument enables us to measure the quantity with more precision. In image processing, resolution refers to the ability of the imaging sensor to record the smallest measurable detail in a visual presentation. High resolution of an image is important in image processing as it helps us derive precise and accurate information for various applications.

Remote sensing images are characterized by four types of resolutions: spatial, spectral, radiometric, and temporal resolution.

- *Spatial resolution:* In digital imaging sensors, the analog images produced by the optical system are spatially sampled by the detector. Spatial resolution is a measure of the sensor's ability to record closely spaced objects such that they are distinguished as separate objects. If the imaging scenes are oversampled with a spatial frequency higher than the Nyquist frequency, it results in a high spatial resolution image. However, in practice, most digital image sensors undersample the analog scene. As a consequence, the resulting resolution is determined by the spatial sampling frequency. In remote sensing, this refers to the area of land space represented by one pixel in an image. It can be thought as the projection of the photo detecting element on to the ground. Thus, resolution is directly related to the area on the ground that represents a pixel in the detector. A sensor with a 1 m × 1 m spatial resolution can give finer details of the scene compared to a sensor with a 10 m × 10 m spatial resolution. Thus, high spatial resolution allows for sharp details and fine intensity transitions across all directions. For representing an object, a high spatial resolution image has more pixels compared to a low resolution (LR) image. In other words, as the spatial resolution increases, the associated file size increases. To capture a high spatial resolution, the camera needs a high density image sensor with closely spaced photo detectors.

  Different applications require varying spatial resolutions. For applications such as large area change detection, it is cost-effective to use medium-resolution imagery with large swath widths to observe areas where changes of interest have occurred. Similarly, for planimetric applications, it is recommended that imagery with the highest possible resolution be used to extract various features such as pavements, roads, etc. Different satellites capture images at different resolutions. For example, in Table 1.1, we list the spatial resolution of the various satellites for capturing multi-spectral (MS) and panchromatic (Pan) images.

- *Spectral resolution:* It refers to the frequency or spectral resolving power of a sensor and is defined as the smallest resolvable wavelength difference detected by the sensor. Spectral resolution represents the width of the band within the electromagnetic spectrum that can be

Table 1.1 Spatial resolution of some satellites		
Satellite	Multi-spectral image	Panchromatic image
Landsat	30 m × 30 m	15 m × 15 m
SPOT 2, 4	20 m × 20 m	10 m × 10 m
Ikonos	4 m × 4 m	1 m × 1 m
OrbView3	4 m × 4 m	1 m × 1 m
Quickbird	2.4 m × 2.4 m	0.6 m × 0.6 m

sensed by a sensor. As the bandwidth becomes narrower, the spectral resolution becomes higher. Spectral resolution plays an important role in satellite imaging. High spectral resolution images captured by remote sensing cameras provide detailed information about mineral resources and geographical structures of the earth or any other planet under observation. They can be acquired by capturing images in a narrow spectral range. These images consists of pixels that represent the spectral response within the band. For example, in the case of vegetation, maximum reflectance occurs at the near-infrared (NIR) region. Hence, images captured in the band of NIR give more details of vegetation compared to images captured in red or green spectral bands. A set of images captured at different spectral bands can be used to monitor land and other natural resources, including vegetated areas, wetlands, and forests. In Table 1.2, we display the spectral resolutions of different MS bands and Pan images provided by two satellites namely, the Landsat enhanced thematic mapper plus (ETM+) and Quickbird.

- *Radiometric resolution:* Pixels carry information of the image intensity in the form of binary digits called 'bits'. The intensity at any location in a real world scene may take a real value over a range. However, in a digital image, it is not possible to represent this entire range. In practice, this range is divided into finite levels and the real world intensity is quantized and assigned the nearest quantization level. Radiometric or brightness resolution refers to the smallest change in brightness that can be represented in an image. Each radiometric level is assigned a binary code and the increase in the brightness resolution requires more number

Table 1.2 Comparison of the spectral resolutions of Landsat ETM+ and Quickbird sensor's bandwidth (μm)

Spectral band	Landsat ETM+	Quickbird
Panchromatic	0.52–0.90	0.45–0.90
Blue (band-1)	0.45–0.51	0.45–0.52
Green (band-2)	0.52–0.60	0.52–0.60
Red (band-3)	0.63–0.69	0.63–0.69
Near-infrared (band-4)	0.75–0.90	0.76–0.90

of brightness levels and hence, more number of bits for each pixel. A binary image has two levels; black and white; hence, it requires only one bit for each pixel. A gray scale image is usually quantized using 256 gray levels with each level represented using 8 bits. Similarly, if each color plane of an RGB image requires 8 bits, then at least 24 bits are needed for representing each pixel. For illustration purpose, we display the radiometric resolution of different satellites in Table 1.3.

Table 1.3 Radiometric resolution of some satellites

Satellite	Radiometric resolution (bits)
Landsat	8
IRS	7
SPOT	8
Quickbird	11
Ikonos	11
OrbView3	11

• *Temporal resolution:* The term 'temporal resolution' is related to video signals. A video of an event is a sequence of images (frames) captured at regular and short time intervals between them. Temporal resolution, also known as frame rate, is the measure of the capability of the instrument to display the smallest movement/motion of the moving objects in the video. Thus, it refers to the number of frames captured per second. A video captured with low temporal resolution exhibits flicker or transitions of the moving objects in the scene/event. With high temporal resolution, the movement of the moving objects appears smooth and continuous. For a given duration of time, a high temporal resolution video requires more memory for storage and large bandwidth for transmission. In remote sensing, temporal resolution refers to the frequency at which a given geographical area is imaged. Higher temporal resolution enables monitoring the occurrence of rapid changes such as forests, floods, etc. This also improves the probability of obtaining cloud-free imagery over areas that experience frequent cloud cover. The revisit period of different satellites are listed in Table 1.4.

Table 1.4 Temporal resolution of various satellites

Satellite/Sensor	Revisit period (days)
Landsat	16
IRS	5
SPOT	5
Quickbird	3
Ikonos	3
OrbView3	<3

There exists a trade-off while selecting a sensor. For example, if we want a high spatial resolution, then the requirement is to keep low instantaneous field of view (IFOV) which reduces the energy of the reflected light acquired by the sensor causing reduction in signal-to-noise ratio. Thus, the captured image is degraded. One can improve the spatial resolution by capturing the image using higher spectral width for the sensor. However, this is possible only at the cost of poor spectral resolution since it requires higher bandwidth to get more energy. Thus, in order to have sensors with optimum performance, we are required to make the suitable choice as per the requirement. High spatial resolution images have better details which help in accurate measurement in the image. On the other hand, images with high spectral resolution give better classification of different regions which are benefitted by accurate identification of the object. In this work, we address the problem of reconstructing remotely sensed images that posses both high spatial and high spectral resolutions.

1.1.1 Multi-spectral images

Objects appear different through a red lens, or through blue or green lenses. Satellite sensors record reflected energy in the red, green, blue, or infrared bands of the spectrum for the purpose of better analysis of data. The process of acquiring images in different bands is called multi-spectral (MS) imaging. The improved ability of multi-spectral sensors provide a basic remote sensing data resource for quantitative thematic information, such as the type of land cover. Resource managers use this information from multi-spectral data to monitor fragile lands, vegetated areas, wetlands, forests, etc. Such data provides unique identification characteristics leading to a quantitative assessment of the earth's features.

In the area of remote sensing, we are interested in recognizing an object or a feature from the images that are captured using sensing devices. These features include vegetation, soil, rocks, minerals, water/ocean, snow, and artificial features. The recognition of such objects requires the sensor to have high spectral resolution. Remote sensing satellites are fitted with a camera that has a multi-channel detector with a few spectral bands. Each detector is sensitive to radiation within a narrow wavelength band. The resulting MS image contains both brightness and spectral (color) information of the targets being observed. Most MS sensors can record reflected energy in the red, green, blue or infrared bands of the spectrum. The improved ability of these sensors provides a basic remote sensing data resource for various kinds of applications. Examples of multi-spectral satellite systems include the following: Landsat TM, MS scanner (MSS), SPOT high resolution visible multi-spectral (HRV-XS), Ikonos MS, QuickBird MS.

In order to capture MS images, the light reflected from the scene is passed through filters with different spectral characteristics. These filters decompose the light into different spectral components which are then collected by multi-channel detectors and converted into a digital image. Since the optical power is divided into several components, the power available to each detector is reduced. This leads to poor signal-to-noise ratio making it necessary to acquire the MS images at low spatial resolution. Thus, multi-spectral images are characterized by high spectral resolution, that is, narrow bandwidth and low spatial resolution. As an example, in Fig. 1.1, we show images of MS bands captured by QuickBird. The spectral range of these bands are

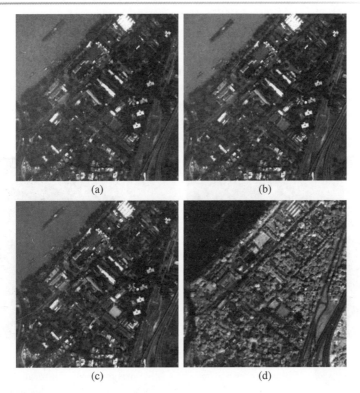

(a)   (b)

(c)   (d)

Figure 1.1 Multi-spectral (MS) images with spatial resolution of 2.4 m × 2.4 m corresponding to the Sundarbans, India, captured using Quickbird: (a) blue (band-1, 0.45–0.52 μm), (b) green (band-2, 0.52–0.60 μm), (c) red (band-3, 0.63–0.69 μm), and (d) near-IR (band-4, 0.76–0.90 μm). (Courtesy: www.glcf.umd.edu)

as follows: blue $(0.45-0.52 \ \mu m)$, green $(0.52-0.60 \ \mu m)$, red $(0.63-0.69 \ \mu m)$, near-infrared $(0.76-0.90 \ \mu m)$. Each spectral band can be used in different kinds of analysis. Band-1 (blue) images are useful for representing water bodies, land, soil, vegetation, etc. Band-2 (green) images enable us to inspect the health of vegetation. Band-3 (red) images help in discrimination of vegetation, delineation of soil, and geologic boundaries. Band-4 (NIR) images identify crops, emphasize land–water contrasts, etc.

In order to visualize the image in RGB color format, it is necessary to combine the red, green, and blue bands. The resulting image is said to have natural color composition (NCC). However, in the case of vegetation where there is a maximum reflectance occurring at the NIR region, we need to observe those effects in color images. This can be accomplished by combining near-IR (NIR), red, and green bands in RGB color image format, which is referred to as false color composition (FCC) since the represented color is not the true color perceived by us. Examples of NCC and FCC images are displayed in Fig. 1.2.

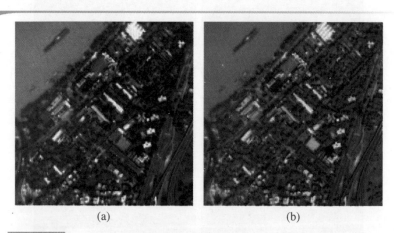

(a)   (b)

Figure 1.2   Color composition of MS image: (a) Natural color composition (NCC) and (b) false color composition (FCC). (Courtesy: www.glcf.umd.edu)

1.1.2 Panchromatic image

A panchromatic (Pan) sensor is a single channel detector sensitive to radiation within a broad wavelength range. Since the wavelength range coincides with the visible range, the resulting image is called Pan (all inclusive) image. The physical quantity being measured is the apparent brightness of the targets. Since the amount of light falling on the Pan sensor is higher when compared to that of MS sensors, the signal-to-noise ratio (SNR) is higher in a Pan image if both Pan and MS images are captured at the same spatial resolution. This makes it possible to capture the Pan image with a high spatial resolution without compromising on the SNR. Examples of Pan imaging systems are as follows: Ikonos Pan, Quickbird Pan, SPOT Pan, Landsat ETM+ Pan. In Fig. 1.3, a Pan image captured using Quickbird satellite is depicted. Here, one can see that the details are clearly visible in the Pan image. Such a high spatial resolution image when used with a low spatial resolution MS image

Figure 1.3   Panchromatic (Pan) image with a spatial resolution of 0.6 m × 0.6 m corresponding to the same geographical area as shown in Fig. 1.1 acquired using Quickbird. The spectral range of the Pan sensor is 0.45–0.90 μm.

(i.e., fused MS image) will help in improving the accuracy of classification and interpretation. The spectral range of the Pan image is 0.45–0.90 μm.

1.1.3 Hyper-spectral images

Typically, MS images consist of 3 to 10 noncontiguous spectral bands spread across the visible and infrared regions of the electromagnetic spectrum; each band having a width of around 100 nanometers. This width of the band determines the spectral resolution of the sensor. Greater the width, lower is the spectral resolution and vice-versa. As stated earlier, spectral resolution of the sensor determines its discrimination ability and having a higher spectral resolution results in better discrimination among objects. An improved version of the multi-spectral imaging sensor is the hyper-spectral (HS) imager [211]. It collects information in the form of reflectance spectrum in hundreds of contiguous bands (generally with a spectral range of 10 nm) simultaneously in the visible to mid-infrared portion of the spectrum, that is, 400–2500 nm. Enabled by recent advances in the manufacturing process, state-of-the-art

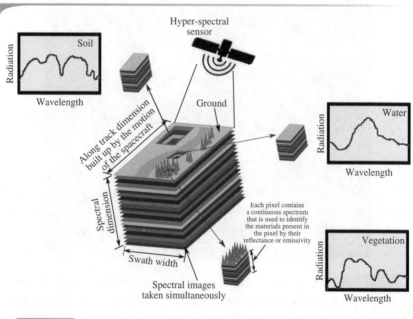

Figure 1.4   Illustration of hyper-spectral image cube.

Table 1.5 Hyper-spectral imaging systems

	AVIRIS [97]	HyDICE [199]	HyMAP [183]	AIMS [23]	Prob-1 [141]	Hyperion [234]	CHRIS [27]	HySI [133]
Introduction year	1987	1995	1996	1997	1997	2000	2001	2008
Platform	airborne	airborne	airborne	airborne	airborne	spaceborne	spaceborne	spaceborne
Nominal altitude (km)	20	6	5	3	2.5	705	550-670	100
Spatial resolution (m)	20	3	10	2	5	30	17 & 34	80
Spectral resolution (nm)	10	10	17	3	10	10	1.3-11.3	15
Spectral range (μm)	0.4–2.5	0.4–2.5	0.4–2.5	0.4–0.88	0.4–2.5	0.4–2.5	0.415–1.05	0.4–0.95
Number of spectral channels	224	210	128	143	128	220	18 & 62	64
Swath width (km)	12	0.9	6	3	3	7.7	0.13	20

hyper-spectral imaging sensors are able to capture remote scenes with better spectral resolution and reasonably good spatial resolution. Hyper-spectral imagers acquire images with spatial resolution of about 4 m × 4 m to 20 m × 20 m having much finer spectral resolution (10 nm spectral width of more than 200 contiguous bands.) The resulting data product is sometimes called a hyper-cube, as depicted in Fig. 1.4, which forms a three-dimensional (two spatial dimensions and one spectral dimension) image cube. The front face of this data cube provides two-dimensional, spatially sampled information, and the third dimension provides spectrally sampled information along the depth of the data cube. Each band provides a narrow-band image of the scene as seen by the sensor. Each pixel in the resulting image cube is associated with a complete spectral measurement of reflectance, called the spectral signature [138], which can be interpreted to identify the material/object present in the scene. Table 1.5 briefly describes a few hyper-spectral imaging systems with their specifications.

The main advantage of an HS image over the MS image is that the former has accurate spectral information, which benefits in many applications such 'as unmixing [33], change detection [220], object recognition [166], scene interpretation [139] and classification [151]. Being spectrally over-determined, HS images provide ample spectral information to identify and differentiate spectrally unique materials [211, 138]. Hence, they are used in a wide range of military and civilian applications that include target detection and tracking of objects, precision agriculture (e.g. monitoring the types, health, moisture status and maturity of crops), agriculture planning, forest inventory, mineral exploration, coastal management (e.g., monitoring of phyto-planktons, pollution, bathymetry changes) and urban planning.

1.2 Low Spatial Resolution Imaging

In order to check the quality of remotely sensed imagery, both spatial and spectral resolutions are very important. Images with high spatial and spectral resolutions provide the required information for many remote sensing tasks. Instantaneous field of view is one of the important factors that limits the spatial resolution of the sensors used in a remote sensing camera.

- *Instantaneous field of view (IFOV):* It is the angular cone of collected energy by a remote sensing camera. The narrower the IFOV, smaller is the area of the land mass covered by sensor and hence, lesser the amount of light energy collected by the sensor, resulting in a noisy image. If we use a sensor with wide IFOV, it covers a large area on the earth and hence, results in increase of light energy. Keeping the IFOV small, one can still increase the amount of light falling on the sensor by increasing the spectral width of the sensor. This can result in high spatial resolution, which is the case in Pan images. In the case of an MS image, it is necessary to keep the spectral width narrow. This decreases the SNR. Hence, we must increase the IFOV of a sensor to obtain an acceptable SNR. A sensor with a wide IFOV acquires an image at lower spatial resolution. Therefore, the sensor hardware in the satellite is constructed to capture low spatial resolution MS images. To overcome this inherent low spatial resolution limitation of MS images, one can use an algorithmic approach, that is, Pan-sharpening (multi-resolution image fusion) to combine the MS and Pan images into a single image. The resulting image has both high spatial and spectral resolutions.

In addition to IFOV, the following are other important factors that are related to low cost cameras that capture low spatial resolution natural images.

- *Imaging system:* Digital imaging systems consist of focusing lens, optical sensors, processor chip, electronic circuits and other mechanical subsystems. While an image is captured using low cost sensors, the original image goes through a sequence of degradations. These include blur, down-sampling, and additive noise. There is a natural loss of spatial resolution caused by optical distortions such as insufficient sensor density, out-of-focus capture and diffraction limit. The observations may be blurred due to optical aberration, relative motion between camera and object, limited shutter speed and atmospheric turbulence. Blur may also be introduced due to relative motion between the system and scene. Such distortions occur when one captures natural images; it may even occur when an MS sensor captures the scene. Note that for MS, we are forced to capture the images at reduced spatial resolution.

- *Density of charge coupled devices (CCDs):* An optical sensor converts optical energy into an electrical signal. In modern digital cameras, two sensors are widely used in order to capture the images. These are charge coupled devices (CCDs) and complementary metal-oxide semiconductor (CMOS) sensors. These sensors consist of an array of photo-detectors. The output voltage generated by the photo-detector depends on the amount of light falling on it. The spatial resolution of an image captured using a camera is determined by the number of photo-detector elements in the sensor. A low cost sensor with lesser number of photo-detectors produces an image having low spatial resolution with distortion. This is because of the lower sampling rate. One can increase the spatial resolution of the image by increasing the number of photo-detectors. As this number increases, the chip size also increases causing an increase in the effect of capacitance, which limits charge transfer rate. A solution to this is to decrease the size of photo-detectors in the same chip area. Reduction in size of photo-detector elements results in decrease in light falling on it and hence, SNR becomes prominent. Thus, there exists a lower limit to reducing the size of the photo-detector element. Therefore, new approaches towards increasing spatial resolution are required to overcome the inherent limitations of the sensors and optical imaging systems. The high cost of high precision optics and larger size of photo-detector elements, which increase the weight of the sensor are important factors in many commercial applications. Hence, a promising approach would be to use algorithmic approaches that obtain high spatial resolution using the available low spatial resolution observations.

In remote sensing, earth observing satellites provide MS and Pan data having different spatial, spectral, temporal and radiometric resolutions as illustrated in Tables 1.1–1.4. The need for a single image having the combined information from both MS and Pan images has increased. MS images with high spatial and spectral resolutions provide feature enhancement by increasing the accuracy of classification and change detection. The designing of a sensor to provide both high spatial and spectral resolutions is limited by the trade-off between spectral and spatial resolutions. Fortunately, there exist a number of image processing techniques that combine the available high spectral resolution MS images with a high spatial resolution Pan image to obtain an image that has both high spatial and spectral resolutions.

1.3 Image Fusion in Remotely Sensed Images

Due to the trade-off between spatial and spectral resolutions of the sensors and other constraints such as bandwidth and on-board storage capabilities of satellites, most commercial remote sensing satellites such as Quickbird, Ikonos and Worldview-2 capture a single panchromatic image and a set of multi-spectral images. A Pan image has high spatial resolution with low spectral resolution while MS images have higher spectral but lower spatial resolution. For example, Ikonos provides a Pan image with 1 m × 1 m spatial resolution and an MS image with a 4 m × 4 m spatial resolution. These two images are required for the accurate description of the captured scene. Since the Pan image has high spatial resolution, it describes subtle details in the scene such as roads, cars, etc. Hence, it provides detailed information of objects and features on the earth's surface. The MS sensors provide multi-band images with color information but with low spatial resolution. They are better suited for the discrimination and/or identification of land type. Moreover, MS images provide the necessary spectral information for the applications such as classification and hence, different objects can be easily identified. These two types of images allow identifying different regions on the ground using the spectral signature on one hand and using the geometrical information on the other. In many remote sensing applications, spatial information is as important as spectral information. In other words, it is necessary to have images that have the spectral resolution of multi-spectral images and the spatial resolution of a panchromatic image. A sensor with a high resolution for both is hardly feasible [139]. It is always a subject of interest in the remote sensing community to merge these images.

Given the low spatial resolution MS images and high spatial resolution Pan image, *Pan-sharpening* or *multi-resolution image fusion* uses an algorithmic approach to enhance the spatial resolution of MS images to make it similar to a Pan image. Ideally, the fused image should have the spatial resolution of the original Pan image and the spectral resolution of a given low resolution (LR) MS image. Such a fused image can lead to better land classification, map updating, soil analysis, feature extraction, etc. The goal of multi-resolution image fusion is to integrate complementary and non-redundant information to provide a composite image that could be used for better understanding of the entire scene.

1.4   Multi-resolution Image Fusion: An Ill-posed Inverse Problem

One of the limitations of low spatial resolution imaging is the mechanism used in the image acquisition process. This mechanism includes the lens subsystem along with the optical sensors, which may result in degradation due to out-of-focus and diffraction limit. Distortions may also rise due to optical aberration or atmospheric turbulence. In addition to this, the speed of the shutter and relative motion between camera and object also affect the quality of the captured image. Thus, the observed images are degraded; degrading also includes aliasing due to down sampling. In order to solve the image reconstruction problem, one can formulate a mathematical model that represents the image acquisition process. This model, known as observation or forward model, relates the original image to the observed image(s). The accurate formulation of the observation model plays an important role in the success of any image reconstruction approach. The most commonly used forward models incorporate translation, blur, aliasing and noise in the formulation.

Image fusion algorithms attempt to reconstruct the high spatial resolution MS image from the given low resolution MS image and a high resolution Pan image. Note that each MS image is sampled at a rate less than Nyquist rate so as to cover larger area leading to low spatial resolution. This causes high frequency distortion leading to aliasing effect. Obtaining a high resolution image from the given low resolution image is an inverse problem wherein the original information is retrieved from the observed data. A schematic representation of the inverse problem is shown in Fig. 1.5. Solving the inverse problem requires inverting the forward transformation. It is difficult to invert the forward model without amplifying the noise present in the observed data and multiple solutions are possible because there are more number of unknowns than knowns. Such problems are called ill-posed inverse problems. While solving the image fusion problem, the forward model of high resolution (HR) to low resolution (LR) transformation can be reduced to matrix manipulations. Hence, it is logical to formulate the fusion problem in a restoration framework as a matrix inversion. Knowing the forward model alone is not sufficient to obtain a satisfactory solution. Some form of constraints on the space of solutions must be included. The procedure adopted to stabilize the inversion of ill-posed problems is called regularization. Regularization based approaches solve ill-posed inverse problems by making them better-posed using prior information about the solution. It is a systematic method for adding more information to the reconstruction system. The Bayesian reconstruction

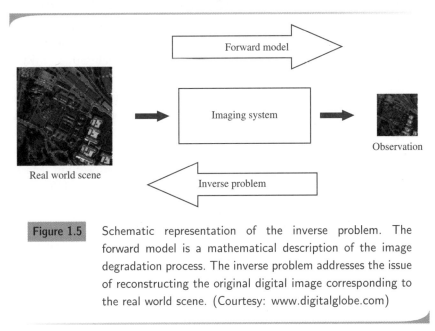

Figure 1.5 Schematic representation of the inverse problem. The forward model is a mathematical description of the image degradation process. The inverse problem addresses the issue of reconstructing the original digital image corresponding to the real world scene. (Courtesy: www.digitalglobe.com)

approach is commonly employed for solving these problems. This method is used when a posterior probability density function of the original image, given the observation, can be established. Bayesian estimation distinguishes between the possible solutions by using an priori model for the fused image. The major advantages of the Bayesian approach are its robustness and flexibility in modelling noise characteristics, *a priori* knowledge about the solution and solving using optimization techniques. In case of convex optimization, efficient gradient based methods can be used to obtain the solution which otherwise would require computationally expensive methods such as simulated annealing. In our work of image fusion, we make use of the high spatial resolution Pan image in order to make the problem better-posed.

1.5   Indian Remote Sensing Satellites

In this section, we briefly describe the history of Indian remote sensing satellites. The mission of creating Indian remote sensing satellites began in the year 1972, when the Government of India established a body called the Department of Space (DOS) to look after different activities related to the space program. The technologies of space applications are carried out through the constituent units of the Indian Space Research Organisation (ISRO), which is an autonomous institution established specifically for the space program. Over the years, ISRO has developed and operationally established an intense space applications program; it has a constellation of Indian national satellite (INSAT) systems serving the communication, broadcasting and meteorological observation needs. It has also established the Indian remote sensing series of satellites (IRS), which provide earth observation data to Indian and global users. In addition to this, the national remote sensing agency (NRSA) was established in the year 1975 at Hyderabad, for establishing and operating earth stations that receive and disseminate remotely sensed satellite data to various users as well as to serve and apply the same for various national developmental needs.

Following the successful demonstration flights of Bhaskara-1 and Bhaskara-2 satellites launched in 1979 and 1981, respectively, India began to develop indigenously built Indian Remote Sensing (IRS) satellites to support the national economy in the areas of agriculture, water resources, forestry, ecology, geology, watersheds, marine fisheries and coastal management. The first indigenously built satellite, IRS-1A, was launched in 1988 with many improvements over Bhaskara-2 in terms of orbit and attitude control as well as spatial and spectral resolutions of the payloads. Subsequent to IRS-1A, the satellites, namely IRS-1B, IRS-P2, IRS-1C, IRS-P3, IRS-1D and IRS-P4 (Oceansat) were launched in 1991, 1994, 1995, 1996, 1997 and 1999, respectively. In 2001, India launched a technology evaluation satellite (TES) that had a number of state-of-the-art technologies with a higher resolution, 1 m × 1 m imaging system. IRS-P6, launched in 2003, has among other improvements, a better multi-spectral imaging capability compared to earlier missions.

The IRS-P5 (Cartosat-1), which was launched in 2005, provides data with higher resolution for cartographic and precision mapping applications. This satellite carries two state-of-the-art Pan cameras that can take gray scale stereoscopic images of the earth in the visible region of the electromagnetic (EM) spectrum. The swath covered by these high resolution Pan cameras is 30 km and their spatial resolution is 2.5 m × 2.5 m. Cartosat-2 is an earth observation satellite in a sun-synchronous orbit and the second of the Cartosat series satellites was launched in 2007. The swath covered by the high resolution Pan camera on this satellite is 9.6 km and the spatial resolution is less than 1 m × 1 m. This satellite can be steered up to 45 degrees along as well as across the track. In addition, Cartosat-2A, Cartosat-2B, Cartosat-2D and Cartosat-2E are a series of other recent Cartosat satellites which were launched in 2008, 2010, February 2017 and June 2017, respectively. The most recent Cartosat satellite, that is, Cartosat-2E carries two primary instruments: Pan camera and the high resolution multi-spectral sensor. The Pan camera is capable of acquiring gray scale images in a selected portion of the visible and near-infrared spectrum (500–850 nm) at a resolution of 0.65 m. The multi-spectral sensor is a four-channel radiometer, which is sensitive across the entire visible spectrum and part of the near-infrared spectrum (430–900 nm); it acquires images at a resolution of 2 m.

In order to fulfill the requirements of ocean applications, IRS-P4 of OceanSat-1 was launched in 1999; it was the first Indian satellite built specifically for ocean applications. This satellite carried an ocean color monitor (OCM) and a multi-frequency scanning microwave radiometer (MSMR) for oceanographic studies. Oceansat-2, launched in 2009, is ISRO's first in the series of Indian remote sensing satellites dedicated to ocean research, and it provides continuity to the applications of Oceansat-1. The main objectives of Oceansat-2 are to study surface winds and ocean surface strata; observation of chlorophyll concentrations; monitoring of phytoplankton blooms; study of atmospheric aerosols and suspended sediments in the water. Furthermore, Resourcesat-1 (also known as IRS-P6) is an advanced remote sensing satellite built by ISRO, intended to not only continue the remote sensing data services provided by IRS-1C and IRS-1D, but also to vastly enhance the data quality. The other satellites in this series are Resourcesat-2 and Resourcesat-2A, which were launched in 2011 and 2016, respectively. The recent satellite, that is, Resourcesat-2A provides the same services as the other Resourcesat missions. It provides regular micro and macro information on land and water bodies, farm lands and crop extent, forests, mineral deposits, coastal information, rural and urban spreads, besides helping in disaster management.

The data acquired from IRS satellites is available at eight ground stations across the globe. The IRS mission forms a strong base for India's satellite remote sensing program by providing continuity of services and establishing worldwide leadership through the operation of a constellation of state-of-the-art remote sensing satellites serving the global community. One of the biggest achievements in the Indian remote sensing program is the operational capability of the launch vehicle PSLV used to launch India's own earth observation satellites. It may be of interest to mention here that the IRS system is the largest constellation of remote sensing satellites for civilian use in operation in the world today, with 11 operational satellites. All these satellites are placed in polar sun-synchronous orbit and provide data with varying spatial, spectral and temporal resolutions. The Indian Remote Sensing (IRS) program completed 25 years of successful operations on March 17, 2013. Moreover, the Indian government established the national natural resources management system (NNRMS) for which the DOS is the nodal agency, providing operational remote sensing data services. Data from the IRS satellites are received and disseminated by several countries all over the world. With the advent of high-resolution satellites, new applications in the areas of urban area, infrastructure planning and other large-scale applications for mapping have been initiated.

Starting from the early seventies, the Indian Remote Sensing program has come a long way with a focus on practical applications in the context of national needs. Political support ensured the sustainability of the program. With data from improved sensors and the use of geographic information system (GIS), the use of remote sensing has emerged as an integral component of the decision-making process at various levels in the country. The application of satellite remote sensing in India is an example for many developing countries; it demonstrates how relevant advanced technology can be for the development of a country.

1.6 Applications of Image Fusion

Image fusion is a specific category of data fusion which began in the 1950s. Due to the rapid the advancement of technology and the invention of new sensors, a larger collection of data is possible where the available information is complementary in nature. Hence, instead of processing individual sensor output, it is always desirable to merge the data from different sensors in order to increase the throughput of the system. The data fusion process includes the combination and utilization of data originating from different sources with an aim to obtain information with 'greater quality'. The meaning of 'greater quality' depends upon the application [242, 18]. When the given data is in the form of the an image, the resultant fusion process is called image fusion. The objectives of fusion differ with the applications. For example, in the medical community, feature enhancement is often required in order to carry out the diagnosis process. The diagnosis could be improved by fusing different images obtained from computed tomography (CT), magnetic resonance imaging (MRI) and positron emission tomography (PET). Similarly, an RGB camera mounted with a thermal sensor provides images that are very useful in detecting security threats in public places or military areas. Fusion of these complementary images enhance the capability of the surveillance systems. A single imaging sensor is often unable to provide complete information of the scene. The process of fusion aims at integrating the complementary information provided by the different sensors for a better representation of the situation than which would have been possible by using any of the sensors individually.

Remote sensing techniques have proven to be powerful tools for the monitoring of the earth's surface and atmosphere on a global, regional and even local scale, by providing important coverage, mapping and classification of land cover features such as vegetation, soil, water and forests. The volume of remote sensing images continues to grow at an enormous rate due to advances in sensor technology for both high spatial and temporal resolution systems. Consequently, an increasing quantity of image data from satellite sensors have become available, including multi-resolution images, multi-temporal images, as well as images of multi-spectral bands. The goal of multiple sensor data fusion is to integrate complementary and non-redundant information to provide a composite image, which could be used for a better understanding of the entire scene. Image fusion has been widely used in many fields of remote sensing, such as object identification, classification and change detection. Change detection is the process of identifying differences in the state of an object or phenomenon by observing it at different times. It is an important process in monitoring and managing natural resources and urban development because it provides quantitative analysis of the spatial distribution of the population of interest. Image fusion for change detection takes advantage of the different configurations of the platforms carrying the sensors. The combination of these temporal images in the same place enhances information on changes that might have occurred in the observed area. Sensor image data with low temporal resolution and high spatial resolution can be fused with high temporal resolution data to enhance the changing information of certain ground objects.

MS images with high spatial resolution are desired in many remote sensing applications. High resolution MS images lead to better analysis, classification and interpretation; fusion technique can be considered to improve the spatial resolution of the land area. The fused images of fields can lead to accurate estimates of types of crops, while those of geographical land area help in better segmentation of regions containing forests, rivers, roads and other geographical structures.

Remote sensing satellites capture the same geographical area at regular intervals depending on the temporal resolution of that satellite. The availability of multi-temporal datasets over the same scene makes it possible to extract valuable temporal characteristics of surface cover types that may be of interest to applications requiring the monitoring of spectral or spatial characteristic changes over time. It also helps in crop monitoring, assessing climate change and monitoring during periods of natural disaster.

One of the shortcomings of the MS image is the limited number of bands in the electromagnetic spectrum with wide spectral width of the individual band. Hyper-spectral imaging image provides densely sampled and almost continuous spectral information over the given wavelengths. Essentially it captures minor variations in the scene reflectance. Although the hyper-spectral data results in better classification of the regions, the processing and analysis of the same requires large computational time since it includes a very large number of images. In this book, we address the fusion of MS and Pan images captured using a multi-spectral sensor in order to enhance the spatial resolution of the MS image. This process is also known in the literature as multi-resolution image fusion or *Pan-sharpening*. We also address the Pan-sharpening of hyper-spectral images in brief. Pan-sharpening of hyper-spectral images is discussed in Section 2.4.

1.7 Motivation

Images with high spectral and spatial resolution provide accurate details of the earth. This information is required in many remote sensing tasks such as classification, change detection, etc. However, due to hardware limitation, the acquired MS image has low spatial resolution though it has high spectral resolution. Similarly, a Pan image has high spatial resolution with poor spectral details. Thus, there exists a need for a single image having complementary information from both the MS and the Pan images. This has motivated us to propose an algorithmic approach to combine MS and Pan image pixels that can better represent the information of both the images.

1.8 Organization of the Book

In this book, we address new approaches to image fusion. We first consider this problem by using detail extraction from the Pan image. We then address the fusion problem using a model based approach. The effect of aliasing is considered in the model by estimating the degradation matrix. We then use the regularization framework to obtain the fused image. Along with the smoothness prior, we also propose a new prior called Gabor prior in order to extract the high frequency details from the Pan image. Finally, we propose a super-resolution technique for natural images based on our fusion model. The organization of the book is as follows:

The literature survey for different fusion methods is described in Chapter 2. Different approaches for extraction of details along with the various injection models for carrying out Pan-sharpening are explained in this chapter.

In Chapter 3, two new approaches for image fusion, by using different edge-preserving filters, are proposed. We chose the guided filter and difference of Gaussians (DoGs) for detail extraction. Since the Pan and MS images correspond to the same scene captured with the sensor, there exists a definite relation between their detail bands. We assume a linear relationship between the observations and make use of the relationship to obtain fusion using filters. The comparison of the results obtained using these proposed fusion approaches is shown with various state-of-the art methods.

The filter based methods presented in Chapter 3 do not take care of aliasing that arises due to undersampling of MS images. In Chapter 4, we present a model based approach that takes care of aliasing due to undersampling of MS observations. The LR MS image is modelled as a blurred and noisy version of its ideal HR fused image. The degradation between LR and HR MS images is determined by first estimating an initial approximation to the fused image. Results obtained using the proposed model based approach are compared and discussed with other existing approaches.

One of the requirements of our model based approach is the need for learning the initial estimate from low resolution and high resolution image pairs. Further, in earlier approaches on fusion, the degradation matrix entries were estimated by modelling the relationship between the Pan derived initial estimate of the fused MS image and the LR MS image. This estimate may be inaccurate since it depends on the low spatial resolution Pan data. In order to increase the accuracy, one needs to derive the initial estimate using the available LR MS image only. With this motivation, we next tackled the problem of image fusion using the concepts of self-similarity and sparse representation theory. We obtained the degradation estimation and proposed a new prior based on Gabor filters in order to extract details from a Pan image. The details of this are given in Chapter 5.

Finally, in Chapter 6, as an application of image fusion, we propose a super-resolution technique applied on natural images obtained using real camera. Considering the similarity with the fusion problem, we extend the fusion technique proposed in the previous chapter to super-resolve natural images. Here, we propose a regularization framework for obtaining super-resolution. Since for natural image super-resolution, we do not have a high resolution image, such as Pan, as an observation, we make use of a database of LR–HR pairs in order to extract the missing high frequency details for the SR image. A contourlet based learning is used to obtain the initial SR estimate which is then used for obtaining the degradation as well as Markov random field (MRF) parameter. Similar to the fusion problem, the final solution is reconstructed using a maximum *a posteriori* MRF (MAP–MRF) framework.

At the end, we provide conclusion and possible future directions in Chapter 7.

Chapter 2

Literature Review

In many remote sensing applications, the spatial information of a fused image is as important as the spectral information. In other words, it is necessary to have images that have the spectral resolution of multi-spectral (MS) images and the spatial resolution of a panchromatic image. A sensor with spatial and spectral resolution, at the same time is hardly feasible [139]. The coarse spatial resolution of MS images is the result of a trade off due to physical and technical constraints. The quantity of light energy which arrives onto the detector is proportional to the width of its spectral range and hence, is smaller in the MS sensor than in the Pan sensor. It is therefore necessary to increase the energy that impinges onto the MS detector to obtain acceptable signal-to-noise ratio. However, this is not possible due to technological limitations. Further, if the MS images had high spatial resolution, the amount of data to transmit would be larger. The difficulties in on-board storage and data transmission to the ground also restrict the spatial resolution of MS images. This makes the remote sensing satellite sensors acquire MS images with low spatial resolution and the Pan image with high spatial resolution. Thus, the MS images have high spectral but low spatial resolution and the Pan image has high spatial but low spectral resolution.

The goal of multi-resolution fusion or Pan-sharpening is to combine the high spatial resolution of the panchromatic image with the high spectral information of the MS image. The fused MS image should have high spatial resolution in order to aid in detection and classification tasks. It should also contain the same spectral (color) information as the original multi-spectral data for better identification of targets. In other words, the fused image should possess both high spatial and high spectral qualities.

In the remote sensing community, multi-resolution image fusion or Pan-sharpening is a challenging problem. During the last two decades, a great amount of research has been carried out in this field. SPOT 1, the satellite launched in 1986 provided Pan and MS images with spatial resolution of 10 m × 10 m and 20 m × 20 m, respectively. Since then, the problem of multi-resolution image fusion has drawn significant attention from the remote sensing community to develop algorithms for better fusion. In 1999, the first review article on the different fusion methodologies was presented by Pohl et al. [187]. In this paper, authors described different fusion techniques which they divided into different categories based on arithmetic operations, wavelet transforms and principal component analysis (PCA) transform. This article also includes the different applications of image fusion such as in land usage studies, flood monitoring, and applications in geology.

Multi-resolution image fusion techniques can be classified in a number of ways. Schowenderdt [205] classified these methods based on spatial and transform domains. In the methods based on spatial domain, the processing is performed directly on the pixel intensity values. However, in the transform domain methods, the test images are first converted to domains such as Fourier or discrete cosine transforms, etc., and the processing takes place in the transform domain itself. Here, inverse transform is necessary to obtain the final fused image in the spatial domain. Fusion methods can also be grouped based on the approaches used in obtaining the final fused image. One such classification is reported by Wald [244], where the author classifies the fusion approaches into three different groups: projection substitution, relative spectral contribution and the fusion methods based on the ARSIS concept (short for Amélioration de la résolution spatiale par injection de structures which means to improve the spatial resolution by structure injection). Wang et al. [250] discuss the framework of general image fusion (GIF), which consists of the classification as well as comparison and comparative analysis of the existing fusion methods.

With the increase in the availability of hyper-spectral (HS) data, various Pan-sharpening techniques that were initially proposed for fusion of MS and Pan images are now being extended for Pan-sharpening of HS images by using HS and MS and/or Pan images. In the literature, several approaches for increasing the spatial resolution of HS images, by using fusion approaches, have been proposed. Loncon et al. [155] make a comparative study of HS Pan-sharpening methods obtained using HS and Pan images, which is considered a special case of HS–MS fusion. Similarly, Palubinskas [181] and Mookambiga and Gomathi [167] review the different HS–MS fusion (or hyper sharpening) methods. Recent reviews of these methods are presented by Yokoya et al. [268]. In this article, various state-of-the-art HS–MS fusion methods have been implemented and compared on the common datasets. Here, we briefly review the existing fusion methods for hyper-spectral images.

To understand the concepts behind different multi-resolution image fusion techniques in a better way, we classify them here into three different categories as projection substitution methods, multi-resolution analysis (MRA) based methods and model based approaches. In the following sections, we describe the different fusion methods under these categories for MS Pan-sharpening as well as HS sharpening. Note that in this book, the terms 'Pan-sharpening' and 'multi-resolution image fusion' are used interchangeably.

2.1 Projection Substitution Based Techniques

Multi-spectral data captured by a remote sensing satellite has a collection of several monochromatic images. Each of this image refers to a band which is captured using a sensor with a particular spectral range. For example, Landsat-7 satellite captures MS images having seven bands in the spectral range 0.45 to 1.25 μm. One can visualize the MS image by considering any three bands as red, green and blue images in the RGB color space format. However, the same can also be projected onto other color space such as intensity hue saturation (IHS), where I describes the luminance component of the scene, H refers to the contribution of the colors and saturation component represents the purity of the colors. The human visual system also works on the principle of IHS color space to identify/describe the objects being imagined by us. The IHS transformation converts the given RGB image into an IHS color space where the intensity component corresponds to the spatial information of the image, and the hue and saturation components together represent the spectral details of the scene [152]. Since IHS transformation separates the spatial and spectral details, one can use the same to fuse the MS and Pan images, that is, the spatial component in the IHS color space can be manipulated using a mathematical operation without disturbing the color details. This category of the fusion classification not only includes the fusion methods based on IHS [43, 204, 91, 107, 185, 241, 119, 92] but also includes methods based on PCA [49, 70, 50, 264], which were proposed in the early 1990s.

In these approaches, one has to use a suitable interpolation technique to make the size of the MS image same as the Pan image before the suitable fusion method is applied. Moreover, since the MS and Pan images are complementary, it is required to perform radiometric corrections on the Pan image using histogram matching between the intensity component of the upsampled MS image and the Pan image. The histogram matched Pan image is then substituted into the intensity component in the IHS color space to get the Pan-sharpened image in the IHS color space. The final fused image is obtained after taking the inverse IHS transform in the last step. An alternative to the IHS transform is the PCA, which transforms the intercorrelated bands into a set of uncorrelated bands. After this, the first principal component, that is, PC^1 is replaced with the Pan image since it represents an image with the highest variance. Histogram matching of Pan to PC^1 is mandatory before substitution because the mean and variance of PC^1 are different than those of the Pan image. In addition to fusion methods based on IHS and PCA under this category of classification, we also include fusion methods based on the concept of relative spectral contribution [244]. In this concept, it is assumed that the spatially degraded Pan image is a linear combination of acquired MS images. This assumption is based on the observation that the spectral response functions of the Pan image overlaps with the various bands of the MS image. Some of the common methods that fall under this category are Brovey [71, 88] and P+XS [1] fusion methods.

One of the drawbacks in the IHS based fusion methods is that it can be applied on any three MS bands only. Due to this, the Pan image `does not correspond to a better representation of the luminance component in the entire set, which affects the quality of fused image severely. Literature shows that the performance of fusion methods based on IHS, PCA transform and relative spectral contribution is highly dependent on the correlation between the I component of the MS and the Pan images [226]. Although these fusion methods result in a fused image with better preservation of geometrical structures [280, 212, 238] that are well suited for applications such as cartography, visual analysis and target recognition [238, 185]; the major drawback in these fusion methods is the spectral or color distortion, which may be localized to certain land areas [245, 185]. The reason behind this spectral distortion is due to the modification or alteration of the low frequency details present in the MS image during the injection of high frequency details from the Pan image [244, 214]. In addition to this, if the spectral responses of the MS bands are not perfectly overlapped with that of the Pan image, the performance of the fusion techniques based on PCA or IHS and relative spectral contribution results in poor fused data [94].

In order to overcome the three-band limitation of the IHS fusion method, Tu et al. [230, 231] have proposed a framework to use more than three bands for fusion using IHS transform. This work is considered to be a pioneer in extending the IHS transform for further use in multi-resolution image fusion. This fusion method is referred to as generalized IHS (GIHS) or fast IHS (FIHS) in the literature. Here, weights are fixed to compute the intensity component. In order to improve the quality of the fused image, Tu et al. [231] have modified the framework of the FIHS method.

Unlike the FIHS method [231] in which fixed weights are used to compute the intensity component, Garzelli and Nencini [85] have estimated the weights and the intensity components are computed using a genetic algorithm. They also used the same algorithm to compute the appropriate gain constants that are multiplied with the extracted details of the Pan image before injecting them into the upsampled MS image. Although this method obtains better Pan-sharpened images, it suffers from computational issues since it requires population based optimization techniques such as genetic algorithms to estimate the weights. The computational complexity of the FIHS fusion method [231] is lesser than that of transform based fusion methods. Gonzalez et al. [94] utilized the spectral response functions of MS and Pan images in order to compute the intensity component of the

IHS transform, which further reduced the computational burden of the FIHS method. They verified their fusion method by conducting experiments on images captured using the Ikonos satellite. The disadvantage of this method is that one has to know the spectral responses of the given images in order to obtain better fusion performance. Similar to Gonzalez et al.'s method [94], the approach proposed by Dou et al. [64] also has lesser computational complexity. In this case, the radiometric properties of MS and Pan data are used in selecting high frequency details from the Pan image and those details are injected into the upsampled MS image. In addition to this, the weights on the extracted Pan details are also computed before injecting it to the MS image. Gonzlez-Audcana et al. [94] also verified the potential of their method using the images acquired by Ikonos satellite. Although the fusion methods proposed by Gonzalez et al. and Dou et al. [94, 64] have the advantage in terms of reduced computational complexity, they require knowledge of the spectral response functions of the data and this restricts their usefulness to only limited sensors.

Choi et al. [55] obtained better solutions for fusion when compared to Tu et al.'s FIHS technique [231] by applying adaptive component substitution. Here, the final fused image is obtained after estimating the initial low and high resolution component images by computing statistical parameters such as correlation coefficient (CC) and standard deviation between MS and Pan images. An adaptive IHS method proposed by Rahmani et al. [192] estimates the different weights used in the component substitution. In addition, in this case, the final fused image is obtained by inserting the edge details from the Pan image estimated using the exponential edge detector.

Aiazzi et al. generalized the IHS fusion model to include projection substitution techniques [13]. Here, a generalized intensity component is modelled as the weighted average of the MS bands, which is similar to the concept of fusion methods based on relative spectral contribution. The weights are obtained as regression coefficients between the MS observations and the spatially degraded Pan image with an aim of capturing the spectral responses of the sensors. These weights are then used in obtaining the intensity component from the MS bands, which is then injected into the upsampled version of the MS image to be fused in order to obtain the final fused image.

Choi [56] introduced a trade-off parameter in order to control the amount of injected details from Pan to MS image. The author formulated the fusion problem as a minimization problem in which the difference between upsampled and fused MS images is minimized. At the same time, the fused image should be as close as possible to the high spatial resolution Pan image. The trade-off between these two constraints control the spatial and spectral distortions in the final fused image. The range of the trade-off parameter is from one to infinity and it varies the fused image from only the MS image (no spatial details from Pan image) to the fused image obtained using FIHS method [231], respectively. They concluded that the spatial and spectral resolutions cannot be enhanced simultaneously. An improvement to this model is proposed by Tu et al. [233] wherein the trade-off parameter is automatically adjusted. The idea of trade-off parameter is further extended by Lillo-Saavedra and Gonzalo [153] who used wavelet transform to obtain the trade-off parameter.

Laben and Brower proposed a method based on the Gram–Schmidt (GS) orthogonalization procedure in order to obtain the fused image [136]. This approach is patented by Eastman Kodak and implemented in the environment for visualizing images (ENVI) software package. In this method, the fused image can be obtained by selecting one of the different versions of the spatially degraded Pan image. Later, Aiazzi et al. [13] have modified this preprocessing step of Pan image by using the multiple regression weights estimation on the MS bands which had been proven to be an effective fusion method using GS orthogonalization. Another fusion method based on the concept of the matting model was proposed by Kang et al. [124]. This model decomposes the given MS image into three components, that is alpha channel, spectral foreground and background. Similar to the concept of the IHS method, the alpha channel is substituted by the Pan image and inverse operation is then applied to obtain the fused image. A fusion approach that uses the smoothing filter based intensity modulation (SFIM) was proposed by Liu [154]. This method modulates the intensity values of low spatial resolution MS images based on the ratio of the Pan image and its degraded version. The proposed method was shown to perform better than the fusion techniques based on Brovey transform by Eshtehardi et al. [71] and IHS transform by Tu et al. [231]. In order to remove the distortion in fusion caused due to the bicubic interpolation in Liu's method [154], a new fusion method was proposed by Khan et al. [127] which uses the non-linear upscaling operation instead of bicubic interpolation that gives a sharper and better correlated upscaled image. The frequency details from the Pan image was extracted using a pair of upscaling and downscaling filters which are then added to the upscaled image. An adaptive Pan-sharpening method based on smoothing filter intensity modulation (SFIM) was also proposed by Tu et al. [232].

Though the aforementioned fusion algorithms have certain advantages, they result in a fused image with some degradations in terms of spectral as well as spatial contents. The IHS transform based approaches enhance the texture features, however they make use of interpolated versions of MS images. Due to this interpolation prior to the replacement of the high frequency details from the Pan image, there is spatial degradation in the fused images. The projection substitution based fusion techniques also result in spectral distortion due to the dissimilarity between intensity component and the Pan data [226]. The IHS based methods require much less computational burden when compared to fusion methods based on transform domain and are easy to implement. However, they still suffer from spatial and spectral distortions.

2.2 Multi-resolution Based Techniques

In the last decade, image fusion techniques based on multi-resolution analysis (MRA) have become significant due to their ability to capture the information present at different scales. These methods work on the following principle: extract the high frequency details not available in the MS images from the Pan image and inject those details in the MS image. This concept of detail extraction and injection was pioneered by Chavez [48] and was based on high pass filtering (HPF). Here, the author extracted the high frequency details from the Pan image by taking the difference of the Pan and its low pass filtered version usually blurred with the box type filter. These extracted details are then injected into the upsampled MS image to obtain the fused image. Chavez et al. compared the fusion methods based on IHS, PCA and HPF and showed the better performance of HPF method when compared to IHS and PCA based fusion techniques [49]. Later the improvement in terms of detail extraction and injection was effectively handled by the development of MRA, that is, wavelet, contourlet, etc., to carry out the data fusion task.

MRA calculates the approximation of signals at various scales, which is done by using wavelet basis functions. The theory of wavelets was introduced in the beginning of the last century and since 1980, it has been applied to perform signal processing tasks. Due to its desirable properties such as multi-scale decomposition and time-frequency localization, it is a very promising tool in various signal and image processing applications. While performing fusion with MRA, the details extracted from an image using the wavelet transform can be injected into that of another image using a number of methods. For example, the method can be based on substitution, addition, or a selection based on either frequency or spatial context. The first effective MRA in this domain was a decimated discrete wavelet transform (DWT), which was a orthogonal, non-redundant and non-symmetric directional transform. It captured detail information present at horizontal, vertical and diagonal directions at each stage of decompositions. Various approaches have been proposed for fusion that are based on the use of DWT [198, 265, 83, 280, 196, 266]. In these methods, first, histogram matching is performed between the Pan image and each band of MS images. The histogram matched Pan image and each band of the interpolated MS image are then decomposed separately using DWT. Finally, the approximation and detail layers obtained at different levels of decompositions of MS and Pan images are used in obtaining the fused image. Here, the extracted details from the Pan image may be added to or they may be substituted for MS image pixels to obtain the fused image. Inverse DWT is performed on the modified MS image to obtain the final fused image in the spatial domain. It has been found that the fusion results obtained by using DWT with additive or substitution fusion rule perform similarly in terms of quality of final Pan-sharpened image [93]. Although MRA using DWT provides an effective tool to carry out data-fusion tasks, the process of detail injection may result in spatial distortions such as blurring, ringing as well as aliasing effects in the fused images, which are mainly due to the shift variant property of DWT [11, 12, 174]. However, multi-resolution representation of the image using DWT makes the fusion results better when compared to that of HPF or IHS based methods which do not use such hierarchical description to describe the image.

In order to avoid the problem of shift variance of DWT, researchers in the fusion community use either 'a trous' wavelet transform (AWT) or a Laplacian pyramid (LP) to decompose the image. Unlike the DWT, which is critically subsampled, the AWT and LP are oversampled, which allow an image to be decomposed into nearly disjointed bandpass channels in the frequency domain without losing the spatial connectivity of its high frequency contents such as edges regions. Use of AWT or LP leads to a stack of image layers obtained from different band pass filters with same dimensions and reduction in resolution by a factor of 2 for each level. The AWT is a non-orthogonal, redundant, undecimated and symmetric directional transform. It was first proposed by Kronland-Martinet et al. [132] for music synthesis. The term 'a trous' (meaning 'with holes') was introduced by Dutilleux [70] who described its theoretical analysis. Various fusion schemes using AWT are presented by Nunez et al., Otazu et al. and Ranchin et al. [174, 178, 197]. Nunez et al. used AWT with additive fusion rule to obtain the fused image by making use of three MS bands [174]. This approach was later generalized for more than three bands and is often referred to as additive wavelet luminance proportional (AWLP) [178]. Otazu et al. [178] also proposed a model for multi-resolution fusion using the spectral response function of the MS and Pan images provided by the manufacturer. Ranchin et al. proposed a framework for fusion using AWT with different detail injection methods [197]. Gonzalez-Audicana et al. compared the fusion results obtained using DWT and AWT and concluded that AWT outperforms DWT [93].

In addition to AWT, the MRA based on LP also represents an undecimated transform [36]. The theory of LP was introduced prior to MRA by Burt and Adelson [38] for compact image representation. Similar to AWT, LP is a bandpass image decomposition derived using Gaussian pyramid (GP) which is a multi-resolution image representation. This can be regarded as an AWT in which the image is recursively low pass filtered and downsampled to generate a low pass approximation image, which is re-expanded and subtracted pixel by pixel from the original image to yield the detail layer. The LP was used by Aiazzi et al. and Ranchin et al. [7, 197] to obtain the multi-resolution fusion of MS and Pan images while Wilson et al. [256] used it to obtain the fusion of hyper-spectral data. One of the benefits from the AWT and LP based Pan-sharpening methods is that by generalization of these methods, it is easy to fuse MS and Pan images having non-integer or even fractional resolution difference. One such implementation is proposed by Aiazzi et al. [11], where the authors propose the fusion of the MS and Pan images having non-octave or fractional resolution ratio. The generalization of these works are proposed by Aiazzi et al. [8, 9, 10], who use the idea of multi-rate signal processing [236]. The common characteristic of the AWT and LP is that they are redundant multi-resolution transforms which are well suited for image fusion as demonstrated by Aiazzi et al. and Gonzalez-Audicana et al. [11, 93]. It is interesting to note that the use of undecimated DWT (UDWT) as MRA to decompose the image may also be useful to obtain the fused image since it is also an oversampled transform. However, the computational cost along with complexity issues are high when it is intended to fuse images having non-octave or fractional resolution ratio.

A number of fusion methods based on MRA framework that use various methods for details extraction and injection are modelled in a generic way by using the ARSIS concept [196, 197]. Thomas et al. and Wald [226, 244] classify the fusion methods based on MRA using the ARSIS concept into three different models. The first is the multi-scale model (MSM) that performs hierarchical description of the information content related to the spatial contents in an image. Examples of MSM include DWT, LP, AWT and UDWT which have already been discussed earlier. In addition to these, it also includes Gaussian pyramids (GP) [227], HPF [49] and iterative filter banks [34]. The second one in the ARSIS concept is the inter band structure model (IBSM) which deals with the relationship between the approximation and/or details of MS and images. It uses a radiometric transformation such as gain or offset of spatial structures when injecting details from Pan to MS image. The final model is the high resolution IBSM (HRIBSM) which is concerned with the procedure of injecting the extracted details from Pan to MS image. For example, the fusion method proposed by Aiazzi et al. [12] consider the modulation transfer function (MTF) of MS images during the injection process. Note that fusion implementations with MSM, IBSM and HRIBSM affect the quality of the different fusion methods.

Many authors have also elaborated the examples of successful implementation of image fusion using AWT and LP as MSMs in the ARSIS concept and the results are compared using different IBSMs. IBSM aims to make the fused image most similar to the original MS image. Ranchin and

Wald demonstrate the use of two local models for image fusion by making use of details instead of approximations [196]. The need for such IBSM in the fusion process is discussed by Garzelli and Nencini [84]. They show the effect of both global and local IBSMs on the results of the fused image using redundant transforms, that is, AWT and LP and conclude that the local IBSM outperforms when compared to the global one. They use the local IBSM as proposed by Aiazzi et al. [11] which consists of space-varying gain. Here, Pan detail coefficients are multiplied with the gain constant to achieve local equalization of the MS and Pan sensors.

Few researchers have worked on fusing Pan and MS images where the resolution difference is not a power of 2, for example fusion of Pan image of systeme pour l' observation de la terre (SPOT) satellite and MS bands of Landsat thematic mapper (TM) satellite. Blanc et al. [34] use the ARSIS concept with iterated rational filter banks to Pan-sharpen the MS image. They compare their results with the method based on DWT which is designed for non-integer resolution factor and show that DWT performs poorly in the non-integer case. Use of the multi-band DWT to merge SPOT Pan and Landsat TM MS images is discussed by Shi et al. [215]. Using the framework of the ARSIS concept, Aiazzi et al. [11] also propose the generalized LP using context based decision (GLP-CBD) to merge the data of non-integer or fractional resolution difference between the Pan and MS images.

In order to exploit the benefits of projection substitution based fusion techniques several Pan-sharpening approaches have been proposed by combining MRA and projection substitution. Nunez et al. [174] combine the IHS transform and the wavelet based MRA to obtain a fused image. A fusion method that uses PCA and wavelet transform is discussed by Tseng et al. [229]. King and Wang [131] and Chibani and Houacine [54] combine the IHS with bi-orthogonal and redundant wavelet transforms, respectively in order to obtain the Pan-sharpened image. Hong and Zhang [111] use integrated IHS and wavelets to fuse the MS and Pan images; they demonstrate their results on images acquired from Quickbird and Ikonos satellites. Gonzalez et al. [91] discuss the framework to merge the MS and Pan images by integrating wavelet transform with IHS and PCA methods, respectively. Recently, a detail injection model based on MTF [12] was used in the fusion approach proposed by Nunez et al. [174] to obtain the fusion [129]. The main advantage of combining MRA and projection substitution methods is that a fused image with better perceptual and quantitative measures is obtained.

Though wavelet transform preserves spectral information efficiently, it is weak at preserving spatial fidelity due to limited directionality. Moreover, the isotropic wavelets have scant shift-invariance and multi-directionality and fail to provide an optimal solution for the highly anisotropic edges and contours that are encountered in images. Moreover, due to limited directionality, the edge extraction and injection may not correspond to those in true MS images. In order to solve these limitations, the MRA based fusion methods using transforms such as curvelet [39] and contourlet [61,59] have also been proposed. Curvelet has the property of anisotropy; it has higher directional property which makes it better suited for image fusion than the wavelet transform. Choi et al. [57] fused the MS and Pan images using the ARSIS concept with curvelet transform. They compared their fusion results with that of IHS and wavelet based methods. Similarly, Nencini et al. [170] proposed a fusion approach based on curvelet transform for resolution factor of 2 and 4 for Quickbird and Ikonos datasets. They used the curvelet transform to extract the high frequency details from the Pan image and inject them into the corresponding details of MS bands. They evaluated perceptual and quantitative tests by comparing the fusion results with traditional methods.

The construction of a curvelet transform requires a rotation operation; it also corresponds to a partition of the 2D frequency plane based on polar coordinates. This property makes the idea of curvelet transform simple in the continuous domain but causes problems in the implementation for discrete images. Similar to the curvelet transform, the contourlet transform (CT) proposed by Do and Vetterli [61] has the properties of wavelet transform. In addition, it also possesses characteristics such as multi-directionality and anisotropy which capture the details present in different directions. It employs LP [60] and directional filter bank (DFB) [26] to capture and link the discontinuities into geometric structures. The disadvantage of CT is that it is shift variant because of subsampling operation used in it. The shift invariance version of CT, called non-subsampled CT (NSCT), [59] performs better in fusion due to the absence of decimation but it suffers from redundancy. The fusion methods based on CT and NSCT are explained by Shah et al., Shi et al. and Mahyari and Yazdi [210,213,159]. Shah et al. [210] obtained the fusion of MS and Pan images using PCA and NSCT. Here, after applying the PCA on upsampled MS images, they choose a principal component (PC) image that has high correlatedness with the Pan image. The selected component and histogram matched Pan image are then decomposed using the NSCT. The detail coefficients of the Pan image are then replaced with the corresponding selected component in the CT domain in order to obtain the fused image. A similar approach is presented by Shi et al. [213], where the transformed image corresponding to the first PC and Pan images are decomposed using NSCT and details are injected based on the local variance of Pan and first principal component images. Mahyari and Yazdi [159] consider both spectral and spatial similarity while fusing. They decompose the Pan and MS images using NSCT; the detail coefficients of the Pan image are then injected to the MS image based on spatial similarity measure. Similar to the method proposed by Shah et al. [210], they inject detail coefficients at all levels from the Pan to the MS image.

In addition to the standard DWT, the complex wavelet transform (CWT) is a complex-valued two-dimensional wavelet transform which provides multi-resolution, sparse representation, and useful characterization of the structure of an image [208, 77, 78]. Steerable filter banks [219] proposed by Simoncelli was one of the first non-adaptive designs that provided an elegant way to obtain flexible orientation specificity with redundant representation. Attempts have been made to achieve near shift-invariance and improved directionality using the idea of near-analytic transform designs such as CWT with small redundancy. Salient features of these complex transform designs are shiftability, that are, near shift-invariance, increased directionality and the availability of phase information. Nguyen and Oraintara [172] proposed a shiftable complex directional transform by combining Laplacian pyramid and complex directional filter bank. Here, in order to obtain the analyticity, the dual-tree structure of real DFBs is constructed where the fan filters used in two trees are constrained to satisfy Hilbert pair criteria and certain conditions on phase responses. The same authors in [173] addressed the implementation issues such as border artefacts and the constraints on the designed finite impulse response (FIR) filters. However, these FIR filters are truncated versions of infinite impulse response (IIR) filters and the transform is approximately shift-invariant. Portilla and Simoncelli [190] proposed complex-valued steerable filter banks for texture synthesis application and utilized the same for finding features based on local phase and energy. Use of subsampled M-directional DFBs (MDFBs) and CWTs in many image processing applications result in suboptimal performance due to the use of downsamplers. Down-sampling stages used in these transforms lead to large reconstruction error (caused by aliasing), limited directional flexibility, difficulty in filter design, etc. Subsampled complex-valued transforms are used for the same [114, 191, 203]. Ioannidou and Karathanassi [114] use DT-CWT [208], while Zhnang et al. [191] and Saeedi and Faez [203] use shiftable complex directional transform [172]. Note that all these MRA based fusion approaches are non-adaptive and to the author's best knowledge, use of spatially adaptive transform based fusion approach has not been explored yet.

In the literature, a number of methods are discussed that use different approaches for fusion. In order to compare these methods, the data fusion committee of the IEEE Geoscience and Remote Sensing Society (GRS-S) sponsors a yearly 'Data Fusion Contest' focusing on one specific application each year. The Data Fusion Contest 2006 was held with an aim to identify the best fusion algorithm. Fusion techniques those were based on projection substitution as well as MRA were included in this contest. Outcomes of this contest are presented by Alparone et al. [18]. An important observation of the evaluation results was that two best performing algorithms, GLP-CBD [11] and AWLP [178] based on MRA using AWT and LP, respectively share a common philosophy of taking into account the imaging sensor related physical models in the algorithm. These techniques are widely used as state-of-the-art methods. However, AWLP and GLP-CBD methods have the limitation that the quality of the fused image depends on the size of the target present in an image. Depending on the size of the target, either AWLP [178] or GLP-CBD [11] performs better. Luo et al. [157] have proposed an approach to use either AWLP [178] or GLP-CBD [11] based on the target size. They have shown that AWLP performs better when the target size is small and GLP-CBD performs better when the target is larger.

2.3 Model Based Fusion Approaches

While a majority of image fusion methods adopt a projection substitution, MRA or a combination of these two, techniques independent of these frameworks have also been proposed in the literature. The most relevant techniques to our discussion here are the methods that are based on the *model based approach*, where the multi-resolution image fusion is posed as a problem of minimizing a cost function based on a model for the imaging sensor. All the approaches addressed earlier do not use an explicit relation between the observed and fused images. The model based fusion methods are partly motivated by image restoration and super-resolution research which use the image formation model and obtain the solution by formulating it as an inverse optimization process.

The image formation involves the degradation of the true high resolution MS image. Because much information is lost in the this process, estimating a true MS image from its degraded version is an ill-posed inverse problem where the solution is not unique. This means that according to the degradation process, many different high resolution MS images can produce the same low resolution MS image. Regularization theory is an effective framework to obtain the better solution for the ill-posed problem. Similarly, Bayesian framework has also been proven to be an important tool to solve such inverse problems. Within this framework, the fused image is extracted from a Bayesian posterior distribution in which prior knowledge and artificial constraints on the fusion results are incorporated. These model based fusion methods utilize image formation models and regard the fusion process as an inverse optimization problem. During recent years, several model based fusion techniques have been proposed which are based on a regularization theory and/or on a Bayesian framework. Generally, there are two types of image formation models used in these methods: first is based on the LR MS formation which relates the high resolution MS image to its LR version and the second is the formation of a Pan image which relates the given Pan image to the true MS image.

The main advantage of a Bayesian formulation is that the problem gets converted into a probabilistic framework. Using this idea, Fasbender et al. [76] have proposed the fusion of MS and Pan images captured using the Ikonos satellite. They use the LR MS and Pan image formation models and assume that the resulting error components follow Gaussian distribution. In a Bayesian framework, it is also required to define the prior knowledge of the fused image. Here, authors used a non-informative model for the fused image since the fused data itself is unavailable, that is, the probability density function of the fused data is uniform. The weighting coefficient between spectral and spatial details is also introduced in the same Bayesian formulation in that method. Within the Bayesian framework, maximizing a posterior distribution in the form of maximum *a posteriori* (MAP) has resulted in improved solutions in many areas of image processing. A MAP estimation for enhancing the resolution of hyper-spectral data was proposed by Hardie et al. [105]. In their work, they obtained two terms in the final cost function, the first term is due to the result of the LR MS image formation and the second term is due to the correlation between the different data to be merged.

Joshi et al. and Joshi and Jalobeanu [122,121] used the LR MS image formation model where an LR MS image is considered as a blurred and decimated version of the true HR MS image. Using MAP estimation, the final cost function is obtained where appropriate priors are used in order to regularize the final solution. The Pan image formation model is not used in these fusion techniques; instead, the same (i.e., Pan image) is used to estimate the different parameters of the priors with the assumption that all the MS bands have spatial structures similar to the Pan image. Joshi et al. [122] have used the auto-regressive prior for fusion and different parameters of this prior were estimated using the Pan image. It is well known that the Markov random field (MRF) based modeling for capturing the spatial correlation among pixels is the most general model and is often used as a prior during regularization while solving ill-posed problems. In the area of image processing and computer vision, many researchers use MRFs as a convenient way of modelling contextual entities such as image pixels, depth field, and other correlated features. Joshi and Jalobeanu [121] have modelled the final fused image as an MRF; they have used an edge-preserving inhomogeneous Gaussian MRF (IGMRF) prior in the regularization framework. They estimated IGMRF prior parameters using the available Pan image. Since the final cost function in the methods proposed by Joshi et al. and Joshi and Jalobeanu [122,121] is convex, a simple gradient based iterative optimization method is used to obtain the final solution. Using MRF based prior, Aanaes et al. [6] have also solved the multi-resolution fusion problem. Here, the spatial neighborhood weights for the MRF are computed from the Pan image to transfer edge information from the Pan to the fused image.

The LR MS image formation model without decimation is used by Li and Leung [149] who have assumed that the interpolated LR MS image is a degraded version of its fused MS image and hence, they do not consider downsampling operation in their model. Along with the LR MS image formation, they also use the Pan image formation where the original Pan image is modeled as a linear combination of all the bands of the fused MS image. The final cost function is derived using discrete sine transform and the solution is obtained by using the constraint least squares method. A similar model was also employed by Zhou et al. [281] where the gradient field of a modified Pan image is used for spatial enhancement. The modified Pan is obtained using an intensity modulation based fusion method, that is, SFIM proposed by Liu [154]. Here, the author has used the local correlation coefficients between the MS and Pan images to adjust the amount of spatial and spectral details in the fused image. Finally, Zhou et al [281]. obtained the Pan-sharpened or fused image by optimizing the cost function using the gradient descent optimization method.

Zhang et al. [273] have addressed the fusion problem using adjustable model based approach. They modelled the LR MS image as a decimated, blurred and noisy version of its true MS image. Along with this they also included the regularization term related to the modelling of the Pan image which accounts for the spatial detail preservation. A Huber edge-preserving prior is used in the MAP framework to regularize the final solution. The regularization parameters are also estimated to take care of the amount of spectral and spatial details in the Pan-sharpened image. Although this method results in better fusion quality, it uses a prior which requires fine tuning to get better fused image.

Aly and Sharma [22] have proposed a model based approach for Pan-sharpening using the image formation models of LR MS and Pan images. Here, the Pan image formation term in the final cost function includes a high pass filter in order to preserve the high frequency details from the Pan image. In addition to this, they also add the regularization prior term which takes care of adding the spatial details of the Pan image to the fused image based on the correlation between Pan and fused images. Since the final cost function is convex, they use the gradient based optimization method to obtain the final fused image.

There are several model based methods that exploit the variational framework in order to obtain the fusion of MS and Pan images. The approach of total variation (TV) was initially introduced for the regularization of inverse problems by Rudin et al. [201] for solving denoising problem. Due to its ability to preserve sharp discontinuities such as edges, it has obtained greater success in applications such as image restoration, denoising, inpainting, etc. The fusion method based on variational framework was first attempted by Ballester et al. [25] who used the geometric information of the Pan image by aligning the same with each band of MS image. In order to get the spectral information for the fused image, they make the assumption that the Pan image is an approximated linear combination of the high resolution MS images. Other fusion methods based on a similar concept are reported by Moeller et al., Palsson et al., and He et al. [165,180,109]. Moeller et al. [165] combined the idea of wavelet transform for a higher spectral quality and used the concept of variational approach in order to obtain the spatial information. Similarly, Palsson et al. [180] utilized the assumption that a linear combination of the fused images gives the Pan image. In addition to this, they also assumed that the decimation of the Pan-sharpened image gives the observed MS image. Using these assumptions, they cast the fusion problem in a regularization framework where TV prior on fused image is used; this encourages images those are piecewise smooth between edges. Similar assumption was used by He et al. [109]. They incorporate the gradient of the Pan image in addition with that of the high resolution MS image in the form of TV prior to obtain the final fused image. An extension of this work is presented by He et al. [110] who included the total variation sparsity priors, also based on the characteristics of the MS and Pan images.

One of the advantages of the variational framework is that the different constraints can be included in the form of different terms in the objective function which is to be minimized. Fang et al. [72] utilized a few constraints such as that the gradient of the Pan image is a linear combination of the gradient of the true MS image, the upsampled MS image is the degraded version of the true MS image and the gradient of the fused MS band is approximated by that of the uspsampled MS image to obtain the final cost function. They proved the effectiveness of the proposed fusion method by conducting subjective as well as quantitative evaluation on two sets of images acquired using Quickbird and Ikonos satellites. The TV prior is also extended to the non-local TV (NLTV) [156,87] method. A Pan-sharpening method based on the NLTV was proposed by Buades et al. [67]. Here, the final cost function consists of two terms: the first term forces the Pan-sharpened image to be consistent with Pan and MS data, and the second corresponds to a non-local regularization term which acts as a neighborhood filter on the Pan image. The Pan image is used to derive non-local relationships among patches describing the geometry of the desired fused image.

Although TV and NLTV regularization may give better fusion results, they suffer from certain implementation issues. A TV prior has L_1 norm in the regularization term. Although this results in edge preservation, the computational complexity is increased due to the non-differentiability of the term with L_1 norm. The difficulty of non-differentiability can be avoided by the small perturbation in the prior [201]. However, this results in the modification of the original cost function and hence, causes deviation in the required solution [148]. In addition to this, the final output also depends on the value of the regularization parameter. Various methods are proposed in the literature to estimate this regularization parameter [58, 82, 104, 168, 176], which are either computationally expensive or yield an approximate solution. It is interesting to note that though there are various approaches proposed in the literature to minimize the cost function using the TV prior, close form solution does not exist for the cost function with TV prior [255]. Unlike the TV prior which utilizes the same weights as its neighbors, NLTV prior incorporates the non-local interaction among the neighboring pixels and computes the weights accordingly. In order to obtain a better solution using NLTV regularization, the accuracy of this weight function is very important. Researchers often use a reference image with features similar to the original image to estimate the weight function since the original image is unavailable [150]. The NLTV prior also suffers from drawbacks such as the selection of the size of the patch for computing the weight function and window size for computing the image gradients which are set empirically [150]. Besides this, the NLTV regularization algorithms designed for a particular penalty are often not applicable to other functionals [263]. Thus, although TV and NLTV regularization may give better fusion results, they suffer from high computational complexity [46] and implementations issues.

Recently, the use of compressive sensing (CS) theory has become very popular due to its ability to recover unknown sparse signals from a small set of linear projections. The key point of CS theory is sparsity regularization which refers to the characteristic of many natural signals; this makes it suitable to solve the inverse problem. Li and Yang [143] introduced the CS theory to obtain the fusion for remotely sensed images. In this method, a dictionary was constructed using sample images having high spatial resolution. They obtain a fused image as the sparse linear combination of HR patches available in the dictionary. Jiang et al. and Li et al. [116, 147] constructed an overcomplete joint dictionary from the available MS and Pan images and extracted the most relevant spectral and spatial information using L_1 minimization. Similarly, Zhu and Bamler [283] use a dictionary constructed with the Pan image and its downsampled LR version and obtain the fusion by exploring the sparse representation of HR/LR multi-spectral image patches. Cheng et al. [53] used the CS framework with dictionary patches learned from the initial high resolution MS image obtained using the AWLP method [178]. They obtained the final fused image using a trained dictionary obtained from K-singular value decomposition (K-SVD). Iqbal et al. [115] created the over-complete dictionary with basis functions of different transforms such as the discrete cosine transform (DCT), wavelets, curvelets and ridgelets; the best bases for MS and Pan images are obtained with convex optimization. The final fused MS image is obtained by merging the best bases coefficients of Pan and MS bands as per values of the local information parameter. In addition to this, Harikumar et al. [106] used the CS theory in order to obtain the initial HR approximation of the final fused image. The final solution is obtained by forming a cost function where truncated quadratic smoothness prior is used to regularize the solution. A graph cut optimization method is used to obtain the Pan-sharpened image. Very recently, methods based on deep machine learning have been proposed [113, 163, 279]. In these works, the authors trained the network by using the relationship between HR and LR patches of the Pan image. By assuming that the relationship between HR/LR MS image patches is the same as that between HR/LR Pan image patches, the HR MS image is reconstructed from the observed LR MS image using the trained deep network.

Regardless of the fusion classification, most of these fusion techniques required the set of MS images to be perfectly aligned with the Pan image, that is the MS and Pan images have to be registered. The discussion on the different effects of image misregistration on different fusion methods is extensively reviewed in [28]. The image interpolation used in many fusion methods may cause the misregistration between the expanded MS and Pan images. The distortion due to the image interpolation is studied by Aiazzi et al. [14] in case of multi-resolution image fusion. It has been found that the visual and quantitative performances of fusion methods largely depend on interpolation accuracy. Here, the authors have proposed the new bicubic interpolation technique which can perfectly align the expanded MS and Pan images. In this book, we present a few new approaches for fusion in which the registered MS and Pan data are used. However, we do not inject the high frequency details into the interpolated version of the MS image in the proposed model based approaches as done in most of the fusion approaches.

2.4 Hyper-spectral Sharpening Methods

In this section, we briefly review the fusion techniques based on hyper-spectral and multi-spectral images. To enhance the spatial resolution of an HS image, first attempt was made by Gomez et al. [90]. They proposed an approach based on the daubheche4 (db4) wavelet transform. However, the performance of this method is based on spectral resampling which often cause difficulties in increasing the spatial resolution of HS image. Chen et al. [52] proposed a generalized framework to fuse HS and MS images. They divided the HS images into the different groups of MS regions and then merged the two images. Similarly, another framework called hypersharpening was proposed by Selva et al. [209] to fuse the available HS and MS images. Fusion was performed with conventional MRA based approach by synthesizing an HR HS band as a linear combination of available MS images using linear regression.

Many researchers have also solved the HS–MS fusion problem using Bayesian formulation which allows the fusion process to be solved using posterior distribution of the fused image. Since the fusion problem is ill-posed, the Bayesian model allows the use of proper prior distribution of the unknown in order to regularize the solution. The first pioneering work using Bayesian framework was proposed by Hardie et al.[105]. Here, the authors arrived at a cost function using a MAP framework; they then used a stochastic model instead of a linear unmixing model to estimate the unknown HS image. The final cost function to find the unknown HS bands using input HS–MS data is in the domain of principal component analysis (PCA). Later, this idea of fusion based on spectral information of both the input images on a subspace domain was utilized by many researchers. For example, many authors in [275, 276, 274, 277] used the same model which was proposed by Hardie et al. [105] in the wavelet domain to fuse the given HS and MS images. Similarly, Figueiredo and Nowak [79] cast the HS–MS images fusion problem in a restoration framework and obtained the high resolution HS image as a deblurring and denoising problem by using expectation–maximization algorithm.

In addition to the aforementioned methods the idea of spectral unmixing was also explored to fuse the given HS and MS images to obtain the fused HS image. Gross and Schott and Guichard and Malgouyres [101, 102] unmixed the LR HS data and sharpened the abundance maps (i.e., enhanced the spatial resolution of the unknown HR fused image) by fusing the HS image with the HR Pan image using constrained optimization. Similarly, Zhukov et al. applied unmixing on LR HS images using the segmentation of available HR images. They increased the spatial resolution of the LR image by assigning the estimated end-member signatures to the corresponding high resolution pixels of the segmentation maps [286]. Recently, this idea of unmixing based HS–MS fusion has been used in many state-of-the-art fusion methods. These methods are based on obtaining the endmember information and the high resolution abundance matrices from the HS and MS data, respectively. The final fused image is obtained as the product of these two resulting matrices. Berné et al. [30] obtained unmixing of LR HS images using non-negative matrix factorization (NMF); they then used the least squares regression to obtain the high resolution abundance maps from the available MS data. Similarly, Yokoya et al. proposed a scheme of coupled NMF (CNMF) to obtain end-member and abundance matrices via alternating spectral unmixing based on NMF under the constraint of relative spectral response functions of two sensors [267].

Recently, many works on hyper-sharpening have been published based on the sparse representation. The success of fusion methods for MS images based on sparse representation is the main reason behind applying it for fusion of HS and MS images. Grohnfeldt et al. [99, 100] have applied the joint sparsity (J-sparseFI) algorithm [284] to fuse HS and MS images. Grohnfeldt et al. [98] used the J-sparseFI algorithm with CNMF to fuse the two images. Similarly, Akhtar et al. [15] proposed a method based on dictionary learning and sparse coding to obtain the end-member and abundance matrices to obtain the fused image. Moreover, other works based on matrix factorization have also been reported in [126, 258, 137]. There are many methods which use the hybrid theory of subspace transformation and regularization in order to overcome the problem of ill-posedness [253, 251, 16] in HS sharpening. Recently, a Sylvester-equation-based explicit solution was integrated into the Bayesian HS–MS fusion methodology. This method is referred to as a fast fusion based on Sylvester equation (FUSE) [252]; it significantly decreases the computational complexity. Simões et al. [218] proposed a method called HS super-resolution (HySure) that is based on vector total variation based regularization of the spatial distribution of subspace coefficients where the subspace is defined by using singular value decomposition (SVD).

Apart from the above methods, there have been many MS fusion methods which are extended for the fusion of HS and MS images by considering Pan-sharpening as a special case of hyper-sharpening. Some of these representative techniques are proposed [13, 154, 12] which are compared by Yokoya et al. [268] with the other hyper-sharpening methods based on Bayesian, unmixing, matrix factorization and sparse representation. According to the reviews reported by Yokoya et al. [268], representative fusion methods ([13, 154, 12]) perform in the same manner as other hyper sharpening methods.

Although a variety of HS–MS data fusion methods have been proposed by many researchers in the remote sensing community in the last decade, the number of available satellite platforms mounting for capturing both HS and MS imaging sensors is still limited resulting in a limited application area of hyper-sharpening products. On the other hand, the data of MS and Pan are available across the globe and can be used widely. Keeping in mind this perspective, in this book, we have limited our discussion to the fusion approaches of MS and Pan data only.

2.5 Conclusion

Multi-resolution image fusion is an emerging research area, for the fusion community, and has acquired the status of a 'matured problem'. Several survey papers have been published that categorize various approaches for Pan-sharpening or multi-resolution image fusion [278, 66, 238, 65, 139, 226, 239, 103, 271, 240]. Similarly, many books have also been published on the fusion techniques and their applications [188, 20, 164, 221, 35, 47].

In this book, we discuss image fusion techniques based on the use of edge-preserving filters and image formation model. Using edge-preserving filters, we extract the high frequency details from the Pan image and inject them into the upsampled MS image. One of the drawbacks of the fusion methods using edge-preserving filters is that the upsampling operation needs to be performed on the MS image before the injection of high frequencies. In our model based approaches, we bring in the idea of using an initial estimate instead of upsampling which is obtained using the available Pan and MS images only. In addition to this, in order to obtain better preservation of the spatial details in the final fused image, we propose a new prior called Gabor prior. Use of Gabor prior ensures that features at different spatial frequencies of the fused image match those of the available HR Pan image. We also extend our image fusion framework to super-resolution (SR) of natural images. The framework of the model based approach is extended to this case and SR results are obtained.

Chapter 3

Image Fusion Using Different Edge-preserving Filters

In this chapter, we discuss image fusion approaches using two edge-preserving filters, namely, guided filter and difference of Gaussians (DoGs). Since the MS and Pan images have high spectral and high spatial resolutions, respectively, one can obtain the resultant fused image using these two images by injecting the missing high frequency details from the Pan image into the MS image. The quality of the final fused image will then depend on the method used for the extraction of high frequency details and also on the technique for injecting those details into the MS image. In the literature on multi-resolution image fusion, various approaches have been proposed based on the aforementioned process that also include state-of-the-art methods such as additive wavelet luminance proportional (AWLP) [178] and generalized Laplacian pyramid-context based decision (GLP-CBD) [13]. Motivated by these works, we first address the fusion problem by using different edge-preserving filters in order to extract the high frequency details from the Pan image. Specifically, we have chosen the guided filter and difference of Gaussians (DoGs) for detail extraction since these are more versatile in applications involving feature extraction, denoising, etc.

3.1 Related Work

A large number of techniques have been proposed for the fusion of Pan and MS images, which are based on extracting the high frequency details from the Pan image and injecting them into the MS image. They were discussed in detail in the chapter on literature survey. These methods broadly cover categories such as projection substitution methods, that is, those based on principal component analysis (PCA), intensity hue saturation (IHS) [50, 231], and multi-resolution approaches based on obtaining a scale-by-scale description of the information content of both MS and Pan images [144, 174]. Among these, the multi-resolution based methods have proven to be successful [226]. Most multi-resolution techniques are based on wavelet decomposition [144, 174], in which the MS and Pan images are decomposed into approximation and detail sub-bands; the detail sub-band coefficients of the Pan image are injected into the corresponding sub-band of the MS image by a predefined rule in which the MS image is first interpolated to make it to the size of Pan image. This is followed by inverse wavelet transform to obtain the fused image. The concept was taken forward in 'a trous' wavelet transform (AWT) based fusion [11] in which the image is first convolved with a cubic spline filter and decomposed into wavelet planes. The GLP-CBD fusion method [11] is an improved and successful version of AWT. It proposes to add the wavelet coefficients not directly but after weighting them with a constant which is computed based on local correlation of MS and Pan images. Another technique known as AWLP [178], which is also based on AWT method, intends to preserve the spectral signature among the bands of the MS image by injecting high frequency values proportional to their original values. A new multi-resolution based technique, which takes into account the characteristics of multiple information sources simultaneously is introduced by Hu and Li [112]. This method is based on bilateral filters [202]. Though this approach takes into account both MS and Pan images while extracting details, no clear relationship is established between these images.

In this chapter, we discuss two separate fusion approaches based on guided filter and difference of Gaussians, respectively. Since the Pan and MS images correspond to the same scene captured with different sensors, there exists a definite relation between their detail bands. We make use of this relationship in our proposed approach using a multistage guided filter which is similar to the fusion methods on the MRA framework. Assuming that this relationship is linear, we derive a multistage guided filter in which the Pan or MS image is used as guidance image while extracting the details from the other images. Since the details extraction process consist of not only the Pan image but also the MS image, the spatial distortion of the MS image is reduced. The proposed method uses a two stage guided filter. The extracted high frequency details are added to the corresponding MS image to obtain the final fused image.

Similar to the guided filter, the other fusion approach is proposed which is based on using Gaussian filters on Pan image to obtain the difference of Gaussians (DoGs) for extracting the edge details from the Pan image. The difference of Gaussians serves as a band-pass filtering to discard all but a handful of spatial frequencies that are present in the Pan image. In the first level, the Pan image is filtered using a Gaussian kernel; the resulting blurred image is subtracted from the original image to get the first level of high frequency details. We then extract the second level of high frequency details by applying the same procedure on the blurred Pan image. The high frequency details obtained in the first and second levels are merged into the upsampled MS image to get the final result. The advantage of the proposed approach using DoGs is the reduction in spatial degradation of the final fused image due to the use of non-subsampled Pan image while fusing.

3.2   Fusion Using Multistage Guided Filter (MGF)

We propose a multi-resolution image fusion approach based on a multistage guided filter (MGF) wherein we extract the details from MS and Pan images. The detail extraction process exploits the relationship between Pan and MS images by utilizing one of them as a guidance image while extracting details from the other. In this way, the spatial distortion of MS image is reduced by consistently combining the details obtained using both types of images. The final fused image is obtained by adding the extracted high frequency details to the corresponding MS image. The results of the proposed algorithm are compared with traditional and state-of-the art fusion methods using the images captured with different satellites such as Quickbird, Ikonos-2 and Worldview-2. Quantitative assessment is evaluated using conventional measures as well as a relatively new index, that is, quality with no reference (QNR), which does not require a reference image. The results and measures clearly show that there is significant improvement in the quality of the fused image using the proposed approach.

3.2.1 Multistage guided filter (MGF)

The guided filter, which is an edge-preserving smoothing filter, has been introduced by He et al. [108]. They successfully experimented the use of the guided filter for a variety of applications including image enhancement, compression, flash/no-flash de-noising, etc. Later, Li et. al. [146] extended its use for fusion of multifocus, multitemporal, and multiexposure images. Motivated by this, we make use of the guided filter explicitly for fusion of remotely sensed images. In order to extract more meaningful details from these images, we extend the guided filter to multistage form. A brief discussion of the guided filter is given here.

A guided filter uses guidance image I as one of the inputs to the filter in addition to input $\wp$. Given the guidance image, the guided filter output Λ is assumed to be a linear transformation of this image. This transformation is given for a local window v_k centered at a pixel k by He et al. [108]

$$\Lambda_i = a_k I_i + b_k, \forall i \in v_k, \tag{3.1}$$

where Λ_i and I_i represent the ith pixel intensity of the filter output and guidance images, respectively. The size of the window v_k is $r \times r$, where r is an integer. The coefficients a_k and b_k are constants in the window v_k. These constants are estimated by minimizing the squared difference between the output image Λ and input image $\wp$ as

$$E(a_k, b_k) = \sum_{i \in v_k} ((a_k I_i + b_k - \wp_i)^2 + \varepsilon a_k^2), \tag{3.2}$$

where ε is a regularization parameter set by the user. The constants a_k and b_k are given by

$$a_k = \frac{\frac{1}{|v|} \Sigma_{i \in v_k} I_i \wp_i - \mu_k \bar{\wp}_k}{\sigma_k^2 + \varepsilon}, \quad \text{and} \quad b_k = \bar{\wp}_k - a_k \mu_k, \tag{3.3}$$

where σ_k^2 and μ_k are the variance and mean of I in v_k, $|v|$ is the number of pixels in v_k, and $\bar{\wp}_k = \frac{1}{|v|} \Sigma_{i \in \wp_i} \wp_i$ is the mean of $\wp$ in v_k. In equation (3.1), the values of a_k and b_k are the same for all the pixels in the window v_k and they are computed for all the overlapping windows in an image. Due to this, the filter output for the ith pixel (Λ_i) has different values for all the overlapping windows over a pixel i. The obtained values of a_k and b_k for the overlapping windows are averaged first and then used in equation (3.1) to compute the filter output. Then, the final guided filter output can be written as

$$\Lambda_i = \bar{a}_i I_i + \bar{b}_i, \tag{3.4}$$

where $\bar{a}_i = \frac{1}{|v|}\sum_{k \in v_i} a_k$ and $\bar{b}_i = \frac{1}{|v|}\sum_{k \in v_i} b_k$.

For the purpose of fusing Pan and MS images, the guided filter is extended to a multistage form. In order to get adequate amount of extracted details, either the Pan or MS image is used as a guidance image for the other. Since the Pan and MS images have different sizes, resampling is done on the MS image to obtain the same size for both. Moreover, it is worthwhile to mention here that since the spatial resolution of the MS images are poor, meaningful high frequency details are extracted from through their intensity component (INT), which is obtained as the weighted average of all the resampled MS bands. Due to the average operation, the computed intensity component has a spectral response similar to the spectral response of the Pan image, which helps in extracting the possible high frequency details from the MS image when it is used as the guidance image. To describe the multistage form of the guided filter, here we use $F(\wp, I)$ notation as the guided filter function with $\wp$ and I as input and guidance images, respectively. At the first stage ($j = 1$), to extract the details from the Pan image, the intensity component INT is used as guidance image (I) and Pan image is used as an input image ($\wp$). This can be represented as

$$\text{Pan}_A^j = F(\text{Pan}, \text{INT}), \tag{3.5}$$

where Pan_A^j represents the guided filtered output or approximation layer with the Pan image as an input image. Similarly, when the Pan image is used as a guidance image (I) with INT image as an input image ($\wp$), the resulting output MS image is given by

$$MS_A^j = F(\text{INT}, \text{Pan}), \tag{3.6}$$

where MS_A^j denotes the approximation layer with intensity component as an input image. The detail layers at this stage can written as

$$\text{Pan}_D^j \;=\; \text{Pan} - \text{Pan}_A^j \text{ and} \tag{3.7}$$

$$MS_D^j \;=\; \text{INT} - MS_A^j, \tag{3.8}$$

For the jth stage $(j > 1)$, the guided filter equations can be depicted as

$$\text{Pan}_A^j \;=\; F\left(\text{Pan}_A^{j-1}, MS_D^{j-1}\right) \text{ and} \tag{3.9}$$

$$MS_A^j \;=\; F\left(MS_A^{j-1}, \text{Pan}_A^{j-1}\right), \tag{3.10}$$

where Pan_A^{j-1} and MS_A^{j-1} are the approximation layers (guided filtered outputs) with Pan and INT component as input images, respectively for the $(j-1)^{\text{th}}$ level. The detail layers for the jth decomposition stage (Pan_D^j and MS_D^j) for the Pan and the MS images can be expressed as

$$\text{Pan}_D^j \;=\; \text{Pan}_A^{j-1} - \text{Pan}_A^j \text{ and} \tag{3.11}$$

$$MS_D^j \;=\; MS_A^{j-1} - MS_A^j. \tag{3.12}$$

3.2.2 Proposed approach using guided filter

The proposed fusion technique is outlined in Fig. 3.1. A two stage guided filter is used to combine the details of the Pan and MS images in a consistent manner. Note that unlike the conventional methods where the information is extracted from the Pan image and injected into the MS image, the details in the proposed method are extracted from both MS and Pan images in which each one functions as a guidance image. The details are then adjusted using a gaining constant to achieve a fused image with higher spatial as well as higher spectral content. Considering an MS image with l different bands and the Pan image (Pan), the proposed fusion technique obtains the fused image (Z) for each band. The steps of the proposed fusion method can be detailed as follows:

1. The low resolution (LR) MS image is re-sampled to the size of the Pan image by using a suitable interpolation technique (bicubic interpolation is normally preferred).

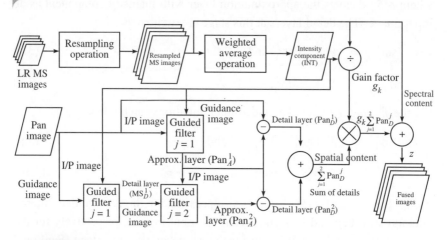

Figure 3.1   Block diagram of the proposed approach using a multistage
guided filter (MGF).

2. Considering the number of MS bands as l, an intensity image INT is
formed using them in order to make same/similar spectral widths for
both MS and Pan images. This is obtained using a weighted average of
the four MS bands [231], that is,

$$\text{INT} = \frac{1}{l} \sum_{k=1}^{l} c_k \cdot MS_k, \tag{3.13}$$

where MS_k, $k = 1,\ldots,l$ denotes the resampled band of the MS image.
$c_k, k = 1,\ldots,l$ are the constants estimated from the spectral response of
MS bands.

3. The intensity component of the MS image (INT) and the Pan image
are used for multistage guided filter decomposition as given in
equations (3.5) to (3.12) and the detail and approximation layers are
obtained. Here, a two stage guided filter decomposition is used.

4. In order to combine the extracted details in a consistent manner, they are
merged band wise using a weighted gain. The gain factor g_k, calculated
separately for each pixel in a band, and the same is given by

$$g_k(i) = \frac{MS_k(i)}{INT(i)} \quad k = 1, \ldots, l, \tag{3.14}$$

where i denotes the pixel location in an image.

5. Finally, the extracted details are merged band wise with the MS image after weighting with g_k as

$$Z_k = MS_k + g_k \sum_{j=1}^{N} \text{Pan}_D^j, \quad k = 1, \ldots, l, \tag{3.15}$$

where N represents the number of stages for the guided filter. Here, the first term (MS_k), that is, the re-sampled MS image contains spectral information while spatial information is carried by the second term, that is, a weighted sum of extracted details.

3.3 Fusion Approach Using Difference of Gaussians (DoGs)

Use of the multistage form of the guided filter to extract details from the Pan image provides improvement in terms of detail extraction. However, due to multistage extension and patchwise computations, it results in increased computations for obtaining the final fused image. In this section, we describe a fast method for multi-resolution image fusion based on the difference of Gaussians (DoGs). The proposed method is based on a two stage form of DoG on the Pan image. First, the Pan image is convolved with a Gaussian kernel to obtain a blurred version and the high frequency details are extracted as first level DoGs by subtracting the blurred image from the original. In order to get the second level DoG, the same steps are repeated on the blurred Pan image. The extracted details at both DoGs are added to the MS image to obtain the final fused image. Experiments have been conducted with different values of standard deviations of Gaussian blur with images captured from different satellite sensors such as Ikonos-2, Quickbird and Worldview-2. The subjective and quantitative assessment show that the proposed technique performs better. It is faster and less complex when compared to recently proposed state-of-the-art techniques.

3.3.1 Difference of Gaussians (DoGs)

Difference of Gaussians (DoGs) involves the subtraction of a Gaussian blurred image from an image which is usually less blurred. The Gaussian blurred image can be obtained by convolving a Gaussian kernel with the input image. The DoG image $\tilde{D}^j(x,y)$ at the jth level can be given as

$$\tilde{D}^j(x,y) = \text{Ł}(x,y,\sigma_1^j) - \text{Ł}(x,y,\sigma_2^j),\tag{3.16}$$

where $\text{Ł}(x,y,\sigma)$ is a blurred image obtained by convolving the input image $I(x,y)$ with the Gaussian kernel $\text{£}(x,y,\sigma_i)$ as

$$\text{Ł}(x,y,\sigma_i^j) = \text{£}(x,y,\sigma_i^j) * I(x,y).\tag{3.17}$$

Here, σ_i^j, $i = 1,2$ are the different values of the standard deviation for the Gaussian kernel at the jth level. Here, $*$ denotes the linear convolution operation. Gaussian blurring suppresses the high-frequency spatial information of the input image. Subtracting one image from the other preserves the spatial information that lies between the range of frequencies that are preserved in the two blurred images. Thus, the DoGs represents a bandpass filter that discards all but the spatial frequencies that are present in the original image. The spreading parameter (σ) of the Gaussian can be chosen to select the edge details within the bandpass region of the Pan image. Fig. 3.2 displays an example of DoGs. In Fig. 3.2(a), we observe the input

(a)   (b)   (c)   (d)

Figure 3.2   Example of DoGs. (a) Input test image, (b) Gaussian blurred image with standard deviation of $\sigma_1 = 4$, (c) Gaussian blurred image with standard deviation of $\sigma_2 = 2$ and (d) DoGs of (b) and (c), shown as inverted pixel intensity values.

test image. Two images blurred with $\sigma_1 = 4$ and $\sigma_2 = 2$ are displayed in Fig. 3.2(b) and (c), respectively. The DoG image is displayed in Fig. 3.2(d).

3.3.2 Proposed approach using DoGs

Difference of Gaussians is widely used for feature extraction and edge detection. In fusion approaches, the high frequency details present in the Pan image are extracted for injecting them in the MS images. In the proposed method, we use the DoGs for extracting these details at two different levels. Since we are interested in extracting high frequency details from the Pan image, the first level of DoG is performed by taking the difference between the original Pan image and its blurred version; the second level of DoG is performed by taking the difference of the second and first level. The extracted details of the first and second levels are merged with the MS image with appropriate weight g_k to get the final result. We conducted the experiments with more than two levels of DoGs but the improvement was not significant with the increased computation cost. Hence, we considered a two stage approach in all our experiments. The block schematic of the proposed method is displayed in Fig. 3.3. The high frequency details extraction from the Pan image using DoGs is shown by the dotted box in Fig. 3.3.

Let the MS image be of size $M \times M$. The high spatial resolution Pan image has a spatial resolution of $qM \times qM$, where q is the resolution difference between the Pan and MS images. The proposed method using DoGs is described in the following steps:

1. The MS image is re-sampled to the resolution of the Pan image using suitable interpolation technique. Here, we use bicubic interpolation since it upsamples the images with reduced artifacts. However, one may use any other suitable interpolation technique as well. The re-sampled MS band is denoted as MS_k, $k = 1, \ldots, l$, where l represents the number of bands.

2. The Pan image ($Pan(x,y)$) is convolved with Gaussian kernel $\pounds(x,y,\sigma_1)$ in order to obtain the blurred version $\pounds_P(x,y,\sigma_1^1)$ which is given as

$$\pounds_P(x,y,\sigma_1^1) = \pounds(x,y,\sigma_1^1) * Pan(x,y). \tag{3.18}$$

3. The first level DoG is obtained by subtracting the blurred Pan image from the original Pan image to obtain the high frequency details as,

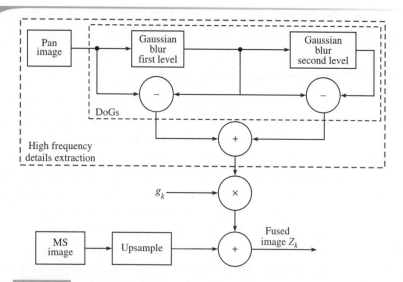

Figure 3.3 Block schematic of the proposed DoGs based approach for k^{th} MS image.

$$\text{Pan}_D^1 = \text{Pan}(x,y) - \text{Ł}_P(x,y,\sigma_1^1). \tag{3.19}$$

4. The Gaussian kernel is again convolved with blurred Pan image $\text{Ł}_P(x,y,\sigma_1^1)$ that gives us the blurred Pan at second level, that is,

$$\text{Ł}_P(x,y,\sigma_2^2) = \text{£}(x,y,\sigma_2^2) * \text{Ł}_P(x,y,\sigma_1^1). \tag{3.20}$$

5. The other possible spatial details at the second level, Pan_D^2, are obtained by performing DoG between $\text{Ł}_P(x,y,\sigma_1^1)$ and $\text{Ł}_P(x,y,\sigma_2^2)$ as

$$\text{Pan}_D^2 = \text{Ł}_P(x,y,\sigma_1^1) - \text{Ł}_P(x,y,\sigma_2^2). \tag{3.21}$$

6. Finally, the extracted details ($\text{Pan}_D^j, j = 1,2$) are combined with the MS image (MS_k) to get the final fused image (Z_k) as

$$Z_k = MS_k + g_k \sum_{j=1}^{2} \text{Pan}_D^j, \quad k = 0,1,\ldots,l. \tag{3.22}$$

Here, g_k represents the gain constant given in equation (3.14).

The same steps are repeated to obtain the fused images for all the acquired MS images.

3.4   Experimental Illustrations

The performance of the proposed fusion methods is evaluated by conducting experiments on the images of different satellite sensors. We use the images captured using Ikonos-2, Quickbird and Worldview-2 satellites. Various details of the data captured using these satellites are listed in Table 3.1. In the experimentations, first MS and Pan images are co-registered. We prepare

Table 3.1   Details of datasets used in experimentation

Satellite	Ikonos-2	Quickbird		Worldview-2
Downloaded from	[2]	[3]	[5]	[4]
Acquired date	February 22, 2003	July 4, 2005	January 28, 2005	October 9, 2011
Area covered	Mount Wellington area near Hobart Tasmania	Area around Boulder city USA	Sundarban India	San Francisco USA
Spatial resolution: MS	4 m × 4 m	2.4 m × 2.4 m		2 m × 2 m
Pan	1 m × 1 m	0.6 m × 0.6 m		0.5 m × 0.5 m
Data format	11-bits	8-bits	11-bits	11-bits
No. of Pan and MS images	1 Pan, 4 bands	1 Pan, 4 bands	1 Pan, 4 bands	1 Pan, 8 bands
Original size: MS	3031 × 3287	828 × 815	4096 × 4096	4096 × 4096
Pan	12124 × 13148	3312 × 3260	16384 × 16384	16384 × 16384

the datasets by cropping the original acquired MS and Pan images into the size of 256×256 and 1024×1024, respectively. Based on Wald's protocol [245], the MS and Pan images are spatially degraded and the experiments are carried out on them to quantitative test the output of the fused results with the true (reference) MS images. In order to do so, we downsample the MS and Pan images by a factor of 4. In all the experiments on the degraded dataset, the size of MS and Pan images are 64×64 and 256×256, respectively. In addition to the degraded dataset experiments, we also conducted the experiments on the un-degraded dataset. Here, the size of MS and Pan images correspond to the size of their originals. The results of the proposed fusion methods are compared with the other approaches on the basis of quality of images in terms of perceptual as well as quantitative measures. The following measures are used for quantitative evaluation for those experiments conducted on degraded images.

- The correlation coefficient (CC) is calculated as,

$$CC = \frac{\sum_{i=1}^{N_1} \sum_{j=1}^{N_2} [Z(i,j) - \bar{Z}][I_{\text{ref}}(i,j) - \bar{I}_{\text{ref}}]}{\sqrt{\sum_{i=1}^{N_1} \sum_{j=1}^{N_2} [Z(i,j) - \bar{Z}]^2} \sqrt{\sum_{i=1}^{N_1} \sum_{j=1}^{N_2} [I_{\text{ref}}(i,j) - \bar{I}_{\text{ref}}]^2}}, \quad (3.23)$$

where I_{ref} and Z denote the reference and fused images with each of size $N_1 \times N_2$, respectively. The $\bar{I}_{\text{ref}}$ and $\bar{Z}$ indicate the mean of reference and fused images, respectively. The correlation coefficient indicates the degree of correlation between I_{ref} and Z. When Z and I_{ref} are the same, the correlation coefficient approaches one.

- The root mean squared error (RMSE) is the intensity difference between two images [178]. It is defined as,

$$RMSE = \frac{1}{N_1 N_2} \sqrt{\sum_{i=1}^{N_1} \sum_{j=1}^{N_2} (I_{\text{ref}}(i,j) - Z(i,j))^2}. \quad (3.24)$$

The ideal value of RMSE is 0 which indicates that the fused image is equal to the reference image.

- ERGAS is an acronym of French expression 'erreur relative globale adimensionnelle de synthese', which translates to 'relative dimensionless global error in synthesis'. It gives a global spectral quality measure of the fused image (Z) [178], which is defined as,

$$ERGAS = 100 \frac{h}{\iota} \sqrt{\frac{1}{l} \sum_{i=1}^{l} (\frac{RMSE^2(i)}{MEAN^2(i)})}, \quad (3.25)$$

where h and ι correspond to spatial resolutions of Pan and MS images, respectively; l is the number of bands of the fused image Z. $\text{MEAN}(i)$ represents the mean value of the ith band of the original MS image and $\text{RMSE}(i)$ indicates the RMSE between the ith band of the original and fused MS images. Note that a smaller value of ERGAS indicates a better fusion result and the ideal value of ERGAS corresponds to zero.

- The average quality (Q_{AVG}) index is defined as the average value of the universal image quality (UIQ) index of each band [178]. UIQ index models the distortion between two images as a combination of distortion due to loss of correlation, luminance and contrast. This index is given as [178]

$$UIQ = \frac{4\sigma_{I_{\text{ref}}Z}\bar{I}_{\text{ref}}\bar{Z}}{(\sigma_{I_{\text{ref}}}^2 + \sigma_Z^2)(\bar{I}_{\text{ref}}^2 + \bar{Z}^2)}, \qquad (3.26)$$

where $\sigma_{I_{\text{ref}}Z}$ denotes the covariance between I_{ref} and Z, $\bar{I}_{\text{ref}}$ and $\bar{Z}$ are the means of I_{ref} and Z, respectively. $\sigma_{I_{\text{ref}}}^2$ and σ_Z^2 are the variances of I_{ref} and Z, respectively. Higher value of UIQ indicates better quality of the fused image. The ideal value of this measure is 1.

In addition to the aforementioned measures, we also perform the quantitative analysis of the fused image by computing a new measure called quality with no reference (QNR), which does not require the reference image.

QNR [19] is defined as

$$QNR = (1 - D_\lambda) \cdot (1 - D_s), \qquad (3.27)$$

where D_s and D_λ are the spatial and spectral distortions of the fused image. The ideal value of QNR is 1. Here, the spatial distortion index (D_s) is calculated as [19]:

$$D_s = \sqrt{\frac{1}{l}\sum_{i=1}^{l}|Q(MS_i, \text{Pan}_{LR}) - Q(Z_i, \text{Pan})|}, \qquad (3.28)$$

where l represents number of MS bands. MS_i and Z_i denote the ith bands of the original and the fused MS images, respectively. Pan is the original Pan image while Pan_{LR} represents the spatially degraded version of the Pan image obtained by passing it through a lowpass filter having normalized cutoff frequency at the resolution ratio between MS and Pan, followed by decimation. $Q(\cdot,\cdot)$ is the quality index defined in equation (3.26). The index D_s attains its minimum value of zero when the quality index are the same for two images. The other quantity, that is, spectral distortion index (D_λ) is calculated as [19]

$$D_\lambda = \sqrt{\frac{1}{l(l-1)} \sum_{i=1}^{l} \sum_{r=1,r \neq i}^{l} |Q(MS_i, MS_r) - Q(Z_i, Z_r)|}. \tag{3.29}$$

Here, D_λ is derived from the difference of inter-band quality index (Q) values calculated using the fused and the original MS bands. The ideal value of D_λ is 0.

The different parameter settings related to our proposed fusion approaches are as follows. In the MGF based fusion method, different sized windows (r) are used for the datasets in the experimentation, while the regularization parameter ε is chosen as 10^{-6} for all the experiments. The values of r are chosen as $2, 7$ and 9 for the experiments on Ikonos-2, Quickbird and Worldview-2 satellite images, respectively. These parameters are selected by trial and error method. In the fusion approach based on DoGs, we use the standard deviation for a Gaussian kernel as 2 and 1 at first and the second stages, respectively, that is, $\sigma_1^1 = 2$ and $\sigma_2^2 = 1$. These values are tuned empirically. We extended the experimentation with more than two levels of DoG; however, the extracted high frequency details after the second DoG level were not very effective in improving the quality of the final fused image. The competence of the proposed fusion methods based on MGF and DoGs are demonstrated by comparing its fusion results with the results of other popular methods such as fast IHS (FIHS) [231], adaptive IHS [192] and AWLP [178].

In the following subsections we present the experimental results obtained using different satellite images. Subsections 3.4.1–3.4.3 discuss the fusion results obtained using the datasets of Ikonos-2, Quickbird and Worldview-2 satellites, respectively. The computational complexity of different fusion methods is the topic of discussion in Subsection 3.4.4.

3.4.1 Experimentations: Ikonos-2 dataset

We evaluate the performance of the proposed methods by conducting experiments on both degraded and un-degraded datasets. Figure 3.4 shows downsampled test MS images for the degraded experiments. We first consider the images captured using Ikonos-2 satellite. The details of data captured using this satellite have been listed in Table 3.1. The downsampled test MS image for this degraded experiment is displayed in Fig. 3.4(a). The fusion results obtained using different methods are displayed in Fig. 3.5 and Fig. 3.6 for degraded and un-degraded datasets, respectively. Here, the results are shown with the color composition of 4, 3 and 2 bands. In Fig. 3.5(a) and Fig. 3.6(a), we display the fusion results obtained using the FIHS

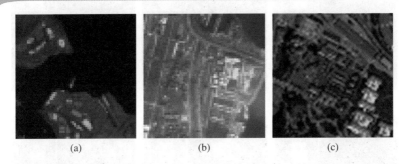

(a)   (b)   (c)

Figure 3.4   Downsampled LR MS images. The LR test MS images of size 64 × 64 obtained using (a) Ikonos-2 satellite shown with the color composition of 4, 3 and 2 bands, (b) Quickbird satellite shown with the color composition of 3, 2 and 1 bands and (c) Worldview-2 satellite shown with the color composition of 5, 3 and 2 bands.

method [231] for degraded and un-degraded cases, respectively. The results of the AIHS method [192] are depicted in Fig. 3.5(b) and Fig. 3.6(b). In addition to this, we have also compared our results with the fusion technique based on wavelet transform [178] and the results for the same are shown in Fig. 3.5(c) and Fig. 3.6(c), respectively. Finally, the results of the proposed fusion approaches using MGF and DoGs are displayed in Fig. 3.5(d, e) and Fig. 3.6(d, e) for degraded and original datasets, respectively. In the experiment of the degraded dataset, the original MS image is available and the same is displayed in Fig. 3.5(f). However, for the un-degraded case, we display the original Pan image in Fig. 3.6(f) in place of the original MS image since we do not have the original MS image. In the results displayed in Fig. 3.5 and 3.6, we show the magnified images corresponding to a small square portion shown with a yellow border in Fig. 3.5(e) and Fig. 3.6(e) and the same are displayed at the top right corner in all the results for better comparison.

The quantitative assessment for these experiments are depicted in Table 3.2.

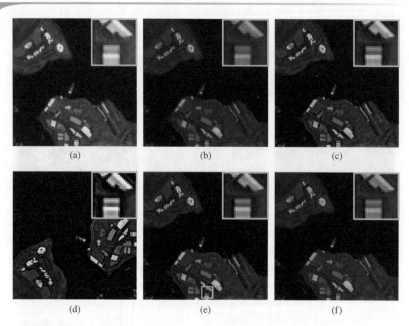

(a)   (b)   (c)

(d)   (e)   (f)

Figure 3.5   Results of the multi-resolution image fusion on the degraded dataset of Ikonos-2 satellite shown with the color composition of 4, 3 and 2 bands. Fusion results of size 256 × 256 obtained using (a) FIHS method [231], (b) AIHS method [192], (c) AWLP approach [178], (d) proposed approach using MGF and (e) proposed method using DoGs. (f) Original MS image of size 256 × 256. The magnified region of a small squared area shown in (e) is displayed at the top right corner. (Courtesy: www.isprs.org)

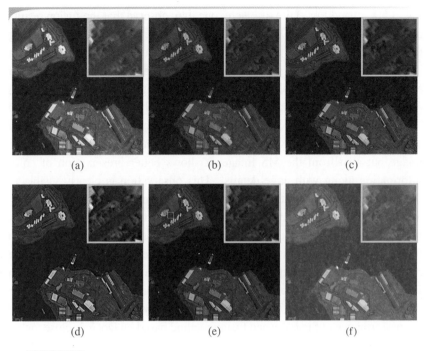

(a)   (b)   (c)

(d)   (e)   (f)

Figure 3.6 Results of the multi-resolution image fusion on the un-degraded dataset of Ikonos-2 satellite shown with the color composition of 4, 3 and 2 bands. Fusion results of size 1024 × 1024 obtained using (a) FIHS method [231], (b) AIHS method [192], (c) AWLP approach [178], (d) proposed approach using MGF and (e) proposed method using DoGs. (f) Original Pan image of size 1024 × 1024. The magnified region of a small squared area shown in (e) is displayed at the top right corner. (Courtesy: www.isprs.org)

The following observations are made from the fusion results displayed in Fig. 3.5 and Fig. 3.6. In the results of the FIHS method [231], which are displayed in Fig. 3.5(a) and Fig. 3.6(a), one can see the preservation of color details along with the spatial contents. Since the approach is based on the spectral response of Ikonos-2 satellite, the results of this method show improvement in the final fused image. By looking at the magnified images, one can compare the results of the FIHS [231] method with the results of the AIHS [192] and AWLP [178] methods, which are displayed in

Fig. 3.5(a–c) and Fig. 3.6(a–c). Here, one may observe that the fusion results obtained using AIHS [192] and AWLP [178] methods lack in preserving the spectral and spatial contents when compared to the FIHS approach [231]. However, one can see an improvement in the results of the proposed MGF based approach, which are displayed in Fig. 3.5(d) and Fig. 3.6(d) for degraded and un-degraded datasets, respectively, over the FIHS method [231]. It is important to note that since the proposed MGF fusion method utilizes the high frequency details which are extracted not only from the Pan image but also from the MS image, it shows better preservation of color information along with edge details. This observation is clearly visible in the magnified images of the proposed MGF fusion method (see Fig. 3.5[d] and Fig. 3.6[d]) which indicates that the results of the proposed MGF fusion method have spatial details such as boundary of houses and streets similar to the Pan image and spectral information close to the original MS image. The results of the proposed fusion method based on DoGs are displayed in Fig. 3.5(e) and Fig. 3.6(e), respectively; its performance is also similar to these methods (AIHS and AWLP). Moreover, it is worthwhile to mention that the performance of the proposed fusion method based on DoGs is close to that of the AWLP method [192], which is a state-of-the-art fusion method.

The quantitative measures for these experiments on degraded and un-degraded datasets are listed in Table 3.2. In this table, we also display the ideal values of these measures within brackets as a reference. Values shown as boldface indicate that they are close to the ideal value. In the experiment of the degraded dataset, the quantitative performance of the proposed fusion method using MGF is better in terms of Q_{AVG} and RMSE. However, for other measures such as CC and ERGAS, the proposed DoGs fusion method performs better when compared to other fusion techniques. For the experiment on the un-degraded dataset, the quantitative evaluation in terms of QNR, D_s and D_λ are better for the proposed fusion approach based on MGF when compared to the other fusion methods. Looking at this quantitative assessment, we can mention the following points. Although the visual assessment of the FIHS method [231] for degraded and un-degraded datasets is better, it lacks in showing better quantitative performance. Moreover, one may notice that though the qualitative performance of the proposed fusion method based on DoGs is close to AIHS [231] and AWLP [178] methods, its quantitative measures have shown improvement in almost all measures except for RMSE. As we can see from Table 3.2, the values of different measures for degraded and un-degraded datasets for the proposed methods are closer to the ideal values when compared to other fusion techniques.

Table 3.2 Quantitative measures for the experiments of the Ikonos-2 dataset shown in Fig. 3.5 and Fig. 3.6

Dataset	Measure	FIHS [231]	AIHS [192]	AWLP [178]	Proposed using MGF	Proposed using DoGs
Degraded	CC(1)	0.980	0.975	0.964	0.973	**0.988**
(Fig. 3.5)	ERGAS(0)	10.929	8.966	5.511	4.160	**4.210**
	$Q_{AVG}(1)$	0.860	0.879	0.896	**0.906**	0.944
	RMSE(0)	21.816	10.544	7.636	**5.645**	8.110
Un-degraded	QNR(1)	0.429	0.583	0.576	**0.640**	0.595
(Fig. 3.6)	$D_s(0)$	0.429	0.287	0.299	**0.228**	0.288
	$D_\lambda(0)$	0.326	0.181	0.177	**0.171**	0.164

3.4.2 Experimentations: Quickbird dataset

The second experiment is conducted on the degraded and un-degraded datasets of the Quickbird satellite which is downloaded from [5]. The details of the data captured using this satellite is presented in Table 3.1. The captured area corresponds to an area of Sundarban, India. In Fig. 3.7 and Fig. 3.8, we display the fusion results with the color composition of 3, 2 and 1 bands. The test MS image for the experiment on the degraded dataset is displayed in Fig. 3.4(b). Similar to the earlier experiments on Ikonos-2 dataset, we compare our fusion results with the recently proposed methods and the same are displayed in Fig. 3.7(a–c) and Fig. 3.8(a–c) for degraded and un-degraded datasets, respectively. The results of the proposed fusion methods based on MGF and DoGs are displayed in Fig. 3.7(d, e) and Fig. 3.8(d, e) for degraded and un-degraded datasets, respectively. For better visualization, a small portion shown in Fig. 3.7(e) and Fig. 3.8(e) with yellow border are magnified and shown in the top right corner of all the results. Looking at the results, the following observations can be made. The results of the FIHS method [231] displayed in Fig. 3.7(a) and Fig. 3.8(a) show poor spectral and spatial contents due to poor injection of details from the Pan to the MS image in this method. Since the detail injection approach uses the model based on spectral response of Ikonos-2 satellite, it results in fused images with distortions when one tries to use it on the data captured using other satellites. These distortions can be seen in the fused images displayed in both Fig. 3.7(a) and Fig. 3.8(a). The other two fusion methods, that is AIHS [192] and AWLP [178], perform better

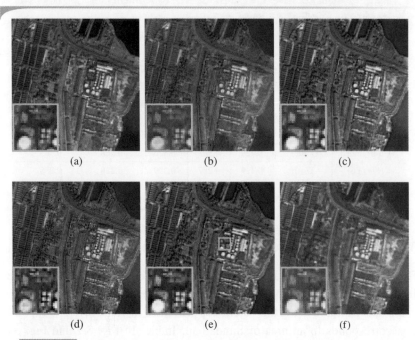

(a)   (b)   (c)

(d)   (e)   (f)

Figure 3.7   Results of the multi-resolution image fusion on the degraded dataset of Quickbird satellite shown with the color composition of 3, 2 and 1 bands. Fusion results of size 256 × 256 obtained using (a) FIHS method [231], (b) AIHS method [192], (c) AWLP approach [178], (d) proposed approach using MGF and (e) proposed method using DoGs. (f) Original MS image of size 256 × 256. The magnified region of a small squared area shown in (e) is displayed at bottom left corner. (Courtesy: www.glcf.umd.edu)

when compared to the FIHS method [231]. Visual observation of the results obtained using the proposed method based on MGF which are displayed in Fig. 3.7(d) and Fig. 3.8(d) indicates that the edges and spectral changes are

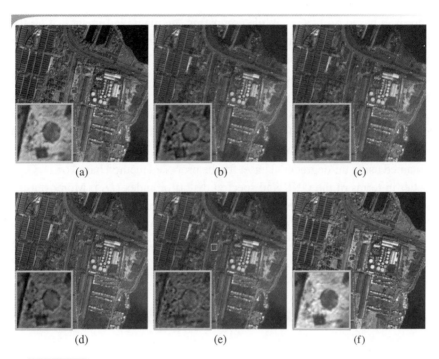

(a)   (b)   (c)

(d)   (e)   (f)

Figure 3.8   Results of the multi-resolution image fusion on the un-degraded dataset of Quickbird satellite shown with the color composition of 3, 2 and 1 bands. Fusion results of size 1024 × 1024 obtained using (a) FIHS method [231], (b) AIHS method [192], (c) AWLP approach [178], (d) proposed approach using MGF and (e) proposed method using DoGs. (f) Original Pan image of size 1024 × 1024. The magnified region of a small squared area shown in (e) is displayed at the bottom left corner. (Courtesy: www.glcf.umd.edu)

better for the proposed fusion method based on MGF when compared to other methods. Similarly, results obtained using the proposed approach based on DoGs (Fig. 3.7[e] and Fig. 3.8[e]) have better preservation of homogenous as well as edge regions. This observation can be easily verified by comparing the magnified images of these results displayed in Fig. 3.7(b, c, e) and Fig. 3.8(b, c, e) for degraded and un-degraded datasets, respectively. Moreover, it is of interest to note that the results of the proposed fusion method based on MGF perform better when compared to that with the other proposed fusion approach based on DoGs. While comparing the magnified images of all the fusion results displayed in Fig. 3.7 and Fig. 3.8, one can say that the results of the proposed fusion approach based MGF and DoGs perform better when compared to that with other methods.

The quantitative analysis for this experiment is depicted in Table 3.3. The values of CC, ERGAS and RMSE measures are better for the proposed method based on MGF. However, Q_{AVG} is highest for the proposed fusion method using DoGs. Similarly, the quantitative evaluation of the results obtained using un-degraded dataset for the proposed method based on DoGs is better in terms of the QNR and spectral distortion index (D_λ). Moreover, the spatial distortion measure (D_s) is lowest for the proposed fusion technique based on MGF. From visual inspection and quantitative analysis, one can conclude that our method on guided filters and difference of Gaussians has noticeable improvement over different regions when we compare the same with the results of other popular fusion methods.

Table 3.3   Quantitative measures for the experiments of Quickbird dataset shown in Fig. 3.7 and Fig. 3.8

Dataset	Measure	FIHS [231]	AIHS [192]	AWLP [178]	Proposed using MGF	Proposed using DoGs
Degraded	CC(1)	0.867	0.917	0.920	**0.942**	0.929
(Fig. 3.7)	ERGAS(0)	6.228	3.996	4.476	**3.874**	4.661
	$Q_{AVG}(1)$	0.892	0.802	0.832	0.845	**0.875**
	RMSE(0)	20.645	13.413	16.037	**12.609**	13.959
Un-degraded	QNR(1)	0.281	0.408	0.410	0.559	0.577
(Fig.3.8)	$D_s(0)$	0.605	0.453	0.447	**0.325**	0.373
	$D_\lambda(0)$	0.288	0.254	0.258	0.171	**0.079**

3.4.3   Experimentations: Worldview-2 dataset

Finally, the last experiment is conducted on the degraded and un-degraded datasets of data captured using Worldview-2 satellite. The original acquired MS and Pan images of this satellite correspond to the area of San Francisco, USA. The spatial resolutions of the images provided by this satellite are highest among the other satellite images which were used in the previous two experiments. The fusion results obtained using different techniques are displayed in Fig. 3.9 and Fig. 3.10, respectively with the color composition of 5, 3 and 2 bands. Similar to the previous two experiments, we display the input MS test image in Fig. 3.4(c) for the experiment on the degraded dataset. In Fig. 3.9(a–c) and Fig. 3.10(a-c), we display the fusion results obtained using different methods such as FIHS [231], AIHS [192] and AWLP [178] for degraded as well as un-degraded datasets. Similar to the earlier experiments on Ikonos-2 and Quickbird satellites, we display the zoomed-in images for a small square area shown in Fig. 3.9(e) and Fig. 3.10(e) with yellow border.

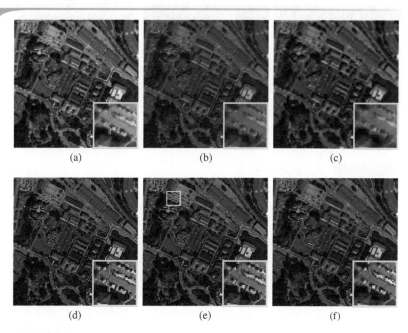

(a) (b) (c)

(d) (e) (f)

Figure 3.9 Results of multi-resolution image fusion on the degraded of dataset Worldview-2 satellite shown with the color composition of 5, 3 and 2 bands. Fusion results of size 256 × 256 obtained using (a) FIHS method [231], (b) AIHS method [192], (c) AWLP approach [178], (d) proposed approach using MGF and (e) proposed method using DoGs. (f) Original MS image of size 256 × 256. The magnified region of a small squared area shown in (e) is displayed at bottom right corner. (Courtesy: www.digitalglobe.com)

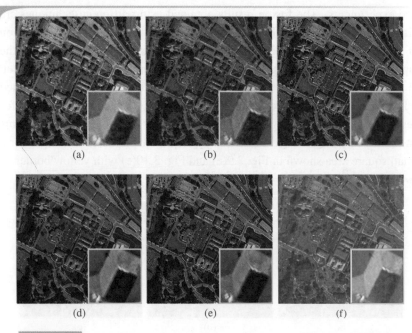

(a)   (b)   (c)

(d)   (e)   (f)

Figure 3.10 Results of multi-resolution image fusion on un-degraded of dataset Worldview-2 satellite shown with the color composition of 5, 3 and 2 bands. Fusion results of size 1024×1024 obtained using (a) FIHS method [231], (b) AIHS method [192], (c) AWLP approach [178], (d) proposed approach using MGF and (e) proposed method using DoGs. (f) Original Pan image of size 1024×1024. The magnified region of a small squared area shown in (e) is displayed at bottom right corner. (Courtesy: www.digitalglobe.com)

By looking at the fusion results obtained using the FIHS method [231], which are displayed in Fig. 3.9(a) and Fig. 3.10(a), we can see that the performance of this method is better for this dataset when compared to the results of AIHS [192] and AWLP [178], which are displayed in Fig. 3.9(b, c) and Fig. 3.10(b, c), respectively. Results of these methods look blurred and also lack of preservation of color details. However, the results of the FIHS fusion method (see Fig. 3.10(a) and Fig. 3.9(a)) appear closer to the original MS image which is displayed in Fig. 3.9(f). Similar observation also holds good for the results obtained using the un-degraded dataset. When we compare the results of our approaches based on MGF and DoGs displayed in Fig. 3.9(d, e) for degraded datasets with the results of all other fusion techniques displayed in Fig. 3.9(a–c), we can observe that performance is improved in terms of the preservation of spatial details with color information. Similarly, we notice the improvement in the results of our methods for the un-degraded case too. One can compare the magnified images of all these results of degraded and un-degraded cases and conclude that the results of proposed fusion techniques using MGF and DoGs have better edge details with spectral information. For example, the zoomed-in images displayed in Fig. 3.10(d–e) show that the fused images in the proposed methods appear sharper and consistent to the Pan image.

The quantitative analysis of these experiments is shown in Table 3.4. For the experiment on the degraded dataset, the measures such as CC and Q_{AVG} are closer to their ideal values for the proposed fusion method based on MGF. Similarly, the ERGAS and RMSE are better for the proposed method using DoGs. For the un-degraded case, all the three measures, that is, QNR, D_s and D_λ are better for proposed fusion method based on DoGs.

Table 3.4   Quantitative measures for the experiments of Worldview-2 dataset shown in Fig. 3.9 and Fig. 3.10

Dataset	Measure	FIHS [231]	AIHS [192]	AWLP [178]	Proposed using MGF	Proposed using DoGs
Degraded (Fig. 3.9)	CC(1)	0.908	0.919	0.916	**0.925**	0.911
	ERGAS(0)	9.031	8.360	7.612	7.334	**7.103**
	$Q_{AVG}(1)$	0.665	0.679	0.675	**0.695**	0.681
	RMSE(0)	30.448	22.320	20.915	19.807	**18.072**
Un-degraded (Fig. 3.10)	QNR(1)	0.4760	0.1587	0.6118	0.6150	**0.6658**
	$D_s(0)$	0.3600	0.5830	0.2390	0.1950	**0.1758**
	$D_\lambda(0)$	0.2550	0.6192	0.1960	0.2360	**0.1921**

It is of interest to note that the proposed fusion method using MGF extracts details from both MS and Pan images and due to this, it results in better fused image. However, in the fusion method using DoGs, the Pan image is used only to extract meaningful details, and performance of this method is slightly poor when compared to the same with MGF fusion method. Although it is worthwhile to mention that the performance of these two fusion methods are considerably improved when compared to the results of other state-of-the-art methods.

3.4.4 Computational complexity

The proposed algorithms as well as those used for comparison are executed on Matlab 7.6 installed on a desktop computer with Intel core 2 Duo processor with 2.4 GHz. The proposed fusion methods are based on simply extracting the details from the Pan image using different filters, and hence, are computationally efficient as compared to different state-of-the-art techniques. However, since the fusion approach based on MGF is based on a multistage filter, it has slightly higher computational complexity when compared to the other approaches. Table 3.5 lists the average time taken to execute the main body of different methods. In this table, one can clearly observe that the average run time for the proposed method based on DoGs is less when compared to other methods.

Table 3.5 Computational complexity of different fusion methods

Method	Average computation time (in seconds)	
	Degraded dataset	Un-degraded dataset
FIHS [231]	0.229	0.570
AIHS [192]	0.789	2.290
AWLP [178]	0.333	0.634
Proposed approach using MGF	1.236	4.896
Proposed approach using DoGs	0.208	0.480

3.5 Conclusion

We have proposed two fusion methods, based on, guided filter and difference of Gaussians. The multistage form of the guided filter is introduced to extract details from Pan and MS images. Similarly, DoGs have been used to extract high frequency details from the Pan image. The extracted details are transferred to the MS image via a weighted average gain factor. The results have been compared with state-of-the-art methods by conducting experiments on images of Quickbird, Ikonos-2 and Worldview-2 satellites. Comparison based on perceptual and quantitative measures clearly shows improvement in the quality of fused image obtained using the proposed fusion methods based on MGF and DoGs. From the displayed results, quantitative measures and the computational complexity analysis, one can say that the performance of the proposed fusion methods based on MGF and DoGs is better, faster and less complex when compared to the state-of-the-art methods.

Chapter 4

Image Fusion
Model Based Approach with Degradation Estimation

Recently, many researchers have attempted to solve the problem of multi-resolution image fusion by using model based approaches, with emphasis on improving the fused image quality and reducing color distortion [273, 121]. They model the low resolution (LR) MS image as a blurred and noisy version of its ideal high resolution (HR) fused image. Solving the problem of fusion by the model based approach is desirable since the aliasing present due to undersampling of the MS image can be taken care of while modelling. Fusion using the interpolation of MS images and edge-preserving filters as given in Chapter 3 do not consider the effect of aliasing which is due to undersampling of MS images. The aliasing in the acquired image causes distortion and, hence, there exists degradation in the LR MS image. In this chapter, we propose a model based approach in which a learning based method is used to obtain the required degradation matrix that accounts for aliasing. Using the proposed model, the final solution is obtained by considering the model as an inverse problem. The proposed approach uses sub-sampled as well as non sub-sampled contourlet transform based learning and a Markov random field (MRF) prior for regularizing the solution.

4.1   Previous Works

As stated earlier, many researchers have used the model based approach for fusion with the emphasis on improving fusion quality and reducing color distortion [6, 149, 105, 273, 143, 116, 283, 76, 121]. Aanaes et al. [6] have proposed a spectrally consistent method for pixel-level fusion based on the model of the imaging sensor. The fused image is obtained by optimizing an energy function consisting of a data term and a prior term by using pixel neighborhood regularization. Image fusion based on a restoration framework is suggested by Li and Leung [149] who modelled the LR MS image as a blurred and noisy version of its ideal. They also modelled the Pan image as a linear combination of true MS images. The final fused image was obtained by using a constrained least squares (CLS) framework. The same model with maximum *a posteriori* (MAP) framework was used by Hardie et al. and Zhang et al. [105, 273]. Hardie et al. [105] used the model based approach to enhance the hyper-spectral images using the Pan image. Their framework takes care of enhancement of any number of spectral bands. Zhang et al. [273] used the same model as Hardie et al.'s for fusion and regularized the solution with a Huber–Markov prior. They also estimated the regularization parameters adaptively with the use of spectral response of the sensor.

    Joshi and Jalobeanu [121] used the LR MS image formation process with a linear model and solved the problem of fusion by applying a discontinuity preserving prior under the regularization framework. An inhomogeneous Gaussian Markov random field (IGMRF) was used as a prior and its parameters were estimated using a Pan image that had high spatial resolution. However, since the learning of the spatial relationship is entirely based on the Pan data, it adds to spectral distortion in the fused image. The fusion performance of this method is also affected due to the approximate parameters estimation using maximum likelihood. Moreover, the method is computationally taxing since IGMRF parameters are estimated at every location in the image. Instead of using approximate IGMRF parameters derived using the Pan image, in this chapter, we make use of a transform domain method in order to extract the high frequency details from the Pan image. In what follows, we briefly explain few fusion techniques that are based on transform domain.

    The favorable time–frequency localization to express the signal locally makes the wavelet a candidate for multi-sensor image fusion. However, wavelet bases are isotropic and represent limited directions. Therefore, they fail to represent the anisotropic edges and contours that are present in the images optimally. To this end, MRA based fusion methods using other transforms such as curvelet [57] and contourlet [210] transform have been also proposed. The contourlet transform (CT) has the characteristics of localization, multi-direction and anisotropy. The CT provides an asymptotic optimal representation of contours and it has been efficiently applied in many image fusion techniques. However, the CT lacks shift-invariance which causes energy content at different levels of decomposition to differ. Hence, its performance while fusing MS and Pan images may be slightly inferior when compared to non-subsampled CT (NSCT). In NSCT, input to filter banks is applied without sub-sampling, which makes it shift-invariant and hence, it performs better. Fusion methods based on these transforms are reported by Shah et al., Shi et al. and Mahyari and Yazdi [210, 213, 159].

Shah et al. [210] obtained enhancement in spectral and spatial information by using principal component analysis (PCA) and non-subsampled CT. Here, all the detail coefficients at different scales of histogram that match the Pan image are injected into the MS image. A similar approach is presented by Shi et al. [213], where the first principal component, that is, PC^1 is also decomposed using NSCT and the details are injected based on local variance of Pan details and PC^1. Mahyari and Yazdi [159] obtained the fused image by using both spectral and spatial similarity. They decomposed the Pan and MS images using NSCT and the detail coefficients of the Pan image are injected into the MS image based on spatial similarity measure. Here, the authors assumed that the spectral frequency bands of the MS images are the same as the NSCT filter bank outputs. All these approaches do not consider the aliasing and blurring present in the low resolution MS image and hence, do not solve the problem of ill posedness, which is inherently present in multi-resolution fusion. Although they use CT, no attempt is made to minimize the aliasing effect by exploiting the relationship between LR and HR MS images.

In this chapter, we present a model based approach that uses subsampled as well as non-subsampled CT for edge preservation. In our work, we first obtain a close approximation (initial estimate) to the final fused image using the available Pan, MS image and the CT/NSCT, which is then used in deriving the relation between LR and HR MS images and also the edges in the final fused image. We assume that the derived initial estimate has the desirable global characteristics of the fused image. The final fused MS image is obtained by regularization for which we use a homogenous MRF prior that requires simple gradient based optimization in order to obtain the final solution. By learning the edge details, we can take care of the edge preservation in the final fused image by regularizing only the non-edge regions, which do not need computationally taxing optimization. This is possible because our method uses CT/NSCT in order to obtain an initial estimate of the fused image that has strong edges. Our approach discussed in this chapter differs from other CT based approaches and has the following advantages.

- Since we consider not only the Pan image but also the MS images while obtaining the initial estimate, it captures the smooth contours (i.e., spatial dependencies) as well as the sharp edges effectively while still preserving the spectral content.

- Use of a homogeneous MRF prior reduces computational complexity. Though the prior is homogeneous MRF, the method still takes care of preserving-edge pixels.

- Use of a Canny edge detector, which is an optimum edge extractor, to locate the edge pixels in the initial estimate and retaining them as edges in the final fused image gives better edge details in the final solution.

- Optimization is carried out only on those pixels which do not belong to edges. This avoids oversmoothing of edge regions.

- Our method uses a degradation matrix estimated using the available MS image and the initial estimate; thus, it avoids the need for assuming the degradation matrix in the MS image formation process. The advantage here is that the degradation matrix is estimated from the given data itself and this leads to an accurate estimation of the fused image.

- The proposed approach preserves edge details without using computationally taxing optimization methods [195, 194].

4.2   Description of the Proposed Approach Using Block Schematic

The block schematic of our proposed multi-resolution fusion is shown in Fig. 4.1 in which an mth low resolution MS image and the Pan image are fused giving Z_m as the fused image. The initial approximation of the fused image (initial estimate) obtained using CT/NSCT is used to recover the high frequency details for the fused MS image. Using the initial estimate and the given LR MS image, the degradation matrix entries are estimated by posing it as a least squares problem. This degradation matrix gives us the relationship between the LR and HR MS images. The discontinuities in the final fused image correspond to the edge pixels in the initial estimate. A Canny edge detector is used to extract those edge details from the initial estimate. The final solution is obtained by using the maximum *a posteriori* Markov random field (MAP–MRF) formulation in which the MRF prior parameter is estimated using the initial estimate image. With this framework, the final cost function consists of a data fitting term and the MRF prior term. Here, data fitting term forms the likelihood function. This cost function is optimized using a gradient based optimization technique in order to smooth only the non-edge regions. Doing so preserves the homogeneity as well as the edges in the final fused image without affecting the spectral content in the MS image.

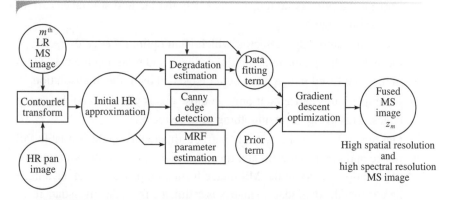

Figure 4.1   Block schematic of the multi-resolution fusion process for fusing an mth MS image and the Pan image. Here, LR and HR correspond to low resolution and high resolution, respectively. The process is repeated for each MS image to obtain a fused image separately for each of the LR observations.

4.3   Background: Contourlet Transform (CT)

In image modelling, simple models are used to capture the defining characteristics of complex natural images. Because of the inherent difficulty in modelling edges and texture directly in space due to their highly complex nature of inter-dependencies between image pixels, models are often constructed in certain transform domains such as Fourier or wavelet domain, where the energy density has a more localized structure. Although these transforms can efficiently capture the intrinsic geometrical structures in natural images in terms of edge details, they have limited directions. *Contourlet transform (CT)* and *non-subsampled CT (NSCT)* [61,59], which are defined using a rich set of basis images, effectively capture smooth contours in various directions that are the dominant features of natural images. A difference between contourlets and other multiscale directional systems is that the CT uses iterated filter banks, which makes it computationally efficient. The NSCT is the shift invariant version of CT that avoids using subsampling. These contourlet transforms not only have the advantages of multi-scale and time-frequency localization properties of wavelets, but they also provide a high degree of directionality and anisotropy. CT and NSCT employ a directional filter bank (DFB) and non-subsampled DFB (NSDFB) that capture the edges in the different directions by linking the point discontinuities into linear structures. More details on CT and NSCT can be found in other works [62, 26, 38, 59].

4.4   Contourlet Transform Based Initial Approximation

Approaches based on multi-scale models (MSMs) are popular among the fusion community. The first MSM which is still widely used by researchers refers to the wavelet transform (WT) based model. It has the properties of multi-scale analysis and time-frequency localization. However, use of WT in the fusion process only preserves the edge details present in the horizontal, vertical and diagonal directions. One can overcome this limitation by using contourlet transform (CT) and non-subsampled CT (NSCT). In our work, we obtain the initial estimate of the Pan-sharpened image using contourlet transform.

We now explain the contourlet transform based method to obtain the initial estimate of the fused image for the given LR MS image of size $M \times M$. It may be mentioned here that though this procedure is explained using CT, it can be easily extended to the non-subsampled case by using the CT without downsampling at every level. The following procedure is used to obtain the initial estimate. The contourlet decomposition is done on the LR MS and the Pan images. We take two level CT on the given low resolution MS image, which is shown in Fig. 4.2(a). Here, sub-band 0 corresponds to the

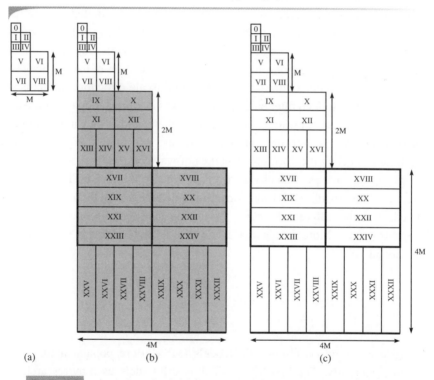

(a)   (b)   (c)

Figure 4.2 Learning the initial approximation to the final fused image (initial estimate) using contourlet transform. (a) Two level contourlet decomposition of an MS image, (b) four level contourlet decomposition of the initial estimate. Here, the shaded area sub-bands coefficients are to be learned from contourlet decomposition of the Pan image and (c) four level contourlet decomposition of the Pan image.

coarsest sub-band. The sub-bands I–IV represent the directional sub-bands for first level contourlet decomposition and the sub-bands V–VIII correspond to those at the second level. Considering a resolution difference of 4 between the Pan and MS, the available Pan image of size $4M \times 4M$ is subjected to four levels of contourlet decomposition (see Fig. 4.2(c)). Looking at both the computation complexity and the need for capturing the high frequency details, we use eight directional filters at the third level and sixteen at the fourth level while decomposing the Pan image. One may also compute the dominant directions of the initial estimate and use an adaptive contourlet based approach in order to learn the edge details [216]. However, due to the adaptive property, computational complexity is increased. We have refrained from doing it since finding the dominant directions can be considered as a significant work by itself. Similar to the MS image, the sub-band 0 represents the coarsest sub-band in Fig. 4.2(c), while the sub-bands I–IV and V–VIII correspond to first and second level decompositions, respectively. The sub-bands IX–XVI and XVII–XXXII correspond to third and fourth level decompositions of the Pan image. In Fig. 4.2(b), we show the four level contourlet decomposition of the initial estimate to be obtained using Pan and MS image decompositions. In the LR MS image, lower frequencies are intact while high frequencies are missing. These missing frequencies can be obtained from the Pan data by using our learning approach. In order to do this, the low frequency details are duplicated in the initial estimate from the sub-bands 0–VIII of the MS image contourlet decomposition. The missing high frequency details, that is, CT coefficients of level 3 and 4, which is shown as the shaded area in Fig. 4.2(b), are obtained by copying the contourlet transform coefficients of the Pan image that correspond to the third and fourth levels (sub-bands IX–XXXII) of the initial estimate. If we denote the sub-band 0 of the MS image contourlet transform decomposition as $\Psi_0 \atop MS$, then one can describe the learning process as follows. The sub-bands 0–VIII of the initial estimate are copied from the sub-bands 0–VIII of the contourlet decomposition of the MS image, that is,

$$\Psi_i \atop \text{INT.} \quad := \quad \Psi_i \atop \text{MS}, \quad i = 0, \text{I}, \text{II}, \ldots, \text{VIII}. \tag{4.1}$$

In the above equation (4.1), $\Psi_i \atop \text{INT.}$ denotes the ith sub-band of the initial estimate for the given MS band image. The sub-bands IX–XXXII of the Pan image contourlet decomposition are copied into the corresponding sub-bands of the initial estimate, that is,

$$\Psi_{\substack{i \\ \text{INT.}}} := \Psi_{\substack{i \\ \text{PAN}}}, \quad i = \text{IX}, \text{X}, \text{XI}, \ldots, \text{XXXII}. \tag{4.2}$$

Here, $\Psi_{\substack{i \\ \text{PAN}}}$ is the ith sub-band of the Pan image contourlet decomposition. Once the contourlet coefficients of the initial estimate are obtained, the inverse contourlet transform is taken to obtain the initial estimate in the spatial domain. This process is repeated for all the MS image bands. It is worthwhile to mention here that it is not possible to obtain the true edge details of the final fused image. Hence, one has to look for those edge details that better approximate the edges in the final solution. Since the CT/NSCT gives better directional details, it is reasonable to assume that the edges in the initial estimate correspond to true edges. A Canny edge detector is then used to obtain the edges from this initial estimate. Here, one may argue about the appropriateness of Canny edge filter for edge preservation. However, it is well known that Canny edge detector is an optimum edge detector and it performs better under noisy conditions. Moreover, it minimizes the amount of false edges due to a number of reasons [169, 217]. In order to set a proper threshold value while extracting the edges from the initial estimate using the Canny edge detector, we first extract the edges of the given Pan image in which a proper threshold is selected to get the edges. The same threshold is then used on the initial estimate. Note that performing edge operation on the Pan is an offline operation.

4.5   Forward Model and Degradation Estimation

Since we cast our problem in a restoration framework, solving such a problem needs a forward model that represents the image formation process. Let l be the number of low-resolution MS images Y_m $(m = 1, 2, \ldots, l)$, each captured with a different spectral band, of size $M \times M$ and Z_m be the corresponding fused HR MS image of size $qM \times qM$, where q is the decimation factor representing the spatial resolution difference between the LR and HR fused images. The forward model for the image formation can be written as

$$\mathbf{y}_m = A_m \mathbf{z}_m + \mathbf{n}_m, \quad m = 1, 2, \ldots, l. \tag{4.3}$$

In equation (4.3), $\mathbf{y}_m$ and $\mathbf{z}_m$ represent the lexicographically ordered vectors of size $M^2 \times 1$ and $q^2 M^2 \times 1$, respectively. A_m is the degradation matrix of size $M^2 \times q^2 M^2$, which accounts for aliasing and blur. In equation (4.3), $\mathbf{n}_m$ is the independent and identically distributed (i.i.d.) noise vector with zero mean and variance $\sigma_{n_m}^2$; it has the same size as $\mathbf{y}_m$. The multivariate noise probability density of $\mathbf{n}_m$ is given by

$$P(\mathbf{n}_m) = \frac{1}{(2\pi\sigma_{n_m}^2)^{\frac{M^2}{2}}} e^{-\frac{1}{2\sigma_{n_m}^2}\mathbf{n}_m^T \mathbf{n}_m}. \tag{4.4}$$

Now, the problem can be stated as follows. Estimate the fused image $\mathbf{z}_m$ given $\mathbf{y}_m$. This is clearly an ill-posed inverse problem and needs an additional constraint in the form of a regularization prior to solve it. In order to obtain the solution by regularization, one has to know A_m. However, this is unknown since we do not have the fused MS image. Since, we already know the approximation (initial estimate) to the fused image, we use it for estimating A_m. One may write A_m as

$$A_m = D_m H_m, \quad m = 1, 2, \ldots, l, \tag{4.5}$$

where D_m is the decimation matrix of size $M^2 \times q^2 M^2$ and H_m is the blur matrix of size $q^2 M^2 \times q^2 M^2$, which is assumed to be space invariant. While solving the fusion problem, H_m is usually considered as an identity matrix [121]. However, in this work, a non-identity blur matrix is assumed. When one assumes aliasing as the averaging of appropriate HR pixels, then for a decimation factor of q, the corresponding decimation/aliasing matrix can be written as [206]

$$D_m = \frac{1}{q^2} \begin{pmatrix} 1\,1\ldots 1 & & & \mathbf{0} \\ & 1\,1\ldots 1 & & \\ & & \ddots & \\ \mathbf{0} & & & 1\,1\ldots 1 \end{pmatrix}. \tag{4.6}$$

In our work, we consider decimation which has a different form for D_m as given in equation (4.7). By considering the LR pixel as a linear combination of q^2 HR pixels with appropriate weights $a_i, i = 0, 1, \ldots, q^2$, we choose D_m as

$$D_m = \begin{pmatrix} a_1^m\, a_2^m \cdots a_{q^2}^m & & & \mathbf{0} \\ & a_1^m\, a_2^m \cdots a_{q^2}^m & & \\ & & \ddots & \\ \mathbf{0} & & & a_1^m\, a_2^m \cdots a_{q^2}^m \end{pmatrix}, \qquad (4.7)$$

where $|a_i| \leq 1, i = 1, 2, \ldots q^2$. Note that equation (4.7) replaces the averaging effect (equal weights) as given in equation (4.6) by unequal weights. This matrix using unequal weights models the distortion caused due to aliasing that happens because of undersampling of the MS image. It is of interest to compare the fusion results obtained using equation (4.7) and equation (4.6); we discuss just such a comparison in the experimental section for $q = 4$. By assuming a space invariant blur, the blur matrix H_m has the form

$$H_m = \begin{pmatrix} H_0^m & H_{qM^2-1}^m & H_{qM^2-2}^m \cdots & H_1^m \\ H_1^m & H_0^m & H_{qM^2-1}^m \cdots & H_2^m \\ \vdots & \vdots & \vdots & \cdots & \vdots \\ H_{qM^2-1}^m & H_{qM^2-2}^m & H_{qM^2-3}^m \cdots & H_0^m \end{pmatrix}, \qquad (4.8)$$

where $m=1, 2, \ldots, l$ and each H_j can be written as

$$H_j^m = \begin{pmatrix} h_{j,0}^m & h_{j,q-1}^m & h_{j,q-2}^m \cdots & h_{j,1}^m \\ h_{j,1}^m & h_{j,0}^m & h_{j,q-1}^m \cdots & h_{j,2}^m \\ \vdots & \vdots & \vdots & \cdots & \vdots \\ h_{j,q-1}^m & h_{j,q-2}^m & h_{j,q-3}^m \cdots & h_{j,0}^m \end{pmatrix}. \qquad (4.9)$$

Here, $h_{..}$ are the values of the point spread function (PSF) for blur. Since we consider a space invariant blur, H_m is block circulant. The multiplication of D_m and H_m results in an A_m matrix which is given by

$$A_m = \begin{pmatrix} A_1^m & A_2^m & \cdots & A_{q^2M^2-1}^m & A_{q^2M^2}^m \\ A_{q^2M^2-q+1}^m & \cdots & A_1^m & A_2^m \cdots & A_{q^2M^2-q}^m \\ \vdots & \vdots & & \vdots & \vdots \\ \cdots & \cdots & \ldots A_1^m & \cdots & \cdots \end{pmatrix}. \qquad (4.10)$$

As an example, if we consider $M = 2$ and $q = 2$, the A_m matrix has a size of 4×16 and can be written as

$$A_m = \begin{pmatrix} A_1^m & A_2^m & A_3^m & A_4^m & A_5^m & A_6^m & A_7^m & A_8^m & A_9^m & A_{10}^m \\ A_{15}^m & A_{16}^m & A_1^m & A_2^m & A_3^m & A_4^m & A_5^m & A_6^m & A_7^m & A_8^m \\ A_9^m & A_{10}^m & A_{11}^m & A_{12}^m & A_{13}^m & A_{14}^m & A_{15}^m & A_{16}^m & A_1^m & A_2^m \\ A_7^m & A_8^m & A_9^m & A_{10}^m & A_{11}^m & A_{12}^m & A_{13}^m & A_{14}^m & A_{15}^m & A_{16}^m \end{pmatrix}$$

$$\begin{pmatrix} A_{11}^m & A_{12}^m & A_{13}^m & A_{14}^m & A_{15}^m & A_{16}^m \\ A_9^m & A_{10}^m & A_{11}^m & A_{12}^m & A_{13}^m & A_{14}^m \\ A_3^m & A_4^m & A_5^m & A_6^m & A_7^m & A_8^m \\ A_1^m & A_2^m & A_3^m & A_4^m & A_5^m & A_6^m \end{pmatrix}. \qquad (4.11)$$

We estimate the entries in equation (4.10) using the available LR MS image and initial HR estimate image. Since the matrix in equation (4.10) has lasser number of rows than the number of columns, least squares with the constraint as minimum norm has been used for the estimation of A_m. In the literature, various algorithms are proposed to estimate the same. However, we use the technique given by Katsikis and Pappars [125], which is computationally very efficient compared to other methods. Inclusion of a non-identity blur matrix leads to under determinant set of equations. It is worthwhile to mention here that we are not assuming the known entries for D_m and H_m matrices; instead, we estimate them from the available data, that is, by using LR observation and the initial estimate (Z_m^0). Many researchers consider an identity matrix for blur which is not true in practice. Hence, the estimated A_m matrix as used in our approach is closer to the true degradation.

4.6 MRF Prior Model

In order to obtain a regularized estimate of the high-resolution fused image, we define an appropriate prior term using MRF modelling. MRF provides a convenient and logical approach to model context dependent entities such as pixel intensities, depth of the object and other spatially correlated features [145]. Conditional random fields (CRFs) also have been used as priors in solving many of the problems in image processing applications. Though it is a good idea to use CRF on fused MS images that depend on the LR resolution MS image, it is difficult to obtain true dependency between them. Moreover, when we model an entity using CRF, the parameter estimation requires the use of a computationally taxing partition function [135]. In this work, we prefer to use an MRF model which does not require LR observations for parameter estimation. The computational complexity is also reduced additionally by the use of a homogeneous MRF where a single MRF parameter is estimated. An MRF prior for the unknown fused HR image can be described by using an energy function U expressed as a Gibbsian density given by

$$P(\mathbf{z}_m) = \frac{1}{Z_{m\theta}} e^{-U(\mathbf{z}_m)}, \tag{4.12}$$

where $\mathbf{z}_m$ is the fused HR image to be estimated and $Z_{m\theta}$ is the partition function. One can choose U as a quadratic form with a single global parameter, assuming that the images are globally smooth. A method of specifying the MRF prior involves considering the pairwise cliques c on a neighbourhood and imposing a quadratic cost, which is function of finite difference approximations of the first order derivative at each pixel location. This constitutes a homogeneous and non-edge-preserving smoothness prior. By using first order neighbourhood, the energy function corresponding to the MRF prior for the mth fused image can be written as

$$U(\mathbf{z}_m) = \sum_{c \in C} V_c(\mathbf{z}_m) =$$

$$\gamma_m \sum_{k=1}^{qM} \sum_{l=1}^{qM} [(Z_{m(k,l)} - Z_{m(k,l-1)})^2 + (Z_{m(k,l)} - Z_{m(k-1,l)})^2], \tag{4.13}$$

where γ_m represents the MRF parameter that indicates the penalty for departure from smoothness in $\mathbf{z}_m$. C indicates a set of all cliques. The MRF parameter γ_m is known if the fused image is known. In our work, since the initial estimate is already available, we make use of the same to estimate γ_m. We use maximum pseudo likelihood for estimating it [145].

It is worthwhile to mention a few points on the various fusion techniques proposed using the discontinuity preserving priors. In order to obtain a better fusion, researchers have used different types of discontinuity preserving priors. In these techniques, the resulting cost function may be convex or non-convex. When the cost function is non-convex, computationally taxing optimization techniques are required to obtain the final solution [195, 193, 86]. A Huber–MRF is an edge-preserving prior and it is convex. Hence, it could be a good choice for edge preservation which allows us to minimize the cost function by using a gradient descent technique [207, 273]. However, the performance of this prior is highly dependent on the selection of the threshold used in defining the prior. Moreover, the use of a single threshold cannot take care of preserving the edges having different gradients present in the image. The estimation of this threshold is a very challenging task and it is image dependant. In our approach, we avoid using such threshold based edge preservation.

Similar to a Huber prior, one may argue for the use of total variation (TV) [201] or non local total variation (NLTV) [156, 87] as the discontinuity preserving prior for edge preservation. The TV prior, first proposed by Rudin et al. [201], has L_1 norm in the regularization term. Although this results in edge preservation, the computational complexity is increased due to the non-differentiability of the term which has L_1 norm. Non-differentiability can be avoided by a small perturbation in the prior [201]. However, this results in the modification of the original cost function and hence, causes deviation in the required solution [148]. In addition to this, the final output also depends on the value of the regularization parameter. Various methods are proposed in the literature to estimate this regularization parameter [58, 82, 104, 168, 176] which are either computationally expensive or yield approximate solutions. It is interesting to note that though there are various approaches proposed in the literature to minimize the cost function while using the TV prior, close form solution does not exist for the cost function [255]. Unlike the TV prior which utilizes same weights for its neighbours, NLTV prior incorporates the nonlocal interaction among the neighbouring pixels and computes weights accordingly. In order to obtain a better solution using NLTV regularization, the accuracy of this weight function is very important. Researchers often use a reference image with features similar to the original image to estimate the weight function since the original image is unavailable [150]. The NLTV prior also suffers from drawbacks such as the selection of the size of the patch for computing the weight function and the window size for computing the image gradients and these are set empirically [150]. Besides this, the NLTV regularization algorithms designed for a particular penalty are often not applicable to other functionals [263]. Thus, although TV and NLTV regularization may give better fusion results, they suffer from high computational complexity [46] and implementations issues. Due to these reasons, we have resorted to a very simple approach for edge-preserving fusion. The edges in the final fused image in the proposed method are obtained by extracting them from an initial estimate which itself is dependent on the given high resolution data, that is, the Pan image. The extracted edges are preserved in the final fused image by retaining the edges corresponding to the initial estimate and by applying MRF regularization on the homogenous regions only. This gives an advantage in terms of using gradient based techniques for optimization and preserving the edges in the final solution.

4.7   MAP Estimation and Optimization Process

4.7.1   MAP estimation

The MRF model on the fused image serves as the prior for the MAP estimation in which the prior parameter is already known. The data fitting term contains the degradation matrix estimated using the initial estimate. In order to use maximum *a posteriori* estimation for the mth HR fused image, we need to obtain the estimate as

$$\hat{\mathbf{z}}_m = \underset{\mathbf{z}_m}{\arg\ \max} P(\mathbf{z}_m / \mathbf{y}_m). \tag{4.14}$$

Using Bayes' rule, we can write,

$$\hat{\mathbf{z}}_m = \underset{\mathbf{z}_m}{\arg\ \max} \frac{P(\mathbf{y}_m / \mathbf{z}_m) P(\mathbf{z}_m)}{P(\mathbf{y}_m)}. \tag{4.15}$$

While maximizing over all $\mathbf{z}_m$, the denominator in equation (4.15) becomes a constant. Hence, we can write

$$\hat{\mathbf{z}}_m = \underset{\mathbf{z}_m}{\arg\ \max} P(\mathbf{y}_m / \mathbf{z}_m) P(\mathbf{z}_m). \tag{4.16}$$

Now taking the log we get,

$$\hat{\mathbf{z}}_m = \underset{\mathbf{z}_m}{\arg\ \max} \left[\log P(\mathbf{y}_m / \mathbf{z}_m) + \log P(\mathbf{z}_m) \right]. \tag{4.17}$$

Finally, using equation (4.3) and equation (4.13), we can write

$$\hat{\mathbf{z}}_m = \underset{\mathbf{z}_m}{\arg\ \min} \left[E(\mathbf{z}_m) \right], \tag{4.18}$$

where $E(\mathbf{z}_m)$ is the final cost function to be minimized and can be expressed as

$$E(\mathbf{z}_m) = \frac{\| \mathbf{y}_m - A_m\mathbf{z}_m \|^2}{2\sigma_{n_m}^2} + \sum_{c \in C} V_c(\mathbf{z}_m). \qquad (4.19)$$

In equation (4.19), the first term ensures the fidelity of the final solution to the observed data through the image formation process; it is called the data term. The second term is the smoothness prior.

4.7.2 Optimization process

Since the cost function given in equation (4.19) is convex, it can be minimized using a simple gradient based technique, which quickly leads to the minima. The gradient of this cost is given by differentiating it with respect to $\mathbf{z}_m$ as

$$\nabla E(\mathbf{z}_m) = -2A_m^T(\mathbf{y}_m - A_m\mathbf{z}_m)/2\sigma_{n_m}^2 + 2\gamma_m\hat{\mathbf{g}}_m, \qquad (4.20)$$

where the first term corresponds to differentiation of the data term, while the $\hat{\mathbf{g}}_m$ vector is constructed after differentiating $\sum_{c \in C} V_c(\mathbf{z}_m)$ at every location. The differentiation with respect to $Z_m(i,j)$ of the second term at a (i,j) location is given by

$$\hat{G}_m(i,j) = 2[4Z_{m(i,j)} - Z_{m(i,j-1)} - Z_{m(i,j+1)} - Z_{m(i-1,j)} - Z_{m(i+1,j)}]. \qquad (4.21)$$

Note that $\nabla E(\mathbf{z}_m)$ is a vector of size $q^2M^2 \times 1$. The complete gradient descent optimization process is depicted in algorithm 4.1 where the value of step size α_m decides the rate of convergence. Note that a smaller value of the α_m will lead to slower convergence; for the larger value, the algorithm may not converge. This makes us use a varying step size α_m^n (i.e., step size in n^{th} iteration) and the same is estimated using the method given by Schultz and Stevenson [207] as

$$\alpha_m^n = \frac{[\nabla E(\mathbf{z}_m^n)]^T \nabla E(\mathbf{z}_m^n)}{[\nabla E(\mathbf{z}_m^n)]^T (A_m^T A_m/2\sigma_{n_m}^2 + \gamma_m\nabla^2\hat{\mathbf{g}}_m)\nabla E(\mathbf{z}_m^n)}. \qquad (4.22)$$

Since the optimization process is iterative, the choice of initial guess fed to the optimization process determines the speed of convergence. Use of the available initial estimate as an initial solution speeds up the convergence. Note that we obtain the initial estimate separately for each of the MS observations and the optimization is carried out independently for every LR MS observation. We mention here again that in order to preserve the edges in the final solution, we detect the edges from the initial estimate with the help of a Canny edge detector; we do not perform optimization on those edge pixels. In other words, the edges in the final fused image correspond to the already learned edges in the initial estimate.

Algorithm 4.1: Gradient descent technique

Data: LR MS image ($\mathbf{y}_m$), initial estimate obtained using NSCT/CT ($\mathbf{z}_m^0$),
      A_m and γ_m
Result: Fused MS image ($\hat{\mathbf{z}}_m$)
foreach LR MS image $\mathbf{y}_m$, $m = 1, 2, ..., l$ **do**
    Set $n = 0$;
    repeat
        Find gradient with respect to $\mathbf{z}_m^n$ of cost function given in equation
        (4.19) using equation (4.20);
        Estimate the step size α_m^n using equation (4.22);
        Perform $\mathbf{z}_m^{n+1} = \mathbf{z}_m^n - \alpha_m^n (\nabla E(\mathbf{z}_m^n))$, where α_m^n is the step size of the nth
        iteration;
        $n = n + 1$;
    until $\frac{\|z_m^n - z_m^{n-1}\|^2}{\|z_m^{n-1}\|^2} \leq 10^{-06}$;
    Set $\hat{\mathbf{z}}_m = \mathbf{z}_m^{n-1}$;
end

4.8   Experimentations

In this section, we present results of the proposed method for fusion. The fusion results using CT as well as NSCT are discussed and a comparison is shown with various state-of-the-art approaches. In addition to fusion experiments conducted on both degraded and un-degraded (original) images, we have also conducted experiments to show the effect of estimated decimation matrix entries (equation [4.7]) over the average one (equation [4.6]) and the effect of the estimated MRF parameter on the fusion results. In order to show the effectiveness of the proposed approach, we have conducted experiments on three sets of real images captured using Ikonos-2, Quickbird and Worldview-2 satellites. The detailed information of these satellites data is given in Table 3.1. The spatial resolution difference between the Pan and MS images is 4 for the images captured using these satellites. In Table 4.1, we show the details of setup used for degraded and un-degraded datasets. In all experiments, we use the '9 − 7' Laplacian pyramid (LP) filter bank based CT/NSCT as proposed by Vetterli and Hereley [237]. Along with this LP filter bank, we use *pkva* and *dmaxflat7* directional filter banks for CT and NSCT decomposition, respectively [59, 186]. In order to compare the performance of the proposed approach using CT/NSCT transform with the wavelet transform based approach, we conducted the experiments using wavelet transform instead of CT/NSCT to obtain the initial estimate. The experiments were conducted using MRF prior with the first as well as the second order neighbourhood systems. The performance of the proposed method was compared with other approaches on the basis of quality of images in terms of perceptual as well as quantitative measures. These measures were computed using the fused and the original MS images. In order to make the original available for quantitative comparison, the experiments were conducted on degraded images by using downsampling operation ($q = 4$) on both Pan and MS images. The following quantitative measures were used for performance evaluation of the experiments conducted on the degraded images.

Table 4.1 Details of experimentation setup

	Degraded dataset	Un-degraded dataset
Image size: MS	64×64	256×256
Pan	256×256	1024×1024
Fused image size	256×256	1024×1024
Data format	Same as original data format	
Downsampling operation ($q = 4$)	Every 4×4 pixels of original images are averaged to get corresponding single pixel in downsampled image	Not required
Image format for display of results	24 bits RGB format	

(i) The CC is given in equation (3.23) and it is widely used by the fusion community. It finds the correlation between the original MS band and the fused MS band. Higher values of CC indicate high spectral and spatial quality of the fused images.

(ii) Recently, Zhang et al. [272] have proposed a new image quality assessment called feature similarity (FSIM). FSIM is based on the value of phase congruency (PC) and gradient magnitude (GM) of a local structure. High value of PC indicates highly informative features. To find the FSIM between two images f and $\hat{f}$, first the PC and the GM values for all pixels are computed as given in [272]. Using these, the similarity measures between f and $\hat{f}$ are calculated as

$$S_{PC}(i,j) = \frac{2PC_f(i,j) \cdot PC_{\hat{f}}(i,j) + T_1}{PC_f^2(i,j) + PC_{\hat{f}}^2(i,j) + T_1}, \tag{4.23}$$

and

$$S_G(i,j) = \frac{2G_f(i,j) \cdot G_{\hat{f}}(i,j) + T_2}{G_f^2(i,j) + G_{\hat{f}}^2(i,j) + T_2}, \tag{4.24}$$

where, T_1 and T_2 represent small positive constants. PC_f, $PC_{\hat{f}}$ and G_f, $G_{\hat{f}}$ represent the phase congruency and the gradient magnitude of f and $\hat{f}$, respectively. $S_{PC}(i,j)$ and $S_G(i,j)$ are then multiplied to get similarity $S_L(i,j)$, that is

$$S_L(i,j) = S_{PC}(i,j) \cdot S_G(i,j). \tag{4.25}$$

Finally, the FSIM is computed as done by Zhang et al. [272]:

$$\text{FSIM} = \frac{\Sigma_{i,j\in\Omega} S_L(i,j) \cdot PC_m(i,j)}{\Sigma_{i,j\in\Omega} PC_m(i,j)}. \tag{4.26}$$

Here, Ω represents the entire image region in the spatial domain and $PC_m(i,j) = \max(PC_f(i,j), PC_{\hat{f}}(i,j))$. The range of FSIM is 0 to 1 and a higher value represents better performance.

(iii) The definition of RMSE is given in equation (3.24). It is the average MSE computed over all the fused MS bands. Low value of RMSE indicates minimum difference between the original and the fused image.

(iv) The *erreur relative globale adimensionnelle de synthse* (ERGAS) defined in equation (3.25) gives the global spatial quality in the fused image. The ideal value of ERGAS is zero.

(v) Spectral information divergence (SID) [45] measures the information divergence between the probability distributions generated by the fused MS and the original MS images. It gives the spectral variability of a single mixed pixel from a probabilistic point of view. A smaller SID value indicates better fused image.

(vi) A universal image quality index (Q_{AVG}) is defined in equation (3.26). It models distortion as a combination of three different factors: loss of correlation, luminance distortion and contrast distortion. The highest value of (Q_{AVG}) is 1 and it indicates that the fused image is same as the original image.

Among the aforementioned measures, CC, RMSE, ERGAS, SID and Q_{AVG} indicate spectral distortion [210, 192, 178] while FSIM gives the spatial fidelity of the fused image.

In addition to the experiments of degraded images, the performance of the proposed method is also verified by conducting experiments on un-degraded (original) datasets. In these experiments, the reference fused image is not available for quantitative comparison and hence, we use following measures in which a reference image is not required.

1. The quality with no reference (QNR) is given in equation (3.27). The ideal value of this measure is 1 and it indicates that the fused image is same as the original MS image. This measure is calculated using spatial distortion (D_s) and spectral distortion (D_λ).

2. The spatial distortion (D_s) defined in equation (3.28) gives the spatial detail by comparing the MS and fused images with the Pan image. Its ideal value is 0.

3. The spectral distortion (D_λ) gives the spectral distortion present in the fused image in comparison with the original MS image and its ideal value is 0. Equation (3.29) defines D_λ.

In the following subsections, Sections 4.8.1 and 4.8.2, we show the effect of decimation matrix coefficients and MRF parameter on fusion, respectively. The fusion results of degraded datasets obtained for different satellites are described in Sections 4.8.3 to 4.8.5. In Section 4.8.6, we describe the fusion results obtained for un-degraded datasets. Finally, the computation time involved for different fusion methods is presented in Section 4.8.6.

4.8.1 Effect of decimation matrix coefficients on fusion

Before proceeding to discussing the fusion results using our proposed method based on CT and NSCT, we first show the effect of decimation matrix on

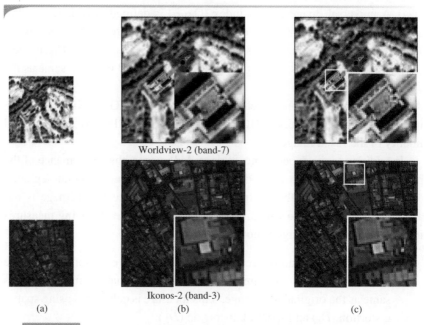

Worldview-2 (band-7)

Ikonos-2 (band-3)

(a)   (b)   (c)

Figure 4.3   Experimental results to show the effect of decimation matrix with equal and unequal weights ($q = 4$). The first and second row show fusion results for images captured using Worldview-2 (band 7) and Ikonos-2 (band 3) satellite sensors, respectively. (a) The downsampled LR MS image. The size of LR MS image is 64 × 64. Fused MS images of size 256 × 256 with (b) equal weights and (c) unequal weights. The zoomed-in version of the small area shown with white color border in (c) are displayed at bottom right corner in (b, c). (Courtesy: www.digitalglobe.com, www.isprs.org)

MS image fusion with estimated unequal weights (equation [4.7]) and equal weights (equation [4.6]) by conducting the experiments on degraded images captured by two different satellites. For this experiment, we display the results of band 7 and band 3 of Worldview-2 and Ikonos-2 satellites, respectively. The matrix with unequal weights were obtained by formulating the problem as a minimization of $||\mathbf{y}_m - D_m\mathbf{z}_m^0||^2$ with respect to sparse entries in D_m, where $\mathbf{z}_m^0$ in the initial estimate is derived from NSCT based learning. The locations of these entries correspond to those used for averaging (i.e., those locations where D_m entries have equal values). Unequal weights of D_m are then obtained using least squares method. The final cost function given in equation (4.19) is then minimized by replacing A_m with D_m in order to obtain the fused image. The fusion results using equal and unequal weights are depicted in Fig. 4.3. In Fig. 4.3(a), we display the low resolution MS images. The fusion results with equal and unequal weights are displayed in Fig. 4.3(b) and Fig. 4.3(c), respectively. For better visualization, we also display the zoomed-in version of a small area at the bottom right corner in the fused images. Looking at these fused images, we can observe that the results with unequal weights have reduced the blurring effect when compared to those of equal weights. One can also see the improvement in quantitative measures as given in Table 4.2. This table shows the mean squared error (MSE) and

Table 4.2   Quantitative measures for fused MS images shown in Fig. 4.3. The values in boldface indicate better performance

Image	Measure	Decimation matrix with equal weights	Decimation matrix with unequal weights
Worldview-2 (band 7)	MSE	0.0478	**0.0394**
	PSNR (in dB)	27.2941	**30.4381**
Ikonos-2 (band 3)	MSE	0.0491	**0.0411**
	PSNR (in dB)	25.9345	**28.8621**

the peak signal-to-noise ratio (PSNR) calculated between the original and the fused MS images. The results shown in Fig. 4.3 confirm that the use of decimation matrix with unequal weights (equation [4.7]) results in better fusion performance when compared to that obtained using equal weights (equation [4.6]). Note that in this experiment, the blur matrix is considered as an identity. However, in this work, we take care of blurring as well as the aliasing by including the non-identity blur matrix and use the estimated degradation matrix (A_m) entries instead of D_m.

4.8.2   Effect of MRF parameter γ_m on fusion

In the proposed approach, first the initial estimate image is obtained using the CT/NSCT transform, MS and Pan images. The final fused image is obtained by casting the problem in a regularization framework and solving the same by using the MAP–MRF approach. In our regularization, we use the MRF smoothness prior given in equation (4.13). Here, γ_m represents the MRF parameter for the mth fused image. It serves as a weight that appropriately penalizes the departure from smoothness in the fused image and its value depends on the entity modelled as MRF. Since the fused image is modelled as MRF and the same is unavailable, the true value of the MRF parameter is not known. However, since we have the initial estimate which represents a close approximation to the final fused image, it can be used to estimate the MRF parameter. If this parameter is not estimated, one may set it empirically; however, doing this increases the computational cost. Since the MRF parameter acts as a regularizing parameter, it is interesting to see the effect of the same on the solution, that is, the fused image. In order to investigate the effect of γ_m on the solution, we conducted an experiment on band 1 of the degraded Quickbird dataset [5] using the proposed approach in which different values of γ_1 are chosen manually. The results of this experiment are displayed in Fig. 4.4 for different choices of γ_1. Figures 4.4(a–c) show the fused images with three different values of γ_1. Comparing the images displayed in Fig. 4.4(a–c), we observe that the fused image shown in Fig. 4.4(a) is smoothed out due to higher value of $\gamma_1 = 0.1$. The fused image in Fig. 4.4(b) looks a bit better when compared to Fig. 4.4(a) but the edges are not preserved well. Although the fused image of Fig. 4.4(c) has minimum smoothness and has prominent edge details, it looks noisy. This is because of the reduction in weightage ($\gamma_1 = 0.001$) for the prior term in equation (4.19). In this case, the final solution relies heavily on the first term (data term) in equation (4.19) forcing it to become noisy since it corresponds to a least squares estimation with much less emphasis on prior. In Fig. 4.4(d), we display the fused image with estimated MRF parameter (γ_1) without using the edge details extracted from a Canny edge detector. What we observe here is the loss of edge details. The entire image appears smooth since the edge regions are also included while minimizing the cost function. In Fig. 4.4(e), we display the fused image with estimated γ_1 but with edge pixels corresponding to those of the initial estimate which were estimated using a Canny edge detector. Thus, we see that Fig. 4.4(e) has better preservation of homogenous and heterogenous regions when compared to other results displayed in Fig. 4.4(a–d).

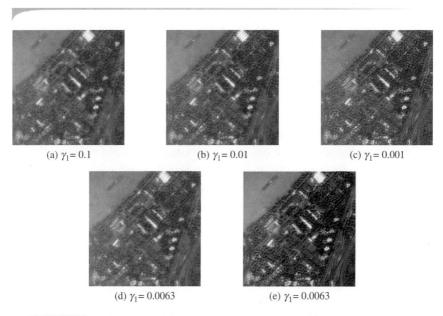

(a) $\gamma_1 = 0.1$ (b) $\gamma_1 = 0.01$ (c) $\gamma_1 = 0.001$

(d) $\gamma_1 = 0.0063$ (e) $\gamma_1 = 0.0063$

Figure 4.4   Effect of γ_1 on fusion result obtained for degraded Quickbird (band 1) satellite image. (a–c) Fused images with manually selected value of γ_1. Fused MS images with estimated γ_1 (d) without using Canny edge detector and (e) with Canny edge detector. (Courtesy: www.glcf.umd.edu)

4.8.3 Fusion results for degraded dataset: Ikonos-2

The Ikonos-2 satellite has one Pan and four MS images (band 1 to band 4) with a spatial resolution of 1 m $\times$ 1 m and 4 m $\times$ 4 m, respectively. These images were downloaded from the Internet [2], which has images of urban as well as non-urban areas. All these images correspond to Mount Wellington area near Hobart Tasmania. They were captured on February

22, 2003 and have a radiometric resolution of 11-bits. The original Pan and MS images are of size 12124×13148 and 3031×3287, respectively. For experimentation, we prepared two datasets from these images by using the cropping operation. These cropped images are then co-registered. Our dataset used for experimentation consisted of a Pan and MS images of size 1024×1024 and 256×256, respectively. We downsampled them by a factor of 4 and conducted the experiments using degraded Pan and MS images of size 256×256 and 64×64, respectively. The radiometric resolution was kept same as the original for these images. Experiments were conducted on the available data without any preprocessing such as converting it into 8-bits or linear stretching etc. MRF parameter was estimated separately for each band using the corresponding initial estimate. The estimated value of the MRF parameter γ_1 for band 1 was 0.00257. As mentioned earlier, the experiments were conducted on first and second order neighbourhood MRF priors. From the results, we observed that using both these neighbourhoods resulted in almost same MSE and also had visually similar results. However, the convergence speed was faster for second order neighbourhood when compared to first order neighbourhood priors. A similar observation was noticed by Xu et al. [259]. Hence, we show the results for second order neighbourhood only. With varying step size value in the gradient descent, convergence was obtained in less than 20 iterations which is fast when compared to using the fixed step size.

The results are shown separately for images containing non-urban and urban areas. In order to accommodate experiments on all the three sets of images, we show the fused results for the non-urban area using bands 3, 2 and 1 while the results on the urban area are shown using the bands 4, 3 and 2. The downsampled LR MS images for different satellites are displayed separately in Fig. 4.5 in which Fig. 4.5(a) and Fig. 4.5(b) correspond to LR MS images for Ikonos-2 satellite. The fusion results for the two cases are shown as color composites in Fig. 4.6 and Fig. 4.7, respectively where the comparison is shown with various state-of-the-art fusion approaches. In both the figures, the magnified portion is shown at the bottom right corner on each of the fused images. Figure 4.6(a) and Fig. 4.7(a) show the fused images obtained using temporal Fourier transform (TFT) [158] method. The results obtained using the approach based on NSCT [213] are displayed in Fig. 4.6(b) and Fig. 4.7(b), respectively. In Fig. 4.6(c) and Fig. 4.7(c), we show the fused images for the approach used by Shah et al. [210]. We also display the fusion results obtained using the method shown by Joshi and Jalobeanu [121] in Fig. 4.6(d) and Fig. 4.7(d). Figure 4.6(e) and Fig. 4.7(e) show the fusion obtained using the adaptive IHS method [192]. The MS fusion images using AWLP method [178] are shown in Fig. 4.6(f) and Fig. 4.7(f). It may be mentioned here that we choose these methods for comparison since they perform the fusion using the edge details in Pan image which follow a similar approach as the proposed method. Finally, the results of the proposed approach using CT and NSCT are depicted in Fig. 4.6(g, h) and Fig. 4.7(g, h), respectively. For visual comparison, we display the original MS images in Fig. 4.6(i) and Fig. 4.7(i), respectively.

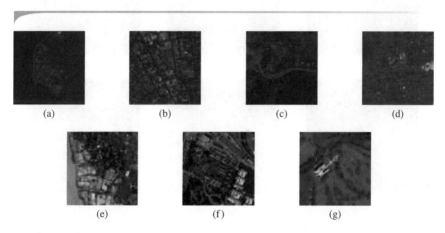

(a)   (b)   (c)   (d)

(e)   (f)   (g)

Figure 4.5   LR test MS images obtained by downsampling the original MS images captured using different satellite sensors. The size of each LR test MS image is 64 × 64. The downsampled MS images for: (a, b) Ikonos-2 satellite with color composition of bands 3, 2, 1 and bands 4, 3, 2 respectively, (c, d, e) Quickbird satellite with color composition of bands 3, 2, 1 and bands 4, 3, 2 corresponding to area around Boulder city, USA, and bands 3, 2, 1 corresponding to Sundarban, India, respectively and (f, g) Worldview-2 satellite with color composition of bands 5, 3, 2 and bands 7, 5, 3, respectively.

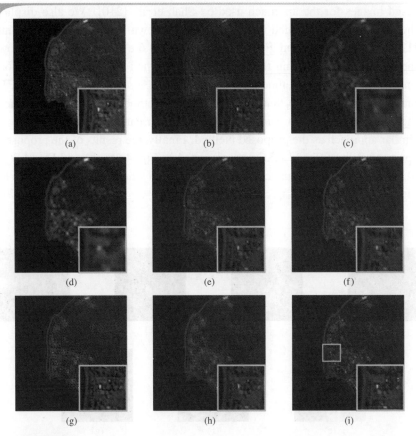

(a)   (b)   (c)

(d)   (e)   (f)

(g)   (h)   (i)

Figure 4.6 MS fusion results for downsampled Ikonos-2 satellite images consisting of non-urban area shown as color composites of bands 3, 2 and 1 ($q = 4$). Fused images obtained using (a) temporal Fourier transform (TFT) based approach [158], (b) approach by Shi et al. [213], (c) approach by Shah et al. [210], (d) approach by Joshi and Jalobeanu [121], (e) adaptive IHS approach [192], (f) AWLP [178], (g) proposed approach using CT and (h) proposed approach using NSCT. (i) Original MS image. The magnified image for a small square region with a green border shown in (i) is displayed at the bottom right corner of all the images. (Courtesy: www.isprs.org)

Looking at the results displayed in Fig. 4.6 for the non-urban area, the following points can be noticed. One can see that the fused image using TFT method (see Fig. 4.6[a]) although showing improvement in spatial information, has spectral distortions. This can be seen in the magnified region in which the artefacts are clearly visible. The approaches based on NSCT [213, 210] (Fig. 4.6[b] and Fig. 4.6[c]) fail in both spectral and spatial information preservation. Similarly, we can observe the poor enhancement of details in Fig. 4.6(d)[121]. Further, the AWLP approach [178] (Fig. 4.6[f]) preserves the spectral details but improvement of spatial details is lacking. This may be because of the non usage of prior information. Although the adaptive IHS method (see Fig. 4.6[e]) gives better fused image perceptually, the results of the proposed approach shown in Fig. 4.6(g, h) are better both in terms of perception and quantitative measures. We can see from the magnified details that in the proposed method, the area nearer to the sea have better preservation of spatial details when compared to the same in Fig. 4.6(a–f). Here, we can also observe that the proposed approach with NSCT (Fig. 4.6[h]) has less spatial and color distortion and also appears closer to the original MS image (Fig. 4.6[i]) when compared to the result using CT (Fig. 4.6[g]).

The quantitative comparison using all 4 bands for the non-urban area (Fig. 4.6) is given in Table 4.3 that also has the ideal value for each measure as a reference. The values marked in boldface indicate that their value is closer to the ideal. It is clearly observed that the proposed method has better CC when compared to all other methods except for band 3. For this band, though the CC value for the proposed method is less, it is still closer to the adaptive IHS technique [192] which has the highest value. The FSIM measure is based on phase congruency (PC) and is highest when there is significant pixel intensity difference between neighbouring pixels. Hence a higher value of this indicates that the edges are well preserved. From Table 4.3, one can observe that the proposed method with the NSCT has a high value of FSIM when compared to other approaches. The other spatial measures such as RMSE and ERGAS are also indicated in Table 4.3. As expected for these measures, the proposed approach shows better performance when compared to all the other approaches. The SID measure which indicates the spectral distortion present in the image is better when compared to other methods. The Q_{AVG} which quantifies spatial as well as the spectral details is also highest for the proposed

Table 4.3 Quantitative measures for fused MS images shown in Fig. 4.6. The boldface indicates values closer to the ideal

Measure	Image	Ideal value	TFT method [158]	Approach in [213]	Approach in [210]	Approach in [121]	Adaptive IHS [192]	AWLP method [178]	Proposed using CT	Proposed using NSCT
CC	Band 1(B)	1	0.8042	0.8672	0.8403	0.8404	0.9093	0.8469	0.9232	**0.9250**
	Band 2(G)	1	0.8814	0.8868	0.8630	0.8597	0.9211	0.9324	**0.9557**	0.9489
	Band 3(R)	1	0.9385	0.8994	0.8929	0.8837	**0.9655**	0.9596	0.9628	0.9633
	Band 4(NIR)	1	0.9519	0.9565	0.9312	0.9259	0.9646	0.9673	**0.9782**	0.9719
FSIM	Band 1(B)	1	0.8304	0.9269	0.8977	0.8907	0.9438	0.8809	0.9550	**0.9574**
	Band 2(G)	1	0.9104	0.9171	0.8577	0.8735	0.9536	0.9322	0.9621	**0.9673**
	Band 3(R)	1	0.9349	0.9160	0.8397	0.8476	0.9513	0.9500	0.9525	**0.9530**
	Band 4(NIR)	1	0.8881	0.8977	0.7629	0.7924	0.8749	0.9171	0.9173	**0.9230**
RMSE	Band 1–4	0	9.08	4.53	5.08	9.55	3.48	3.81	3.07	**3.01**
ERGAS	Band 1–4	0	7.57	4.16	4.59	6.52	3.12	3.28	2.88	**2.83**
SID	Band 1–4	0	0.0530	0.0075	0.0386	0.0840	0.0394	0.0386	0.0061	**0.0057**
Q_{AVG}	Band 1–4	1	0.4989	0.9008	0.8960	0.5303	0.9003	0.8962	0.9104	**0.9146**

method. From Table 4.3, we can say that the proposed method using CT and NSCT performs better in terms of quantitative measures when compared to other methods except for the correlation coefficient which is marginally less than the adaptive IHS approach for band 3. However, we can see that fusion using adaptive IHS is visually poor when compared to the proposed method.

Similar observations can be made for Fig. 4.7 which depicts an urban area. Here, we display the magnified portion separately as seen at the bottom right corner. We see that all other approaches except the AWLP method [178] show inferiority in terms of visual perception when compared with our approach. However, looking at the magnified portion which consists of the areas around large building, one can say that preservation of spatial details in the proposed approach are better when compared to the AWLP approach [178]. A careful observation shows that distinguishing a region such as the one shown in the magnified area from other regions is more easier in the proposed methods, indicating better preservation of spectral features. Interestingly, one can also see that artefacts are less dominant in Fig. 4.7(h) indicating that NSCT performs better due to non subsampling property. The quantitative comparison for the results on urban area is shown in Table 4.4. As indicated, the proposed method performs better in terms of quantitative measures when compared to other approaches. We see from Table 4.4 that the CC measures for both CT and NSCT are better among all other approaches. Similarly, we can see the improvement in the FSIM for the proposed method when compared to other methods; the values of RMSE and ERGAS are also closer to the ideal value. The measures that show the spectral details preservation, that is SID and Q_{AVG} are also better when compared to other methods. We mention here that the use of NSCT improves the RMSE and ERGAS when compared to the CT method; however, this improvement is not significant for other measures. From the results displayed in Fig. 4.6 and Fig. 4.7 and the quantitative measures shown in Table 4.3 and Table 4.4, we can see that the proposed method performs well in terms of both perceptual as well as quantitative assessment for the results on images of Ikonos-2 satellite.

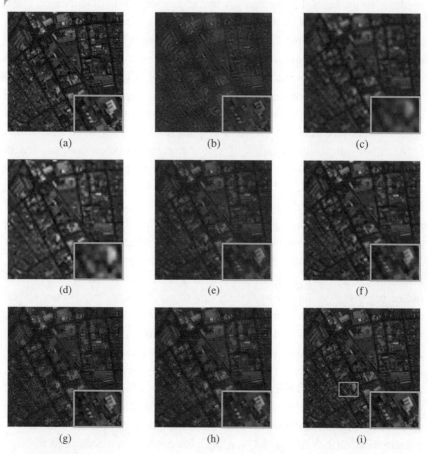

Figure 4.7 MS fusion results for degraded dataset of urban area images captured using Ikonos-2 satellite shown as color composites of bands 4, 3 and 2 ($q = 4$). Fused images obtained using (a) TFT based approach [158], (b) approach by Shi et al. [213], (c) approach by Shah et al. [210], (d) approach by Joshi and Jalobeanu [121], (e) adaptive IHS approach [192], (f) AWLP [178], (g) proposed approach using CT and (h) proposed approach using NSCT. (i) Original MS image. The magnified image for a small square region with a green border shown in (i) is displayed at the bottom right corner of all the images. (Courtesy: www.isprs.org)

Table 4.4 Quantitative measures for fused MS image results shown in Fig. 4.7. The boldface indicates values closer to the ideal

Measure	Image	Ideal value	TFT method [158]	Approach in [213]	Approach in [210]	Approach in [121]	Adaptive IHS [192]	AWLP method [178]	Proposed using CT	Proposed using NSCT
CC	Band 1(B)	1	0.8892	0.8359	0.8107	0.8121	0.9405	0.9323	0.9406	**0.9441**
	Band 2(G)	1	0.9215	0.8553	0.7988	0.8009	0.9487	0.9380	0.9543	**0.9543**
	Band 3(R)	1	0.9415	0.8702	0.7860	0.7890	0.9493	0.9322	**0.9498**	0.9497
	Band 4(NIR)	1	0.8787	0.8589	0.7121	0.7155	0.9016	0.8925	0.9032	**0.9200**
FSIM	Band 1(B)	1	0.8303	0.8568	0.7611	0.7893	0.9043	0.9115	**0.9155**	0.9083
	Band 2(G)	1	0.9118	0.8496	0.7203	0.7728	0.8860	0.9083	0.9255	**0.9294**
	Band 3(R)	1	0.9324	0.8607	0.7131	0.7736	0.8760	0.8972	**0.9394**	0.9320
	Band 4(NIR)	1	0.9049	0.8035	0.6618	0.7572	0.8228	0.8719	0.9091	**0.9164**
RMSE	Band 1–4	0	11.65	12.99	14.02	15.19	9.56	9.49	9.04	**7.87**
ERGAS	Band 1–4	0	5.44	6.07	6.52	6.27	4.46	4.42	4.25	**3.69**
SID	Band 1–4	0	0.0257	0.0144	0.0182	0.0312	0.0145	0.0139	0.0125	**0.0116**
Q_{AVG}	Band 1–4	1	0.4945	0.7135	0.7390	0.7276	0.7558	0.7454	0.7582	**0.7695**

4.8.4   Fusion results for degraded dataset: Quickbird

We now consider images captured using Quickbird satellite, which provides Pan and MS images with spatial resolutions of 0.6 m × 0.6 m and 2.4 m × 2.4 m, respectively. These images were downloaded from the website [3]. This satellite data covers an area around Boulder city, USA. These images were captured on July 4, 2005 and their radiometric resolution is of 8-bit. The Pan and MS images were of size 3312 × 3260 and 828 × 815, respectively. After the cropping operation, the Pan and MS images had a size of 1024 × 1024 and 256 × 256, respectively. Their LR versions, that is the downsampled images are of size 256 × 256 and 64 × 64, respectively.

The results for this experiment are shown in Fig. 4.8 and Fig. 4.9, respectively. In Fig. 4.8, we show the fusion results with color composites of bands 3, 2 and 1 covering the forest area, while Fig. 4.9 shows the fused images with color composites of bands 4, 3 and 2 and it consists of a semi-urban area. The LR MS images are shown in Fig. 4.5(c) and Fig. 4.5(d). The fused images obtained for all other approaches except the proposed method are shown in Fig. 4.8(a–f) and Fig. 4.9(a–f). In Fig. 4.8(g, h) and Fig. 4.9(g, h), we show the results obtained using the proposed method using CT and NSCT. Finally, we display the original MS images in Fig. 4.8(i) and Fig. 4.9(i). For better visual clarity, we also show the magnified regions in all the fused results.

Similar to the experiments on Ikonos-2 images, here also we observe better preservation of spatial details in Fig. 4.8(a) but with spectral distortion. The results shown in Fig. 4.8(b–d), do not show comparable performance with the result of the proposed method. The MS fused images shown in Fig. 4.8(e) and Fig. 4.8(f) using the adaptive IHS and AWLP show the improvement in spectral information but they do not preserve the spatial content well. From the magnified region consisting of road and tree areas, one can see that the proposed approach using NSCT (see Fig. 4.8[h]) has better spatial and spectral contents when compared to AWLP [178] as well as adaptive IHS method [192]. A closer look indicates that the proposed approach using NSCT has better edge details; moreover, the texture is close to the original MS image when compared to AWLP and adaptive IHS methods. Similar observations can be made from the images displayed in Fig. 4.9, where the improvement in the proposed method is evident in the magnified region. In Fig. 4.9(g, h), we

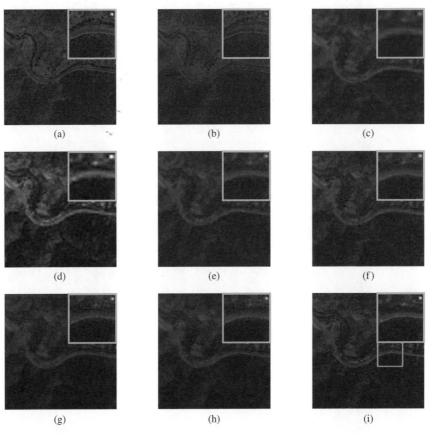

Figure 4.8 MS fusion results for a degraded dataset of forest area captured using Quickbird satellite shown as color composites of bands 3, 2 and 1 ($q = 4$). Fused images obtained using (a) TFT based approach [158], (b) approach by Shi et al. [213], (c) approach by Shah et al. [210], (d) approach by Joshi and Jalobeanu [121], (e) adaptive IHS approach [192], (f) AWLP [178], (g) proposed approach using CT and (h) proposed approach using NSCT. (i) Original MS image. The magnified image for a small square region with a green border shown in (i) is displayed at the top right corner of all the images. (Courtesy: www.digitalglobe.com)

Table 4.5 Quantitative measures for fused MS image results shown in Fig. 4.8. The boldface indicates values closer to the ideal

Measure	Image	Ideal value	TFT method [158]	Approach in [213]	Approach in [210]	Approach in [121]	Adaptive IHS [192]	AWLP method [178]	Proposed using CT	Proposed using NSCT
CC	Band 1(B)	1	0.7152	0.7223	0.8829	0.8794	0.9274	0.8835	0.9375	**0.9381**
	Band 2(G)	1	0.7854	0.7552	0.8819	0.8786	0.9408	0.9312	0.9458	**0.9465**
	Band 3(R)	1	0.7417	0.7387	0.8871	0.8817	0.9313	0.9266	0.9318	**0.9401**
	Band 4(NIR)	1	0.7901	0.7308	0.8235	0.8282	0.9101	0.9116	0.9150	**0.9223**
FSIM	Band 1(B)	1	0.7581	0.8831	0.8695	0.8235	0.9332	0.9217	**0.9390**	0.9136
	Band 2(G)	1	0.8463	0.8526	0.7895	0.8398	0.8845	0.8870	0.8945	**0.9017**
	Band 3(R)	1	0.8270	0.8467	0.8041	0.8253	0.8698	0.8798	0.8874	**0.8934**
	Band 4(NIR)	1	0.8263	0.7515	0.6792	0.7864	0.8098	**0.9025**	0.8735	0.8765
RMSE	Band 1–4	0	10.49	14.85	7.40	13.21	5.83	5.54	**5.48**	5.56
ERGAS	Band 1–4	0	6.58	6.76	3.85	5.26	3.08	**3.01**	3.04	3.21
SID	Band 1–4	0	0.1051	0.0574	0.0308	0.0492	0.0259	0.0252	0.0236	**0.0233**
Q_{AVG}	Band 1–4	1	0.8786	0.8053	0.9483	0.7536	0.9463	0.9470	0.9492	**0.9575**

Table 4.6 Quantitative measures for fused MS image results shown in Fig. 4.9. The boldface indicates values closer to the ideal

Measure	Image	Ideal value	TFT method [158]	Approach in [213]	Approach in [210]	Approach in [121]	Adaptive IHS [192]	AWLP method [178]	Proposed using CT	Proposed using NSCT
CC	Band 1(B)	1	0.6621	0.6814	0.8676	0.8565	0.9162	0.9169	0.9151	**0.9278**
	Band 2(G)	1	0.7022	0.7061	0.8613	0.8518	0.9270	0.9210	**0.9324**	0.9149
	Band 3(R)	1	0.6507	0.6852	0.8631	0.8559	0.9189	0.9133	0.9303	**0.9313**
	Band 4(NIR)	1	0.6195	0.5609	0.6966	0.7952	0.8746	0.8751	0.8766	**0.8820**
FSIM	Band 1(B)	1	0.7463	0.8242	0.8323	0.8514	0.8856	0.8892	0.8849	**0.8901**
	Band 2(G)	1	0.7933	0.7976	0.7690	0.7862	0.8519	0.8533	0.8559	**0.8590**
	Band 3(R)	1	0.7860	0.8011	0.7848	0.8119	0.8488	0.8437	0.8505	**0.8511**
	Band 4(NIR)	1	0.7589	0.6586	0.6966	0.7617	0.7709	0.8378	0.8414	**0.8451**
RMSE	Band 1–4	0	17.87	17.44	12.43	18.93	10.32	9.61	6.82	**6.64**
ERGAS	Band 1–4	0	8.91	8.20	5.62	8.72	4.35	4.39	2.88	**2.81**
SID	Band 1–4	0	0.2038	0.1088	0.0507	0.1904	0.0686	**0.0318**	0.0490	0.0514
(Q_{AVG})	Band 1–4	1	0.7678	0.7924	0.8981	0.7130	0.9042	0.9011	0.9067	**0.9090**

can compare the performance of the proposed method using CT and NSCT. It is clearly visible that the proposed approach using NSCT performs better in terms of preservation of spatial details as well as in terms of spectral enhancement compared to the method using CT. In conjunction with the results shown in Fig. 4.8 and Fig. 4.9, the quantitative comparisons are given in Table 4.5 and Table 4.6, respectively. The following observations can be made from the values given in the two tables. Looking at Table 4.5, the values of CC for the proposed CT and NSCT methods are better when compared to all the other approaches. Moreover, all the other measures except FSIM for band 4 and ERGAS computed using bands $1 - 4$ are closer to their ideal for the proposed approach when compared to other approaches. These two measures are better for the AWLP method [178]. Similar observations can be made from Table 4.6, in which except for the SID measure, our proposed fusion approach performs better when compared to other approaches. This indicates that barring a few bands, the performance of the proposed approach is better when compared to other methods. As expected, edge enhancement is poor for the AWLP approach since it is based on WT which has limited directionality. From the fusion results displayed in Fig. 4.8 and 4.9 and the quantitative measures shown in the tables, we may conclude that the proposed algorithm performs better on Quickbird images too.

In continuation with the aforementioned experiments on Quickbird images, we also experimented on the images downloaded from another link [5]. These images cover an area of Sundarban, India; the radiometric resolution of these images was of 11-bits. The Pan and MS images are of size 16384×16384 and 4096×4096, respectively. The test images were prepared by cropping and co-registering the images and the experiments were conducted on degraded as well as on un-degraded images. The results of the experiments conducted on degraded images are displayed in Fig. 4.10 and the quantitative comparison for the same is depicted in Table 4.7. One can see that the results of temporary Fourier transform (TFT) [158] and NSCT based [213] methods are very poor. Moreover, the results of the approaches proposed by both Shah et al. [210] and Joshi and Jalobeanu [121] (see Fig. 4.10(c, d)) appear blurred indicating spatial and spectral distortions. We display the results of adaptive IHS and AWLP methods in Fig. 4.10(e) and

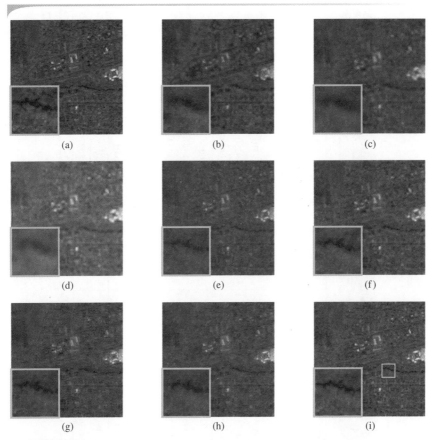

Figure 4.9 MS fusion results for downsampled Quickbird satellite images consisting of a semi-urban area shown as color composites of bands 4, 3 and 2 ($q = 4$). Fused images obtained using (a) TFT based approach [158], (b) approach by Shi et al. [213], (c) approach by Shah et al. [210], (d) approach by Joshi and Jalobeanu [121], (e) adaptive IHS approach [192], (f) AWLP [178], (g) proposed approach using CT and (h) proposed approach using NSCT. (i) Original MS image. The magnified image for a small square region with a green border shown in (i) is displayed at the bottom left corner of all the images. (Courtesy: www.digitalglobe.com)

Table 4.7 Quantitative measures for fused MS image results shown in Fig. 4.10. The boldface indicates values closer to the ideal

Measure	Image	Ideal value	TFT method [158]	Approach in [213]	Approach in [210]	Approach in [121]	Adaptive IHS [192]	AWLP method [178]	Proposed using CT	Proposed using NSCT
CC	Band 1(B)	1	0.5466	0.5756	0.9250	0.9099	0.9137	0.9002	0.9244	**0.9256**
	Band 2(G)	1	0.5505	0.5309	0.9208	0.9071	0.9304	0.9316	9220	**0.9363**
	Band 3(R)	1	0.4581	0.5159	0.9225	0.9146	0.9251	0.9380	9165	**0.9389**
	Band 4(NIR)	1	0.9182	0.5091	0.8967	0.8816	0.9759	0.9614	0.9578	**0.9742**
FSIM	Band 1(B)	1	0.6792	0.7236	0.7730	0.7858	0.8052	0.8076	0.8129	**0.8417**
	Band 2(G)	1	0.7446	0.7559	0.7568	0.7492	0.8485	0.8457	0.8390	**0.8509**
	Band 3(R)	1	0.6972	0.7241	0.7541	0.7392	0.8160	0.8333	**0.8577**	0.8501
	Band 4(NIR)	1	0.8108	0.7156	0.7023	0.6074	0.8976	0.9079	0.8763	**0.9183**
RMSE	Band 1-4	0	19.90	20.01	20.90	21.63	17.47	16.76	14.67	**14.02**
ERGAS	Band 1-4	0	9.89	8.05	5.78	7.12	5.25	5.01	5.76	**4.95**
SID	Band 1-4	0	0.4381	0.4370	0.0320	0.1119	0.0686	0.0381	0.0431	**0.0378**
Q_{AVG}	Band 1-4	1	0.6936	0.5381	0.7930	0.5377	0.8034	0.8827	0.8571	**0.8901**

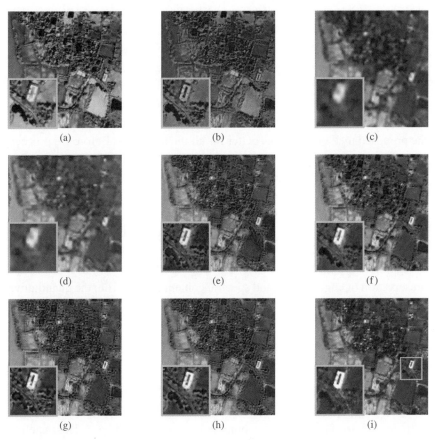

(a)   (b)   (c)

(d)   (e)   (f)

(g)   (h)   (i)

Figure 4.10   MS fusion results for degraded dataset of a semi-urban area of Sundarban, India captured using Quickbird satellite shown as color composites of bands 3, 2 and 1 ($q = 4$). Fused images obtained using (a) TFT based approach [158], (b) approach by Shi et al. [213], (c) approach by Shah et al. [210], (d) approach by Joshi and Jalobeanu [121], (e) adaptive IHS approach [192], (f) AWLP [178], (g) proposed approach using CT and (h) proposed approach using NSCT. (i) Original MS image. The magnified image for a small square region with a green border shown in (i) is displayed at the bottom left corner of all the images. (Courtesy: www.glcf.umd.edu)

Fig. 4.10(f), respectively and they appear perceptually similar to fused results of the proposed method using CT and NSCT shown in Fig. 4.10(g, h). We can see that the spectral improvement of the proposed method is similar to adaptive IHS and AWLP methods. However, we observe that both these methods lack in preserving the spatial information when compared to the proposed method which is visible in the magnified region that show clear edge details for the proposed approach. We include the original MS image in Fig. 4.10(i). From the quantitative measures presented in Table 4.7, it is clear that the proposed method performs better for all the measures. Before we proceed to the next experiment, we would like to mention the following points related to this experiment. In the fusion results shown in Fig. 4.10 for the degraded dataset of the color composition of bands 3, 2 and 1, the original band 1 MS image acquired from the satellite lacks sharpness. The downsampling operation further degrades it. Hence, we notice spectral distortions in the results of this experiment. However, we see that in the proposed method, though there exists spectral distortion, it still performs better in terms of the preservation of edge regions and spectral content as seen from the quantitative measures.

4.8.5   Fusion results for degraded dataset: Worldview-2

Finally, we conduct experiments on the images captured using Worldview-2 satellite sensor which has more than four MS images and also provides images with higher spatial resolution compared to other satellites. This satellite captures a Pan image and eight MS images with spatial resolution of 0.5 m × 0.5 m and 2 m × 2 m, respectively. The images used in this experiment are downloaded from [4]; they cover urban and sem-urban areas of San Francisco, USA. These images were captured on October 9, 2011 and have 11-bits of radiometric resolution. Here also we use the images with the same radiometric resolution without using any correction such as contrast stretching. The dataset consisting of the Pan image of size 1024 × 1024 pixels and the MS images of size 256 × 256 pixels for the experiments. The results are shown in Fig. 4.11 and Fig. 4.12, respectively. In Fig. 4.11, we display the fused images with color composites of bands 5, 3 and 2 and this has the urban area. The results in Fig. 4.12, showing the semi-urban area are displayed by

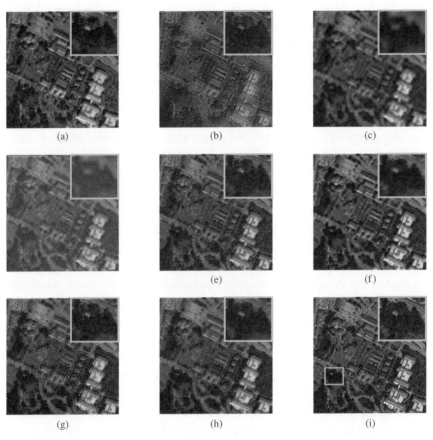

Figure 4.11   MS fusion results for degraded dataset of urban area image captured using Worldview-2 satellite shown as color composites of bands 5, 3 and 2 ($q = 4$). Fused images obtained using (a) TFT based approach [158], (b) approach by Shi et al. [213], (c) approach by Shah et al. [210], (d) approach by Joshi and Jalobeanu [121], (e) adaptive IHS approach [192], (f) AWLP [178], (g) proposed approach using CT and (h) proposed approach using NSCT. (i) Original MS image. The magnified image for a small square region with a green border shown in (i) is displayed at the top right corner of all the images. (Courtesy: www.digitalglobe.com)

choosing color composites of bands 7, 5 and 3. The degraded LR MS images of urban and semi-urban areas are shown in Fig. 4.5(f) and Fig. 4.5(g), respectively. In Fig. 4.11 and Fig. 4.12, we display the fusion results obtained using various approaches along with their original MS images. Similar to the previous two experiments, here also we display the magnified portions, of the region. The results of the proposed approach are shown in Fig. 4.11(g, h) and Fig. 4.12(g, h). Once again, looking at the images in Fig. 4.11, we see that the proposed method preserves high frequency edge details better when compared to other approaches. In the image showing the urban area, we select a region consisting of a house surrounded by trees for magnification. From the magnified regions displayed in Fig. 4.11, we can see that spatial details in the tree and the color of the house are better preserved for the proposed method using NSCT when compared to all other methods. These details appear blurred for the AWLP method [178]. For the adaptive IHS method [192], the same region has poor preservation of edges. Similarly, in Fig. 4.12 also, one can observe the enhancement of spatial details for the proposed method when compared to the other approaches. Once again looking at the magnified portion, we can see that texture preservation is better for the proposed approach based on NSCT. One may notice blur in the fusion results obtained using methods by Shi et al., Shah et al. and Joshi and Jalobeanu [213], [210], [121] (Fig. 4.12[b–d]). In Fig. 4.12(b), we display the result of the fusion method [213] which has significant blur. This is due to the lesser correlatedness between MS and Pan images which yields a saturated fused image when using the method of Shi et al. [213]. Since the method proposed by Shah et al. [210] (Fig. 4.12[c]) is based on a similar concept it also results in blur. The result of the fusion approach proposed by Joshi and Jalobeanu [121] is displayed in Fig. 4.12(d); the approach uses IGMRF parameters. Since it requires accurate registration of Pan and MS images in order to obtain a better fused image, a small error in registration leads to degradation of edge/non-edge regions in the fused image which is clearly visible as a distortion in Fig. 4.12(d).

The quantitative comparisons for the same experiments of urban and semi-urban images are displayed in Table 4.8 and Table 4.9, respectively. As can be seen from Table 4.8, all the quantitative measures are better for the proposed methods. However, in Table 4.9, the CC measure of band 5

Table 4.8 Quantitative measures for fused MS image results shown in Fig. 4.11. The boldface indicates values closer to the ideal

Measure	Image	Ideal value	TFT method [158]	Approach in [213]	Approach in [210]	Approach in [121]	Adaptive IHS [192]	AWLP method [178]	Proposed using CT	Proposed using NSCT
CC	Band 2(B)	1	0.8340	0.8395	0.7781	0.7811	0.9194	0.8955	0.9254	**0.9260**
	Band 3(G)	1	0.8800	0.8574	0.7769	0.7786	0.9367	0.9105	0.9386	**0.9412**
	Band 5(R)	1	0.8778	0.8632	0.8176	0.8164	0.9461	0.9314	**0.9501**	0.9489
	Band 7(NIR)	1	0.8113	0.5223	0.7861	0.7816	0.8747	0.8829	0.8828	**0.8866**
FSIM	Band 2(B)	1	0.8262	0.7916	0.6975	0.7054	0.8527	0.8440	0.8540	**0.8650**
	Band 3(G)	1	0.8659	0.8151	0.6824	0.6700	0.8749	0.8621	0.8909	**0.8949**
	Band 5(R)	1	0.7908	0.8124	0.6825	0.6839	0.8514	0.8584	0.8785	**0.8786**
	Band 7(NIR)	1	0.7169	0.6123	0.6490	0.6186	0.7790	0.7805	**0.7873**	0.7826
RMSE	Bands 2,3,5,7	0	27.26	35.11	31.13	39.73	22.32	21.72	**21.10**	21.30
ERGAS	Bands 2,3,5,7	0	10.23	12.56	12.08	11.35	8.36	8.18	7.88	**7.58**
SID	Bands 2,3,5,7	0	0.7670	0.2816	0.2709	0.2614	0.2541	0.2554	**0.2511**	0.3047
Q_{AVG}	Bands 2,3,5,7	1	0.5141	0.5625	0.6644	0.5588	0.6795	0.6788	0.6819	**0.6837**

Table 4.9 Quantitative measures for fused MS image results shown in Fig. 4.12. The boldface indicate values closer to the ideal

Measure	Image	Ideal value	TFT method [158]	Approach in [213]	Approach in [210]	Approach in [121]	Adaptive IHS [192]	AWLP method [178]	Proposed using CT	Proposed using NSCT
CC	Band 2(B)	1	0.7482	0.8286	0.8824	0.8852	0.9345	0.9329	0.9336	**0.9378**
	Band 3(G)	1	0.9013	0.8322	0.8944	0.8932	0.9677	0.9553	0.9746	**0.9754**
	Band 5(R)	1	0.7687	0.8265	0.8777	0.8789	**0.9427**	0.9363	0.9291	0.9387
	Band 7(NIR)	1	0.8898	0.7228	0.8896	0.8845	0.9319	0.9317	0.9347	**0.9377**
FSIM	Band 2(B)	1	0.7861	0.7846	0.7946	0.7761	0.8336	0.8357	0.8402	**0.8460**
	Band 3(G)	1	0.8721	0.7979	0.7800	0.7577	0.9200	0.8937	**0.9227**	0.9186
	Band 5(R)	1	0.7694	0.7546	0.7573	0.7203	0.8401	0.8424	**0.8440**	0.8364
	Band 7(NIR)	1	0.6912	0.7407	0.6823	0.6843	0.7661	**0.8393**	0.7698	0.7716
RMSE	Bands 2,3,5,7	0	25.62	29.40	22.38	28.85	17.40	15.69	14.82	**14.52**
ERGAS	Bands 2,3,5,7	0	14.59	18.32	12.02	13.37	8.70	8.55	6.88	**6.69**
SID	Bands 2,3,5,7	0	1.5759	0.4488	0.4542	0.5746	0.4892	0.4388	**0.4100**	0.4110
(Q_{AVG})	Bands 2,3,5,7	1	0.7517	0.4780	0.6581	0.6104	0.8374	0.8480	**0.8505**	0.8485

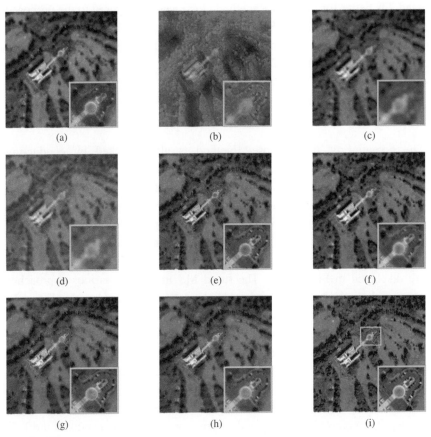

Figure 4.12 MS fusion results for degraded dataset of semi-urban area images captured using Worldview-2 satellite shown as color composites of bands 7, 5 and 3 ($q = 4$). Fused images obtained using (a) TFT based approach [158], (b) approach by Shi et al. [213], (c) approach by Shah et al. [210], (d) approach by Joshi and Jalobeanu [121], (e) adaptive IHS approach [192], (f) AWLP [178], (g) proposed approach using CT and (h) proposed approach using NSCT. (i) Original MS image. The magnified image for a small square region with a green border shown in (i) is displayed at the bottom right corner of all the images. (Courtesy: www.digitalglobe.com)

for adaptive IHS [192] shows minor improvement and the FSIM value for band 7 is better for the AWLP method [178] when compared to the proposed approach. Except CC and FSIM measures, the proposed method using CT and NSCT perform better for other measures. Thus, one can say that our approach works well for Worldview-2 satellite images too.

4.8.6 Fusion results for un-degraded (original) datasets: Ikonos-2, Quickbird and Worldview-2

The potential of the proposed method is also checked by conducting experiments on un-degraded (original) MS and Pan images. The same datasets consisting of images from Ikonos-2 [2], Quickbird [5] and Worldview-2 [4] satellites were used here. Unlike the previous experiments in this case, Pan and MS images were not downsampled which resulted in 1024×1024 and 256×256 sizes, respectively. Similar to the degraded dataset experiments, the radiometric resolution is not altered. The original MS images are displayed in Fig. 4.13. The fused MS images of various approaches along with the proposed method for all the datasets are displayed in Fig. 4.14 to Fig. 4.16. Figure 4.14 shows the fusion results for images of Ikonos-2 satellite showing a semi-urban area while Fig. 4.15 and Fig. 4.16 correspond to results on urban area images captured using Quickbird and Worldview-2 satellites. The size of the fused MS image was 1024×1024. The performance of the proposed approach was compared with the methods used in the earlier experimentations on degraded images. Here, we also include the results of the Brovey method [71] along with other approaches. The results of the TFT based method [158], approach by Shah et al. [210], method by Joshi and Jalobeanu [121], adaptive IHS [192], AWLP [178] and Brovey method [71] are shown in Fig. 4.14(a–f) to Fig. 4.16(a–f). The results of the proposed approach based on CT and NSCT transforms are depicted in Fig. 4.14(h, i) to Fig. 4.16(h, i) for the three datasets. In order to compare the fusion performance of using CT/NSCT for the initial estimate over the use of wavelet transform for the same, we also conducted the experiments using a wavelet transform based initial estimate. Here, we use "db3" wavelet in order to obtain the initial estimate. This initial estimate is used in the regularized framework to obtain the final fused image. The fused images obtained with this initial estimate are displayed in Fig. 4.14(g) to Fig. 4.16(g). In all these results, we also include the zoomed-in versions of a small portion of the image for better visual comparison. The quantitative comparison is presented in Table 4.10 for all the un-degraded images; the quality index with no reference (QNR) [19] was used which does not require a reference image. As stated earlier, the definition of QNR involves two terms: spectral distortion (D_λ) and spatial distortion (D_s). These measures along with their ideal values are displayed in Table 4.10. The boldface value in the table indicates that the value is best among the methods.

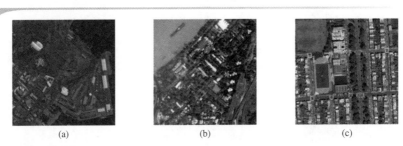

(a)   (b)   (c)

Figure 4.13 Un-degraded (original) MS images captured using different satellite sensors. The size of each MS image is 256 × 256. The MS images for (a) Ikonos-2 satellite with color composition of bands 3, 2, 1, (b) Quickbird satellite with color composition of bands 3, 2, 1 and (c) Worldview-2 satellite with color composition of bands 7, 5, 3. (Courtesy: www.isprs.org, www.glcf.umd.edu, www.digitalglobe.com)

The following observations can be made from the results displayed in Fig. 4.14 to Fig. 4.16. The fused images obtained using TFT method [158], approach by Shah et al. [210] and method by Joshi and Jalobeanu [121] show high spectral and spatial distortions. The other methods such as adaptive IHS [192], AWLP [178] and the Brovey method [71] show improvement in spectral and spatial details. In the results of the Ikonos-2 dataset which is displayed in Fig. 4.14, one may see that the performance of the proposed method is comparable to those of other methods [192, 178, 71]. However, a close observation of these results indicate a small improvement in spatial details in the results of the proposed method when compared to the other methods. The spectral content of the proposed method looks almost similar to other state-of-the-art methods showing better preservation of colors. The quantitative performance for this experiment is listed in Table 4.10 in which

Table 4.10 Quantitative measures for fused MS image results shown in Fig. 4.15 to Fig. 4.16 for un-degraded images. The boldface indicates values closer to the ideal

Dataset	Measure	Ideal value	TFT method [158]	Approach in [210]	Approach in [121]	Adaptive IHS [192]	AWLP method [178]	Brovey method [71]	Proposed using CT	Proposed using NSCT
Ikonos-2 (Fig. 4.14)	QNR	1	0.5772	0.4804	0.4305	0.6521	0.6662	0.6617	0.6664	**0.6772**
	D_λ	0	0.2639	0.2726	0.2658	0.1848	0.1653	0.1751	0.1683	**0.1543**
	D_S	0	0.2159	0.3396	0.4137	0.2001	0.2017	**0.1979**	0.1988	0.1992
Quickbird (Fig. 4.15)	QNR	1	0.5430	0.5581	0.5524	0.6176	0.6125	0.5955	0.6217	**0.6256**
	D_λ	0	0.2726	0.2190	0.2251	0.1825	0.1919	0.2006	0.1845	**0.1811**
	D_S	0	0.2535	0.2854	0.2871	0.2445,	0.2420	0.2551	0.2376	**0.2360**
World-view-2 (Fig. 4.16)	QNR	1	0.5629	0.5200	0.5635	0.5852	0.5929	0.5859	0.6002	**0.6080**
	D_λ	0	0.2302	0.2298	0.1914	0.1769	0.1804	0.1996	0.1720	**0.1716**
	D_S	0	0.2688	0.3249	0.3031	0.2890	0.2766	0.2680	0.2751	**0.2660**

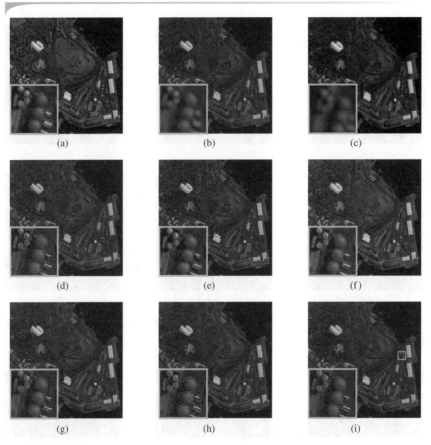

Figure 4.14 MS fusion results for un-degraded dataset consisting of semi-urban area captured using Ikonos-2 satellite shown as color composites of bands 3, 2 and 1 ($q = 4$). Fused images obtained using (a) TFT based approach [158], (b) approach by Shah et al. [210], (c) approach by Joshi and Jalobeanu [121], (d) adaptive IHS approach [192], (e) AWLP [178], (f) Brovey method [71], (g) wavelet based initial estimate, (h) proposed approach using CT and (i) proposed approach using NSCT. (i) Original MS image. The magnified image for a small square region with a green border shown in (i) is displayed at the bottom left corner of all the images. (Courtesy: www.isprs.org)

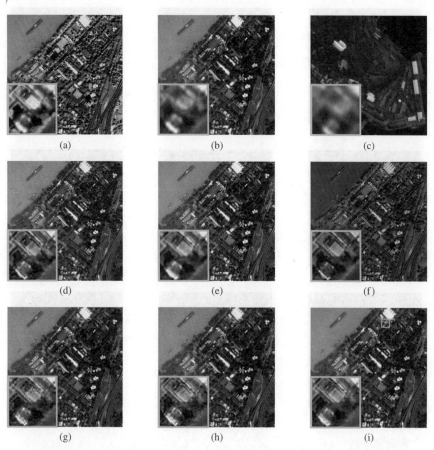

(a) (b) (c)

(d) (e) (f)

(g) (h) (i)

Figure 4.15 MS fusion results for un-degraded dataset consisting of an urban area captured using Quickbird satellite shown as color composites of bands 3, 2 and 1 ($q = 4$). Fused images obtained using (a) TFT based approach [158], (b) approach by Shah et al. [210], (c) approach by Joshi and Jalobeanu [121], (d) adaptive IHS approach [192], (e) AWLP [178], (f) Brovey method [71], (g) wavelet based initial estimate, (h) proposed approach using CT and (i) proposed approach using NSCT. The magnified image for a small square region with a green border shown in (i) is displayed at the bottom left corner of all the images. (Courtesy: www.glcf.umd.edu)

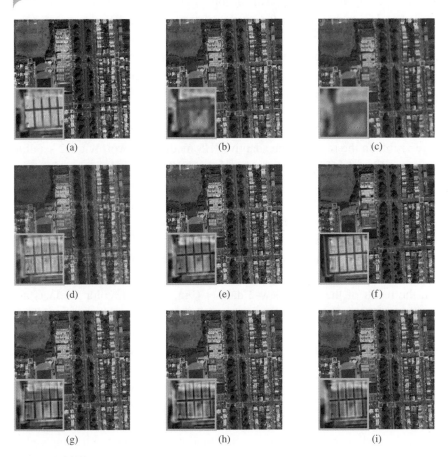

Figure 4.16 MS fusion results for un-degraded dataset consisting of an urban area captured using Worldview-2 satellite shown as color composites of bands 7, 5 and 3 ($q = 4$). Fused images obtained using (a) TFT based approach [158], (b) approach by Shah et al. [210], (c) approach by Joshi and Jalobeanu [121], (d) adaptive IHS approach [192], (e) AWLP [178], (f) Brovey method [71], (g) wavelet based initial estimate, (h) proposed approach using CT and (i) proposed approach using NSCT. The magnified image for a small square region with a green border shown in (i) is displayed at the bottom left corner of all the images. (Courtesy: www.digitalglobe.com)

the values of QNR and spectral distortion D_λ are better for the proposed NSCT based fusion approach and the spatial distortion factor D_s is better for the Brovey method. However, one can see that the difference between the values of D_s for the proposed method and the Brovey method is insignificant. The performance of the proposed method is improved in the results of Quickbird and Worldview-2 satellites displayed in Fig. 4.15 and Fig. 4.16, respectively. In Fig. 4.15, we can see that the use of the adaptive IHS method (Fig. 4.15[d]) causes color artefacts as well as spatial distortions. Similarly, black spots are visible in the result of the adaptive IHS method for Worldview-2 satellite images (Fig. 4.16[d]). The results of the AWLP method displayed in Fig. 4.15(e) and 4.16(e) show improvement in spectral and spatial details when compared to the adaptive IHS method. However, spectral distortion and the loss of edges details are less in the proposed method (see Fig. 4.15[i] and Fig. 4.16[i]) when compared to the results of the AWLP method (Fig. 4.15[e] and Fig. 4.16[e]). The fusion results of the Brovey method are shown in Fig. 4.15(f) and Fig. 4.16(f) for Quickbird and Worldview-2 datasets, respectively. In the result of the Worldview-2 dataset (Fig. 4.16[f]), color artefacts are visible when compared to the results of the proposed method using NSCT displayed in Fig. 4.16(i). Thus, we observe that the performance of the proposed method in terms of perceptual quality is better when compared to the other approaches. Similar to the visual performance, the quantitative analysis (see Table 4.10) also shows better performance for the proposed method using NSCT when compared to all the others. From these results on un-degraded datasets and quantitative comparison, one may conclude that the proposed method has better spectral and spatial details when compared to other state-of-the-art methods. It is important to note that the fused image has significant spatial and color distortions if we choose the wavelet transform instead of CT/NSCT for obtaining the initial estimate. In Fig. 4.14(g) to Fig. 4.16(g), we display these fused images which have a blockiness effect as well as color distortion. This may be due to the limited directionality property of wavelet transforms. We mention here that we conducted the experiments using degraded and un-degraded datasets having different resolutions with different types of regions and the obtained results using the proposed method were better when compared to the state-of-the-art approaches. Thus, we conclude that our fusion method performs better on exhaustive datasets.

4.8.7 Spectral distortion at edge pixels

Since our approach is based on extracting the edges from the initial estimate and incorporating them in the final fused image, it would be of interest to check spectral distortion caused due to this. In order to check the same, we compute the spectral distortion measures on edge pixels. It should be noted that if a sudden change in color occurs over a region, it also results in spatial intensity change in the fused image [32]. Hence, the quantitative measures such as CC and D_λ computed on the fused image pixels are useful in evaluating the performance of the fusion method over the edge regions. Ideally, the values of both CC and D_λ must be 1 and 0, respectively which indicates that the fused edges are the same as the original image.

Both CC and D_λ measures are computed over the edge pixels of the selected regions of Figs 4.6–4.12 and they are displayed in Table 4.11 for the degraded case. In Figs 4.6 and 4.7, we observe that the zoomed-in portions of selected regions of non-urban and urban area acquired using Ikonos-2 satellite have significant spectral details. One can observe that the proposed method has lower values of CC and D_λ when compared to other methods. The spectral distortion measures computed for the results shown in Figs 4.8–4.10 correspond to the results of Quickbird satellite. In this also, the values of the spectral distortion measures are better for the proposed method. It is important to note that although Fig. 4.10 shows spectral distortion in all the methods, the proposed method still works better for this dataset. In the images of Worldview-2 satellite, we have chosen a region which has significant spectral change (see Figs 4.11 and 4.12). Similar to earlier experiments of Ikonos-2 and Quickbird, here also the proposed method has lowest spectral distortion which is clearly indicated by the values shown in Table 4.11. One can see from the results displayed in Fig. 4.12(b) that the fusion results of Shi et al. [213] appear highly distorted. This is also reflected in the values of CC and D_λ in Table 4.11 with a high value of D_λ and significantly low values for CC.

Similar to the degraded dataset experiments, we have also performed the quantitative analysis on edge pixels for the results of un-degraded datasets. In this case, since the original MS image is not available, we compute D_λ only since it does not require the original image. These values of D_λ are displayed in Table 4.12 for the results shown in Figs 4.14–4.16. From the zoomed-in images displayed in these figures, one can visually observe that the proposed

Table 4.11 Spectral distortion measures computed on edge pixels of selected regions shown in Fig. 4.6 to Fig. 4.12 for degraded images. The boldface indicates values closer to the ideal

Dataset	Measure	Band	TFT method [158]	Approach in [213]	Approach in [210]	Approach in [121]	Adaptive IHS [192]	AWLP method [178]	Proposed using CT	Proposed using NSCT
Ikonos-2 (Fig. 4.6)	CC	Band 1	0.8170	0.8464	0.8084	0.8173	0.9164	0.9253	0.9236	**0.9372**
		Band 2	0.8579	0.8200	0.8632	0.8516	0.9245	0.9372	0.9406	**0.9453**
		Band 3	0.8878	0.8756	0.8989	0.8425	0.9515	0.9626	0.9570	**0.9679**
	D_λ	Band 1-3	0.2549	0.2107	0.2204	0.2088	0.1484	0.1366	0.1120	**0.0983**
Ikonos-2 (Fig. 4.7)	CC	Band 2	0.9351	0.8445	0.7952	0.8109	0.9556	0.9559	0.9660	**0.9699**
		Band 3	0.9514	0.8846	0.7851	0.7906	0.9553	0.9610	0.9676	**0.9717**
		Band 4	0.8602	0.8601	0.7254	0.7299	0.9252	0.9269	0.9162	**0.9343**
	D_λ	Band 2-4	0.2813	0.2513	0.2389	0.2647	0.1976	0.1890	0.1941	**0.1856**
Quickbird (Fig. 4.8)	CC	Band 1	0.7032	0.7181	0.8966	0.8575	0.9112	0.9116	**0.9271**	0.9251
		Band 2	0.7773	0.7472	0.8760	0.8663	0.9368	0.9284	0.9339	**0.9416**
		Band 3	0.7303	0.7486	0.8861	0.8526	0.9345	0.9303	0.9410	**0.9471**
	D_λ	Band 1-3	0.2459	0.2366	0.2504	0.2524	0.1582	0.1486	0.1363	**0.1238**
Quickbird (Fig. 4.9)	CC	Band 2	0.6928	0.6865	0.8592	0.8471	0.9352	0.9280	0.9373	**0.9469**
		Band 3	0.6740	0.6608	0.8595	0.8419	0.9020	0.9111	0.9415	**0.9458**
		Band 4	0.6042	0.5516	0.7061	0.8076	0.8915	0.9011	0.9134	**0.9180**
	D_λ	Band 2-4	0.5248	0.3479	0.2655	0.1967	0.1261	0.1344	0.1243	**0.1121**

Table 4.11 Contd.

Dataset	Measure	Band	TFT method [158]	Approach in [213]	Approach in [210]	Approach in [121]	Adaptive IHS [192]	AWLP method [178]	Proposed using CT	Proposed using NSCT
Quickbird (Fig. 4.10)	CC	Band 1	0.5322	0.5856	0.8900	0.8768	0.9203	0.9103	0.9165	**0.9308**
		Band 2	0.5670	0.5281	0.9077	0.8932	0.9288	0.9335	0.9356	**0.9413**
		Band 3	0.4647	0.4911	0.9126	0.8994	0.9370	0.9385	0.9255	**0.9397**
	D_λ	Band 1-3	0.2624	0.2154	0.2290	0.2116	0.1620	0.1670	0.1546	**0.1489**
Worldview-2 (Fig. 4.11)	CC	Band 2	0.8641	0.8318	0.8038	0.8048	0.9218	0.9114	0.9331	**0.9439**
		Band 3	0.9146	0.8857	0.7988	0.7838	0.9412	0.9333	0.9475	**0.9522**
		Band 5	0.8745	0.8919	0.7870	0.7894	0.9346	0.9270	0.9387	**0.9393**
	D_λ	Band 2,3,5	0.2198	0.2203	0.2045	0.2153	0.1533	0.1538	0.1499	**0.1415**
Worldview-2 (Fig. 4.12)	CC	Band 3	0.8914	0.8228	0.8629	0.8973	0.9511	0.9489	0.9553	**0.9607**
		Band 5	0.7820	0.7658	0.8593	0.8657	0.9433	0.9323	0.9497	**0.9546**
		Band 7	0.8527	0.6945	0.8810	0.8820	0.9286	0.9280	0.9325	**0.9360**
	D_λ	Band 3,5,7	0.2151	0.5996	0.2436	0.2525	0.1301	0.1346	0.1206	**0.1145**

Table 4.12 Spectral distortion measures computed on edge pixels of selected regions shown in Fig. 4.14 to Fig. 4.16 for un-degraded images. The boldface indicates values closer to the ideal

Dataset	Measure	Band	TFT method [158]	Approach in [210]	Approach in [121]	Adaptive IHS [192]	AWLP method [178]	Brovey method [71]	Proposed using CT	Proposed using NSCT
Ikonos-2 (Fig. 4.14)	D_λ	Band 1-3	0.2384	0.2263	0.2408	0.1596	0.1588	0.1657	0.1516	**0.1415**
Quickbird (Fig. 4.15)	D_λ	Band 1-3	0.2237	0.1928	0.1943	0.1365	0.1358	0.1309	0.1246	**0.1224**
Worldview-2 (Fig. 4.16)	D_λ	Band 3,5,7	0.2451	0.2667	0.2637	0.1645	0.1595	0.1895	0.1419	**0.1394**

fusion method has better preservation of the spectral details. This observation is also reflected by having lowest values of D_λ for the proposed method when compared to the other fusion techniques. This quantitative analysis performed on degraded and un-degraded datasets also clarifies that the fusion techniques based on multi-resolution analysis (MRA) are proven to be effective against spectral distortions when compared to other fusion methods which is also valid for the proposed method since it is based on CT/NSCT.

4.8.8 Computational time

Finally, let us consider the computational expenses of the different fusion approaches. All these methods have been implemented in Matlab 7.6 installed on Intel core 2 Duo processor with 2.4 GHz, 4 GB memory. In Table 4.13, we display the average computation time to obtain a single fused image for a degraded dataset using different fusion methods. Here, TFT, adaptive IHS, AWLP and Brovey methods have less computational time. However, the fusion method by Shah et al. [210] takes more time due the computation of PCA and cross correlation coefficient. The average time to run the proposed CT based algorithm is about 1.4 seconds while it is slightly more (3.5 seconds) for NSCT based approach. This computation time is a bit more compared to the non-regularizing techniques such as TFT, AWLP and Brovey. However, due to the regularization frame work of the proposed approach, the advantages in terms of preservation of edge and color details are possible at the cost of a slight increment in the computational time. In the proposed method, most of the time is used in obtaining contourlet decomposition at different levels as it is implemented in Matlab. However, it can be reduced drastically if the algorithm is implemented using C language and executed on a machine with a graphical processing unit. Note that our approach does not add to time complexity when compared to the method of fusion involving CT/NSCT [210], since the proposed approach does not involve training database. We even avoid using computationally expensive methods such as simulated annealing for preserving the edges. Much of the computational burden is reduced due to the use of a simple optimization method and the use of an estimated MRF parameter while optimizing the cost function. Use of an estimated MRF parameter avoids trial and error based selection of the parameter during optimization and hence, reduces the computational burden.

Table 4.13 Average computation time involved in different fusion approaches

Experiment on	Average computation time to obtain single fused band (in *seconds*)						
	TFT method [158]	Approach in [210]	Approach in [121]	Adaptive IHS [192]	AWLP method [178]	Brovey method [71]	Proposed using CT	Proposed using NSCT
Degraded dataset	0.5075	56.4426	1.9721	0.7892	0.3263	0.3464	1.3934	3.5403

4.9 Conclusion

We have presented a new technique for multi-resolution image fusion using contourlet based learning and MRF prior. In the proposed method, we first obtain the initial high resolution MS image using the available Pan image and the test MS image. Since the initial estimate has high spatial and spectral resolutions, it is used to obtain the degradation between fused MS and test MS images, where the blur is assumed to be a non-identity matrix. We cast the fusion problem in a restoration framework and obtain the final solution by using a regularization framework. The final cost function is obtained using the MAP–MRF approach, where an MRF smoothness prior is used to regularize the solution. The edge details in the final fused image are obtained by applying Canny edge detector on the initial estimate. This gives us the advantage of preservation of edges in the final solution without using discontinuity preserving prior. The MRF parameter is also estimated using the initial estimate image which is used during optimization. The potential of the proposed fusion method is demonstrated by conducting experiments on the datasets acquired using various satellites. These datasets have pixels corresponding to different regions of ground scene. Along with the qualitative analysis, we also show the quantitative performance by computing various measures. Since the final solution is obtained using Canny edge detector and smoothness MRF prior, the proposed method not only recovers the finer details with minimum spectral distortion, it also avoids the use of computationally expensive optimization techniques. The perceptual and the quantitative analysis show that the proposed technique yields a better solution when compared to the state-of-the-art approaches. In this chapter, the initial estimate was obtained using Pan data. In the next chapter, we derive the initial estimate using the LR MS image itself. We also propose the use of a new prior based on the Gabor filter.

Chapter **5**

Use of Self-similarity and Gabor Prior

In this chapter, we introduce a concept called self-similarity and use the same for obtaining the initial fused image. We also use a new prior called Gabor prior for regularizing the solution. In Chapter 4, degradation matrix entries were estimated by modelling the relationship between the Pan-derived initial estimate of the fused MS image and the LR MS image. This may lead to inaccurate estimate of the final fused image since we make use of the Pan data suffering from low spectral resolution in getting the initial estimate. However, if we derive the initial fused image using the available LR MS image, which has high spectral resolution, mapping between LR and HR would be better and the derived degradation matrix entries are more accurate. This makes the estimated degradation matrix better represent the aliasing since we now have an initial estimate that has both high spatial and spectral resolutions. To do this, we need to obtain the initial estimate using only the available LR MS image since the true fused image is not available. We perform this by using the property of natural images that the probability of the availability of redundant information in the image and its downsampled versions is high [89]. We exploit this self-similarity in the LR observation and the sparse representation theory in order to obtain the initial estimate of the fused image. Finally, we solve the

Pan-sharpening or multi-resolution image fusion problem by using a model based approach in which we regularize the solution by proposing a new prior called the Gabor prior.

5.1 Related Work

Before we discuss our proposed approach, we review few works carried out by researchers on image fusion that use compressive sensing (CS) theory since our work also uses sparse representation involved in CS. Li and Yang [143] applied CS to obtain the fusion of remotely sensed images in which a dictionary was constructed from sample images having high spatial resolution. They obtained the fused image as a linear combination of HR patches available in the dictionary. The performance of their method depends on the availability of high resolution MS images that have spectral components similar to that of the test image. Considering this limitation, Jiang et al. and Li et al. [116, 147] proposed constructing an over-complete joint dictionary from available MS and Pan images and extracting the most relevant spectral and spatial information using L_1 minimization. They considered the MS image as the decimation of the original high resolution MS image and considered the Pan as a linear combination of all the bands of the high resolution MS images. On a similar line, Wei et al. [283] used a dictionary constructed with the Pan image and its downsampled LR version and obtained the fusion by exploring the sparse representation of HR/LR multi-spectral image patches. Cheng et al. [53] used the CS framework with dictionary patches learned from the initial high resolution MS image obtained using AWLP method [178]. They obtained the final fused image using a trained dictionary obtained from K-singular value decomposition (K-SVD). Iqbal et al. [115] created the over-complete dictionary with basis functions of different transforms such as discrete cosine transform (DCT), wavelets, curvelets and ridgelets and the best bases for MS and Pan images were obtained using convex optimization. The final fused MS image was obtained by merging the best bases coefficients of Pan and corresponding MS band according to values of the local information parameter.

The drawback of all these CS based fusion approaches is that the dictionary is constructed either using a database or by the use of MS and Pan images. The use of database requires the availability of high resolution

MS images having characteristics similar to the test image. Pan data suffers from the disadvantage of being of lower spectral resolution for dictionary construction. In the present work, we do not need the Pan data to construct the dictionary; instead, the dictionaries are constructed using the LR HR pairs that are obtained using self-similarity of the observed LR MS image patches. Self-similarity is based on the concept of the probability of occurrence of the same or similar patches within and across the scale of image [89]. Literature shows that on an average, 23% best match patches (exactly the same patches) are available across the image for a downsampling factor (q) of 2 [89]. After obtaining similar patches across the scale of LR MS image and their corresponding HR patches, the HR patches for which matches are not found are obtained by using the sparse representation theory that uses the dictionaries constructed from the LR HR patches already found. This constitutes the initial Pan-sharpened image estimate in our approach. The same is used in estimating the degradation between the LR MS image and the unknown fused image. A regularization framework is then used to obtain the final solution in which the proposed Gabor prior extracts the bandpass details from the Pan image to embed it into the final fused image. In this way, the necessary Pan details are transferred to the final fused image. In addition to the term corresponding to Gabor, our regularization also includes an MRF prior that maintains spatial smoothness in terms of patch continuity in the final fused image. The MRF parameter required while regularizing the solution is estimated using the initial estimate, that is the initial fused image. The final cost function is convex which allows us to use a gradient based optimization technique for minimization.

The proposed approach has the following advantages which makes it different from the other CS and regularization based Pan-sharpening approaches.

- Instead of using Pan and MS images, only the LR MS image is used to obtain the initial estimate which results in a better estimate of degradation between the LR and HR images.

- Spatial details in the final fused image are better preserved due to the use of Gabor prior for regularizing the solution. Use of such a prior not only extracts the high frequency edge details from Pan image, it also extracts the bandpass features and hence aids in making the fused image possess these Pan characteristics.

- Use of a homogeneous MRF prior keeps the patch continuity and hence, spatial details in the final fused image are better preserved.

- The proposed approach avoids the use of computationally taxing optimization methods to obtain the final solution.

5.2 Block Schematic of the Proposed Method

The block schematic to obtain the fused MS image Z^m for the mth low resolution MS is shown in Fig. 5.1. As shown in this figure, we first obtain the initial HR approximation to the fused image by using the self-similarity of the mth LR image patches followed by the sparse representation theory on these patches. Assuming that the initial HR approximation or initial estimate is close to the final Pan-sharpened image, we then obtain the patchwise degradation between the Pan-sharpened image and the LR MS image from this initial estimate. Using a model based approach, the degradation matrix estimated for each patch are used in the data fitting term of the final cost function. With maximum *a posteriori* (MAP) framework, our final cost function consists of two prior terms in addition to the data fitting term. Here, we use a Gabor prior that extracts the bandpass details including the high frequency contents from the Pan image and makes the fused image possess

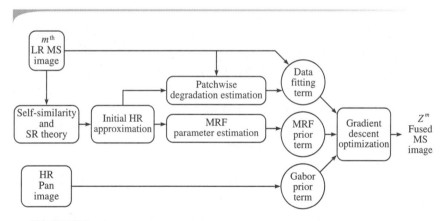

Figure 5.1   Block schematic of the proposed image fusion method for fusing m^{th} MS and the Pan images. Here, LR and HR correspond to low resolution and high resolution, respectively.

these features. Another prior term is based on MRF in order to maintain spatial continuity between patches. Here, the single MRF parameter used in the regularization is estimated using the initial estimate. Finally, gradient descent optimization technique is used to obtain the final Pan-sharpened image.

5.3   Initial HR Approximation

In the proposed method, we obtain an initial HR approximation (initial estimate) which is used in obtaining the degradation or transformation between LR and HR patches of MS and also to obtain the MRF parameter. One may obtain the transformation by using a training set of LR and HR pairs of MS images. However, we do not have the HR MS images since they have to be estimated. We have the Pan image available at high resolution which we may use as HR MS approximation to find the transformations and use them in our optimization to get the final solution. However, this is not a good idea because of the following reasons. (1) Pan has low spectral resolution and hence using it to obtain the transformation cannot serve as an accurate estimate of degradation between LR–HR MS images. (2) Using the same Pan for all LR MS images adds to inaccurate estimates of degradation between LR and HR MS images and (3) the total spectral width of MS images and the Pan image may differ in many of the satellite sensors adding to inaccurate estimates of transformation. This motivates us to obtain initial HR MS estimates separately for each LS MS observation by using the available LR MS itself. By doing so, we obtain initial HR MS images with high spectral as well as spatial resolutions for each LR MS image and hence, the estimated degradation is more accurate. In our work, the initial approximation is obtained by using the concepts of self-similarity and sparse representation. The unmatched patches are estimated using the sparse representation framework.

In Fig. 5.2, we illustrate the concept of self-similarity. Figure 5.2(a) displays the LR MS image (I_0) of Quickbird satellite shown with color composition of bands 3, 2 and 1. The coarser resolution (I_{-1}) for downsampling factor (q) 2 of the same image is displayed in Fig. 5.2(b). In order to obtain the downsampled image, we pass the LR MS image through a Gaussian filter with different Nyquist cutoff frequencies considering the sensors modulation transfer function (MTF) [12] followed by a downsampling operation with a factor of 2 along rows and columns. However, it is a good idea to use the registered pair of LR and its downsampled version when they are available. Consider a patch P_0 of size $w \times w$ which is marked with a green border in I_0. We can observe in Fig. 5.2(b) that the same or a similar patch is also available in its coarser image I_{-1} as P_{-1} which is also marked with green border. Since these two patches form an LR–LR match, parent HR patch (R_0) of P_{-1} (marked with a blue color border in Fig. 5.2(a)) of size $qw \times qw$ is available in the LR MS image itself forming the corresponding LR–HR matched pair, that is P_0 and R_0 constitute an LR–HR matched pair. Note that R_0 represents the matched HR patch for P_0.

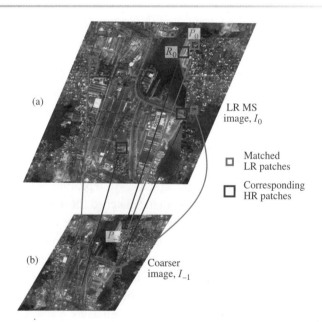

Figure 5.2   Patch recurrence for LR MS image into its coarser resolution image. (a) LR MS image, I_0, and (b) coarser resolution of (a), I_{-1}. Here, patches shown with green border are the matched LR patch pairs and corresponding to these matched pairs, HR patches are shown with blue border in (a).

In order to investigate the possible number of matched LR–HR pairs in different types of satellite images, we carried out the statistical analysis for downsampling factor (q) of 2 and 4.

To do this, we conducted an experiment with different images captured using various satellites such as Ikonos-2, Quickbird and Worldview-2. Here, we use 50 MS images each of size 256×256 for every satellite. The coarser resolution images for $q = 2$ and $q = 4$ are obtained using Gaussian blurring and downsampling operation. In each band of MS image, we consider an LR patch of size $w \times w$ (here $w = 5$) and is searched in its coarser resolution image. The *approximate nearest neighbourhood* (ANN) [24] is used to find the same patch using the sum of squared difference (SSD) distance criteria resulting in an LR–LR match. The threshold value for SSD is set to be 0 for all the datasets. Since the resolution difference is known, the corresponding $qw \times qw$ matched HR patch can be easily located in the LR MS band and this results an in an LR–HR matched pair.

In order to understand this, consider an experiment with resolution difference of 2. We have two images of the MS band having a size of 256×256 and 128×128 pixels, respectively. If a $w \times w$ patch in the MS image of size 256×256 is matched (similar) to a patch centred at a location (l, m) in its coarser resolution of size 128×128, then a patch of size $2w \times 2w$ centred at $(2l, 2m)$ in the MS image of size 256×256 corresponds to a matched HR patch giving a matched LR–HR patch pair. We repeat this procedure for all the non overlapping patches and obtain the matched LR–HR patch pairs in the given band. We then calculate the percentage of LR–HR matched patch pairs by using the total number of available LR patches and matched LR–HR patch pairs for that band. This experiment is performed for all the 50 images of that particular satellite to obtain the different number of matched LR–HR patch pairs; we then compute the average value in order to display the statistics. This statistics is presented in Fig. 5.3 for $q = 2$ as well as for $q = 4$. One can see in Fig. 5.3 that for Ikonos-2 images, out of a total number of 63504 patches, we obtained $23.25\% (\approx 14765)$ and $6.02\% (\approx 3822)$ matched LR–HR patch pairs for $q = 2$ and 4, respectively. It is worthwhile to mention that since there are more patches matched for $q = 2$ than for $q = 4$, we use the coarser resolution image of $q = 2$ only while finding the matches. Hence, in order to obtain the initial estimates for our MS bands where q is 4, we repeat the procedure for

$q = 2$. We can see that on an average, the number of matched LR–HR patch pairs for $q = 2$ and 4 are 23% and 5%, respectively.

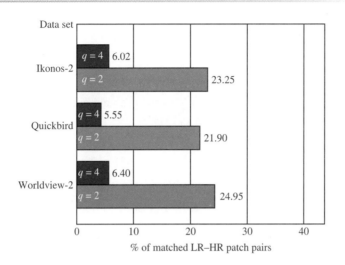

Figure 5.3 The statistics for the number of matched LR–HR patch pairs using the images of different satellites for $q = 2$ and 4.

As already discussed, the ANN is used to find the patch match in the LR and its coarser versions and hence, its HR patch can be found from the LR image itself. To find the initial approximation, we need to find an HR patch for every LR patch by considering non overlapping patches in the LR MS image. We make use of the already found LR–HR pairs to find the remaining HR patches, that is HR patches for the unmatched LR–LR patches. Let N_{best} be the number of matched LR–HR patch pairs in the given LR MS image and corresponding to this, let D_{LR} and D_{HR} be the LR and HR dictionaries of size $w^2 \times N_{best}$ and $q^2 w^2 \times N_{best}$, respectively. Here, $w^2 \times 1$ and $q^2 w^2 \times 1$ correspond to the size of lexicographically ordered pixels in the LR and HR patch, respectively. These dictionaries and sparse representation framework are used to obtain the remaining HR patches. The sparse representation theory described by Bruckstein et al. [37] demonstrates the recovery of the sparse vector. A vector $\mathbf{x}$ in $\Re^{\aleph_1}$ can be represented as

$$\mathbf{x} = \Psi \mathbf{v} \text{ for } \Psi \in \Re^{\aleph_1 \times \aleph_2}, \ \aleph_1 << \aleph_2. \tag{5.1}$$

Here, Ψ is a measurement matrix and $\mathbf{v}$ is a $\aleph_2 \times 1$ vector of weighting coefficients. If the vector $\mathbf{v}$ is sparse in the Ψ domain, then only a few columns of Ψ are required to form vector $\mathbf{x}$. The sparsest solution may be obtained by solving the following problem

$$\min \| \mathbf{v} \|_0, \quad \text{subject to } \mathbf{x} = \Psi \mathbf{v}, \qquad (5.2)$$

where $\| \cdot \|_0$ represents the L_0 norm which counts the number of non-zero elements in $\mathbf{v}$. However, this is an NP hard problem and its solution is often obtained through L_1 minimization as [51],

$$\min \| \mathbf{v} \|_1 \quad \text{subject to } \mathbf{x} = \Psi \mathbf{v}. \qquad (5.3)$$

One can adapt the aforementioned framework to noisy setting, where the measurements are contaminated with a noise η as done by Bruckstein et al. [37],

$$\mathbf{x} = \Psi \mathbf{v} + \eta \quad \text{for } \| \eta \|_2 < \varepsilon. \qquad (5.4)$$

A stable solution can be obtained from

$$\min \| \mathbf{v} \|_1 \quad \text{subject to } \| \mathbf{x} - \Psi \mathbf{v} \|_2 < \varepsilon. \qquad (5.5)$$

An L_1 norm is closest to the L_0 norm, so this substitution is often referred to as convex relaxation [37]. With this new formulation, a solution can be obtained in polynomial time by using greedy pursuits and iterative thresholding methods [37,182,162].

The HR patches for unmatched LR (I_0)–LR (I_{-1}) patches are obtained using the sparse representation framework as depicted in Fig. 5.4. Given an LR patch for which no HR match is available and the LR dictionary D_{LR}, we can estimate the sparse coefficient vector $\mathbf{v}$ using L_1 minimization. This is represented in Fig. 5.4(a). Assuming that both the LR and HR patches have the same sparseness, the estimated sparse vector can be utilized to compute the unknown HR patch as displayed in Fig. 5.4(b). Repeating this for all those LR patches for which no HR matches are available, we obtain LR–HR matched pairs for the complete image. Placing these HR patches at their corresponding locations results in the initial approximation image. It is important to note that if the number of matched LR patches are significant, the quality of the initial estimate would be better since we compute the unmatched LR–HR patches using the linear sparse combination of matched LR–HR patches. The procedure is repeated to obtain an initial estimate separately for each LR MS image.

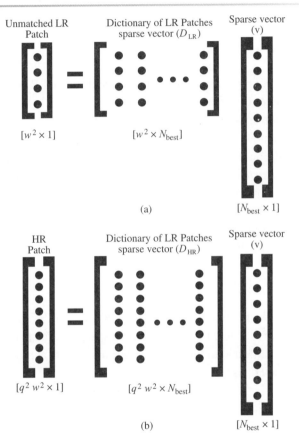

(a) Sparse representation framework to obtain the sparse coefficient vector **v** for unmatched LR patches. (b) The corresponding HR patch estimated using a dictionary of HR patches (D_{HR}) and the spare vector **v** obtained in (a). Here the sparse representation framework is depicted for $q = 2$.

5.4 LR MS Image Formation Model and Degradation Matrix Estimation

The LR MS image is modelled as a blurred and noisy version of the true MS image. This linear model for the ith patch of the mth LR MS image of size $N_1 \times N_2$ can be written as

$$\mathbf{y}_i^m = A_i^m \mathbf{z}_i^m + \mathbf{n}_i^m, \quad m = 1,2,\dots,l, \quad i = 1,2,\dots,N. \tag{5.6}$$

In equation (5.6), l represents the number of bands in the LR MS image and N is the total number of patches, each of size $w \times w$ in the LR MS image Y. The $\mathbf{y}_i^m$ and $\mathbf{z}_i^m$ are the lexicographically ordered vectors of the ith patch for the mth LR MS and unknown Pan-sharpened or fused MS images, respectively. The $\mathbf{n}_i^m$ is the corresponding noise vector which is assumed to be an *independent and identical distribution (iid)* Gaussian with zero mean and unit variance. The degradation matrix for the ith patch of the mth LR MS image is given by A_i^m and it is unknown since we do not have the fused MS image. Since we already know the initial estimate of the fused image, we use it for estimating A_i^m. One may write A_i^m as

$$A_i^m = D_i^m H_i^m, \quad m = 1,2,\dots l, \tag{5.7}$$

where D_i^m is the decimation matrix of size $w^2 \times q^2 w^2$ and H_i^m is the blur matrix of size $q^2 w^2 \times q^2 w^2$, which is assumed to be space invariant. By considering the LR pixel as a linear combination of q^2 HR pixels with appropriate weights, one may choose D_i^m as

$$D_i^m = \begin{pmatrix} a_{i1}^m \, a_{i2}^m \dots a_{iq^2}^m & 0 & 0 \\ 0 & a_{i1}^m \, a_{i2}^m \dots a_{iq^2}^m & 0 \\ \cdot & \cdot & \cdot \\ 0 & 0 & a_{i1}^m \, a_{i2}^m \dots a_{iq^2}^m \end{pmatrix}. \tag{5.8}$$

Moreover, the space invariant blur matrix H_i^m has the form

$$
H_i^m = \begin{pmatrix}
H_{i0}^m & H_{iqM^2-1}^m & H_{iqM^2-2}^m & \cdots & H_{i1}^m \\
H_{i1}^m & H_{i0}^m & H_{iqM^2-1}^m & \cdots & H_{i2}^m \\
\cdot & \cdot & & \cdots & \cdot \\
H_{iqM^2-1}^m & H_{iqM^2-2}^m & H_{iqM^2-3}^m & \cdots & H_{i0}^m
\end{pmatrix}, \tag{5.9}
$$

where $m = 1, 2, \ldots, l$ and each H_{ij} can be written as

$$
H_{ij}^m = \begin{pmatrix}
h_{ij,0}^m & h_{ij,q-1}^m & h_{ij,q-2}^m & \cdots & h_{ij,1}^m \\
h_{ij,1}^m & h_{ij,0}^m & h_{ij,q-1}^m & \cdots & h_{ij,2}^m \\
\cdot & \cdot & & \cdots & \cdot \\
h_{ij,q-1}^m & h_{ij,q-2}^m & h_{ij,q-3}^m & \cdots & h_{ij,0}^m
\end{pmatrix}. \tag{5.10}
$$

Here $h_{...}$ are the values of the point spread function (PSF) for blur. Since we consider a space invariant blur, H_i^m is the block circulant. The multiplication of D_i^m and H_i^m results in the A_i^m matrix which is given by

$$
A_i^m = \begin{pmatrix}
A_{i1}^m & A_{i2}^m & \cdots & A_{iq^2M^2-1}^m & A_{iq^2M^2}^m \\
A_{iq^2M^2-q+1}^m & \cdots & A_{i1}^m & A_{i2}^m \cdots & A_{iq^2M^2-q}^m \\
\cdot & \cdot & & \cdot & \cdot \\
\cdots & & \cdots A_{i1}^m & \cdots & \cdots
\end{pmatrix}. \tag{5.11}
$$

For $w = 2$ and $q = 2$, the A_i^m matrix has a size of 4×16 and can be written as in equation (5.12). In equation (5.13), we give the entries of the A_i matrix estimated for one of the best matched LR–HR patch pair for $w = 2$ and $q = 2$.

$$
A_i^m = \begin{pmatrix}
A_{i1}^m & A_{i2}^m & A_{i3}^m & A_{i4}^m & A_{i5}^m & A_{i6}^m & A_{i7}^m & A_{i8}^m & A_{i9}^m & A_{i10}^m \\
A_{i13}^m & A_{i14}^m & A_{i15}^m & A_{i16}^m & A_{i1}^m & A_{i2}^m & A_{i3}^m & A_{i4}^m & A_{i5}^m & A_{i6}^m \\
A_{i9}^m & A_{i10}^m & A_{i11}^m & A_{i12}^m & A_{i13}^m & A_{i14}^m & A_{i15}^m & A_{i16}^m & A_{i1}^m & A_{i2}^m \\
A_{i5}^m & A_{i6}^m & A_{i7}^m & A_{i8}^m & A_{i9}^m & A_{i10}^m & A_{i11}^m & A_{i12}^m & A_{i13}^m & A_{i14}^m
\end{pmatrix}
$$

$$
\begin{pmatrix}
A_{i11}^m & A_{i12}^m & A_{i13}^m & A_{i14}^m & A_{i15}^m & A_{i16}^m \\
A_{i7}^m & A_{i8}^m & A_{i9}^m & A_{i10}^m & A_{i11}^m & A_{i12}^m \\
A_{i3}^m & A_{i4}^m & A_{i5}^m & A_{i6}^m & A_{i7}^m & A_{i8}^m \\
A_{i15}^m & A_{i16}^m & A_{i1}^m & A_{i2}^m & A_{i3}^m & A_{i4}^m
\end{pmatrix}. \tag{5.12}
$$

$$A_i = \begin{pmatrix} 0.0691 & 0.0778 & 0.0472 & 0.0812 & 0.0590 & 0.0477 & 0.0544 & 0.0677 \\ 0.0590 & 0.0477 & 0.0544 & 0.0677 & 0.0605 & 0.0550 & 0.0474 & 0.0538 \\ 0.0605 & 0.0550 & 0.0474 & 0.0538 & 0.0859 & 0.0469 & 0.0735 & 0.0712 \\ 0.0859 & 0.0469 & 0.0735 & 0.0712 & 0.0691 & 0.0778 & 0.0472 & 0.0812 \end{pmatrix}$$

$$\begin{pmatrix} 0.0605 & 0.0550 & 0.0474 & 0.0538 & 0.0859 & 0.0469 & 0.0735 & 0.0712 \\ 0.0859 & 0.0469 & 0.0735 & 0.0712 & 0.0691 & 0.0778 & 0.0472 & 0.0812 \\ 0.0691 & 0.0778 & 0.0472 & 0.0812 & 0.0590 & 0.0477 & 0.0544 & 0.0677 \\ 0.0590 & 0.0477 & 0.0544 & 0.0677 & 0.0605 & 0.0550 & 0.0474 & 0.0538 \end{pmatrix}. \quad (5.13)$$

We estimate the entries in equation (5.11) using the ith matched LR–HR patch pair. Inclusion of non-identity blur matrix in equation (5.7) makes it an underdetermined system of equations and hence, it cannot be solved using left inverse. We use a minimum norm approach for estimating A_i^m for all i and m. Note that the degradation matrix consists of decimation and blur matrices which means that our model takes care of both aliasing occurring due to LR (downsampling) and blur.

5.5 Regularization Using Gabor and MRF Priors

As discussed in the previous section, the initial estimate is obtained by using the LR MS image itself, thus avoiding the use of Pan to model the LR–HR mapping. Due to this, the spectral details are intact in the initial estimate resulting in a better degradation estimation. The Pan-sharpening problem formulated using equation (5.6) is ill-posed which requires regularization in order to obtain a final solution. To regularize the solution, we need a suitable prior that preserves the spatial features at various frequencies. We also need to take care of the spatial dependencies in the final Pan-sharpened image. In the literature, many researchers have used various edge-preserving priors for Pan-sharpening. However, these priors are only suitable for preserving the high frequency content. Moreover, they are computationally inefficient since they use costly optimization techniques in order to obtain the final solution. In order to capture features of Pan at various frequencies, one may use a Gabor filter, which is a linear filter used to extract the bandpass details present in the signal/image at various frequencies and orientations. Since the Pan image has high spatial resolution, these details can be extracted from the Pan image and used as prior in order to improve the final solution. The Gabor filter has been used for texture representation and synthesis in the computer vision community [123,254]. The impulse response of 2D Gabor filter can be obtained by modulating a 2D sinusoidal using 2D Gaussian function as

$$g(x,y,f,\theta,\sigma_x,\sigma_y) = e^{-\frac{1}{2}(\frac{x'^2}{\sigma_x^2}+\frac{y'^2}{\sigma_y^2})} \cos(2\pi f x'), \tag{5.14}$$

where (x,y) denotes the spatial coordinates and $(x',y') = (x\cos(\theta) + y\sin(\theta), -x\sin(\theta) + y\cos(\theta))$ represents the rotated (x,y) coordinates with angle θ. σ_x and σ_y are the variances in the x and y directions for the Gaussian kernel and f represents the spatial frequency of the sinusoid. The Gabor filter given in equation (5.14) describes the bandpass filter with varying frequency f and orientation θ.

The use of a Gabor prior in the proposed approach is illustrated in Fig. 5.5. It consists of the Gabor filter bank having different frequencies and orientations. The Pan and unknown Pan-sharpened image (to be estimated) are passed through this filter bank. Since the Gabor filter extracts the bandpass features, the outputs of the filter bank for Pan and the unknown Pan-sharpened image correspond to the features at different frequencies and orientations. In Fig. 5.5, we display the Gabor filter bank outputs when an ith patch of the Pan and Pan-sharpened images are applied as input to the filter bank. Here, R represents the number of filters in the Gabor filter bank. Using this setup for prior, in our approach, we seek a Pan-sharpened image which when passed through the Gabor filter bank has the bandpass details similar to that of the Pan image (see Fig. 5.5[b]).

In addition to the Gabor prior, we also use the Markov random field (MRF) prior that preserves the patch continuity. Since our approach is based on patch based learning, the final output may exhibit blockiness which can be taken care of by using MRF as a smoothness prior. The MRF gives the spatial contextual dependency among the neighbouring pixels and the same can be used to preserve the continuity in the final Pan-sharpened image.

By using first order neighbourhood, the MRF prior can be written as

$$\sum_{c \in C} V_c(\mathbf{z}^m) = \gamma^m \sum_{k=1}^{qN_1} \sum_{l=1}^{qN_2} [(Z_{k,l}^m - Z_{k,l-1}^m)^2 + (Z_{k,l}^m - Z_{k-1,l}^m)^2], \tag{5.15}$$

where γ^m represents the MRF parameter that indicates the penalty for departure from smoothness in $\mathbf{z}^m$. C is the set of all cliques. The parameter

γ^m should be estimated using the fused image. However, this is unknown and hence, we use the initial approximation itself to estimate γ^m and use maximum pseudolikelihood [145] for the same. Note that in equation (5.15), Z^m represents the entire image rather than a patch.

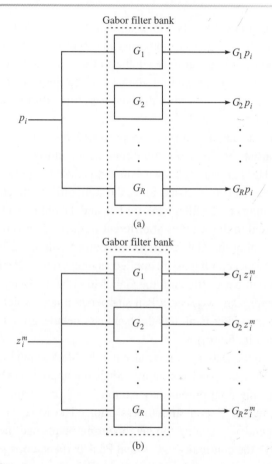

(a)

(b)

Figure 5.5   Illustration of Gabor prior. The outputs of the Gabor filter bank when input is the ith patch of (a) Pan image and (b) unknown Pan-sharpened image.

Using MAP–MRF regularization framework, one can obtain the final cost function for estimating the final fused image for the mth LR MS as

$$\hat{\mathbf{z}}^m = \underset{\mathbf{z}^m}{\arg\min} \left[\varepsilon(\mathbf{z}^m) \right], \tag{5.16}$$

where $\varepsilon(\mathbf{z}^m)$ can be expressed as

$$\varepsilon(\mathbf{z}^m) = \sum_{i=1}^{N} \left(\| \mathbf{y}_i^m - A_i^m \mathbf{z}_i^m \|^2 + \sum_{j=1}^{R} \| G_j \mathbf{p}_i - G_j \mathbf{z}_i^m \|^2 \right) + \sum_{c \in C} V_c(\mathbf{z}^m). \tag{5.17}$$

A_i^m corresponds to the estimated degradation between the ith low resolution MS image patch and the corresponding Pan-sharpened patch. Here, N represents the total number of patches in the LR MS image which is also the number of patches in the Pan-sharpened image. R denotes the total number of Gabor filters in the filter bank. The second and third terms in equation (5.17) are Gabor and MRF smoothness priors, respectively. G_j represents a Gabor filter operator that corresponds to the jth filter impulse response; $\mathbf{p}_i$ denotes the ith patch vector of the Pan image arranged in the lexicographical order.

5.5.1 Optimization process

Since the cost function given in equation (5.17) is convex, it can be minimized using a simple gradient based technique, which quickly leads to the minima. It is worthwhile to mention here that the minimization of the first and second terms in equation (5.17) is performed patchwise; however, the minimization of the last term in the same equation is carried out on the entire image. The gradient of this cost is given by differentiating it with respect to $\mathbf{z}^m$ as

$$\nabla \varepsilon(\mathbf{z}^m) = -2 \sum_{i=1}^{N} \left[(A_i^m)^T (\mathbf{y}_i^m - A_i^m \mathbf{z}_i^m) + \sum_{j=1}^{R} G_j^T (G_j \mathbf{p}_i - G_j \mathbf{z}_i^m) \right] + 2\gamma^m \hat{\mathbf{g}}^m,$$

$$\tag{5.18}$$

where the first two terms correspond to differentiation of the data fitting and Gabor prior terms, while $\hat{\mathbf{g}}^m$ vector is constructed after differentiating $\sum_{c \in C} V_c(\mathbf{z}^m)$ at every location. The differentiation with respect to $Z^m(i, j)$ of the second term at an (i, j) location is given by

$$\hat{G}^m(i,j) = 2[4Z^m_{(i,j)} - Z^m_{(i,j-1)} - Z^m_{(i,j+1)} - Z^m_{(i-1,j)} - Z^m_{(i+1,j)}]. \quad (5.19)$$

Note that $\nabla\varepsilon(\mathbf{z}^m)$ is a vector of size $q^2 N_1 N_2 \times 1$. The complete gradient descent optimization process is depicted in algorithm 5.1 which is similar to algorithm 4.1.

Algorithm 5.1: Gradient descent technique

Data: LR MS image ($\mathbf{y}^m$), initial estimate obtained using self-similarity
and sparse representation theory (($\mathbf{z}^m)^0$), γ^m and patchwise A^m_i,
$i = 1, 2, ..., N$

Result: Fused MS image ($\hat{\mathbf{z}}^m$)

foreach LR MS image y^m, $m = 1, 2, ..., l$ **do**

> Set $n = 0$;
>
> **repeat**
>
>> Find gradient with respect to $(\mathbf{z}^m)^n$ of cost function given in equation
>> (5.17) using equation (5.18);
>>
>> Perform $(\mathbf{z}^m)^{n+1} = (\mathbf{z}^m)^n - \alpha_m (\nabla E(\mathbf{z}^m)^n)$, where α_m is the step size;
>>
>> $n = n + 1$;
>
> **until** $\frac{\|(z^m)^n - (z^m)^{n-1}\|^2}{\|(z^m)^{n-1}\|^2} \le 10^{-06}$;
>
> Set $\hat{\mathbf{z}}^m = (\mathbf{z}^m)^{n-1}$;

5.6   Experimental Results

The effectiveness of the proposed Pan-sharpening approach is verified by conducting the experiments on datasets of different satellites such as Ikonos-2, Quickbird and Worldview-2. The spatial resolution difference between Pan and MS images captured by using these satellites is 4. We conducted the experiments on degraded as well as on un-degraded (original) images. Details of the datasets used for experimentation are given in Table 5.1. The data for the experiments were prepared from the original MS and Pan images using cropping operation. The original MS and Pan images were cropped appropriately to obtain the images of size 256×256 and 1024×1024, respectively and these cropped images were used in all our experiments. These datasets were co-registered before conducting the experiment. It is worthwhile to mention here that we use the datasets with the original radiometric resolution without doing any pre-processing such as contrast stretching. For the accurate and fair comparison, we have used the *Pan-sharpening toolbox* made available by Zeng and Lu [240]. The performance of the proposed fusion method is compared with the following state-of-the-art Pan-sharpening techniques.

Table 5.1 Details of datasets used in experimentation

Satellite	Ikonos-2	Quickbird	Worldview-2
Acquired date	November 16, 2000	January 28, 2005	October 9, 2011
Area covered	Sichuan region China	Sundarban India	San Francisco USA
Spatial MS Resolution Pan	4 m × 4 m 1 m × 1 m	2.4 m × 2.4 m 0.6 m × 0.6 m	2 m × 2 m 0.5 m × 0.5 m
Radiometric resolution	11-bits	11-bits	11-bits
No. of Pan and MS images	1 Pan, 4 MS bands	1 Pan, 4 MS bands	1 Pan, 8 MS bands
Original size: PAN MS	9200 × 7260 2300 × 1815	16384 × 16384 4096 × 4096	16384 × 16384 4096 × 4096

(a) EXP: MS image interpolation by using a polynomial kernel with 23 coefficients [240]

(b) GIHS: *generalised IHS* [230]

(c) GSA: Gram-Schmidt adaptive (GSA) [13]

(d) PRACS: partial replacement adaptive component substitution (PRACS) [55]

(e) AWLP: additive wavelet luminance proportional [178]

(f) MTF–GLP: modulation transfer function–generalised Laplacian pyramid [11] with MTF-matched filter [12] with unitary injection model,

(g) MTF–GLP–CBD: GLP [11] with MTF-matched filter [12] and regression based injection model [18]

(h) Aly and Sharma [22].

The quantitative analysis of the experiments on the degraded dataset was performed by calculating the following different measures:

- $Q2^l$: quality index (i.e., Q4 for four band datasets and Q8 for the Worldview-2 dataset) [17]

- Q_{AVG}: average quality index [248]

- SAM: spectral angle mapper [269]

- ERGAS: erreur relative global adimensionnelle de synthse [243]

- SCC: spatial correlation coefficient [178]

In the case of the un-degraded experiments, quality with no reference (QNR) [19] was computed which does not require a reference image. The QNR measure is a combination of the spectral and spatial distortions which are represented by D_λ and D_s, respectively. We have used the same *Pan-sharpening toolbox* [240] for the estimation of all the aforementioned measures.

5.6.1 Experimental setup

In order to perform the experiments on the degraded dataset, we passed the original Pan and MS images through a Gaussian filter with different Nyquist cutoff frequencies considering the sensor's modulation transfer function (MTF) [12] and downsampling operation. The downsampling factor (decimation) was chosen as $q = 4$ since the spatial resolution difference between MS and Pan images was 4. Thus, the size of the degraded MS and Pan images were 64×64 and 256×256, respectively. However, for un-degraded experiments, they remained same as the original size of the MS and Pan image. We used a patch size (w) of 5×5 while obtaining the initial estimate. We also experimented with a patch size of 7×7, but there was no significant improvement in the visual quality in the estimated image. In order to obtain the unmatched HR patches, we used L_1 minimization with the L_1 *MAGIC* toolbox provided by Candes and Romberg [40]. We obtained the initial estimate for all the datasets; but, due to the space constraint, they are not displayed here. In the Gabor filter bank, we used 8 filters having different frequencies and orientations [282]. Note that they were chosen after extensive experimentation on various satellite images and they remained fixed while experimenting on other satellite images. Here, we chose 2 frequencies and 4 orientations making them 8 pairs with one pair corresponding to each filter. The chosen frequencies were 0.03, 1.50 and the orientations were 0, 45,

90, 145. We experimented with more number of filters in the bank; however, the improvement in the final Pan-sharpened images was not very significant. The step size for gradient descent optimization was chosen as 0.01 for all the experiments. Quantitative measures such as Q4 and Q_{AVG} are generally calculated using non-overlapping windows with different window size, that is, 8×8, 16×16, etc. In our experiments, we fixed this to 32×32 for all the results.

5.6.2 Experimental results on degraded and un-degraded Ikonos-2 datasets

The first experiment was conducted on the degraded and un-degraded images of Ikonos-2 satellite. Details of the data captured using this satellite can be found in Table 5.1. The acquired images in this dataset were downloaded from ftp://ftp.glcf.umd.edu/glcf/China_earthquake_May_2008/IKONOS and it consists of mountainous and vegetation areas of Sichuan region in China; the Pan-sharpening results of the same are displayed using the color composition of 4, 3 and 1 bands. The results obtained using different state-of-the-art approaches in addition to the proposed approach are displayed in Fig. 5.6 and Fig. 5.7 for degraded and un-degraded images, respectively. The interpolated version of the MS image referred as EXP is displayed in Fig. 5.6(a) and Fig. 5.7(a) for degraded and un-degraded datasets, respectively. The Pan-sharpened results of the GIHS method on degraded and original (un-degraded) data are depicted in Fig. 5.6(b) and Fig. 5.7(b), respectively. In Fig. 5.6(c) and Fig. 5.7(c), we display the results of the GSA method. The fusion results obtained using PRACS algorithm are displayed in Fig. 5.6(d) and Fig. 5.7(d). The Pan-sharpening results of the AWLP method are displayed in Fig. 5.6(e) and Fig. 5.7(e). In Fig. 5.6(f, g) and Fig. 5.7(f, g), we display the Pan-sharpening results obtained using MTF–GLP and MTF–GLP–CBD methods, respectively. In Fig. 5.6(i) and Fig. 5.7(i), we display the results of the proposed Pan-sharpening approach. The original image is available for the experiment on degraded data and the same is displayed in Fig. 5.6(j). In order to have a better visual comparison among the results, we also display the enlarged versions of a small area marked with red border shown in Fig. 5.6(j) and Fig. 5.7(i). In Fig. 5.6, this magnified portion contains a road in the mountain region and in Fig. 5.7, it consists of

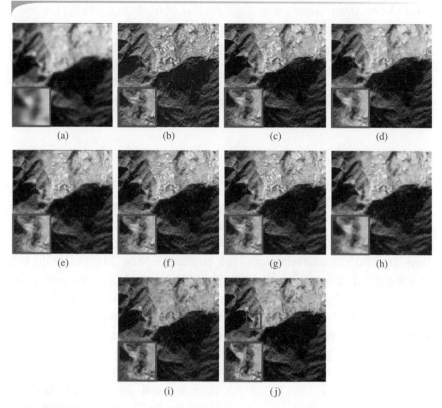

Figure 5.6 Results of Pan-sharpening on the degraded dataset of Ikonos-2 satellite consisting of an urban area shown as color of band compositions 4, 3 and 1 ($q =4$). Pan-sharpened images obtained using (a) EXP, (b) GIHS, (c) GSA, (d) PRACS, (e) AWLP, (f) MTF–GLP, (g) MTF–GLP–CBD, (h) Aly and Sharma, (i) proposed approach. (j) Original MS image. The magnified image of a small square region with a red border shown in (j) is displayed at the bottom left corner of all the images. (Courtesy: www.glcf.umd.edu)

vegetation area. The enlarged portion is shown in each of the images at the bottom left corner. The quantitative measures of this experiment using the degraded dataset are summarized in Table 5.2. For the experiment on the

Table 5.2 Quantitative measures for Ikonos-2 imagery shown in Fig. 5.6 and Fig. 5.7. Here, a boldface value indicates that the value is better amongst the other methods. The numbers in the brackets indicate the ideal values

Dataset	Measure	GIHS	GSA	PRACS	AWLP	MTF-GLP	MTF-GLP-CBD	Aly and Sharma	Proposed
Degraded (Fig. 5.6)	$Q4(1)$	0.5187	0.7022	0.7183	0.7323	0.7374	0.7320	0.8496	**0.8521**
	$Q_{AVG}(1)$	0.5916	0.6968	0.7144	0.7306	0.7260	0.7209	0.8369	**0.8393**
	SAM(0)	5.0595	4.6361	4.6503	4.7700	4.4351	4.4904	**3.5943**	4.0821
	ERGAS(0)	4.8787	4.6051	4.3082	4.5287	4.2335	4.3194	3.1040	**3.0989**
	SCC(1)	0.6084	0.6638	0.6686	0.6575	0.6845	0.6793	0.8624	**0.8701**
Un-degraded (Fig. 5.7)	$D_S(0)$	0.4212	0.3573	0.2858	**0.1724**	0.1997	0.1888	0.3318	0.2350
	$D_\lambda(0)$	0.1721	0.1144	0.0596	0.0874	0.1019	0.0926	0.1167	**0.0488**
	QNR(1)	0.4792	0.5692	0.6716	**0.7552**	0.7187	0.7360	0.5901	0.7276

un-degraded dataset, the reference Pan-sharpened image is not available and hence, the quantitative evaluation is carried out with the help of the QNR index which is included in Table 5.2. The boldface values in the table indicate that they are better amongst the other methods. We also display the ideal value of different measures in the bracket.

The following points can be observed from the results on the degraded and un-degraded datasets of Ikonos-2 satellite. One can see from Fig. 5.6(b) and Fig. 5.7(b) that the results of the GIHS method lack in preserving of color information. Moreover, these results appear blurred. The performance of GSA Pan-sharpening method in terms of preservation of high frequency details and spectral information (see Fig. 5.6[c] and Fig. 5.7[c]) was better when compared with the results of the PRACS, AWLP and MTF–GLP approaches (see Fig. 5.6[d, e, f] and Fig. 5.7[d, e, f]). This can be concluded based on the observation of the zoomed-in portion of these results. However, the results of MTF–GLP–CBD which are displayed in Fig. 5.6(g) and Fig. 5.7(g) show improvement in spectral and spatial contents when compared to the results of the GSA method. The Pan-sharpening results obtained by Aly and Sharma [22] are displayed in Fig. 5.6(h) and Fig. 5.7(h), where one can see that the edge features and spectral details are well preserved when compared to the results of the MTF–GLP–CBD approach. However, the visual comparison of different approaches with the results of the proposed method (see in Fig. 5.6[i] and Fig. 5.7[i]) indicate that the proposed Pan-sharpening method has better preservation of spectral and spatial details. By looking at the magnified portions of the images, one may observe that the edge details of the mountain surface and the color of the roads appear sharp in the results of the proposed method. Similar conclusion can be made for the experiment on the un-degraded dataset which is displayed in Fig. 5.7. In this figure, we display the zoomed-in region which consists of a vegetation area. It can be seen from these magnified portions that the high frequency details in these regions are retained well in the results of the proposed Pan-sharpening method when compared to the other methods.

Quantitative measures for this experiment are shown in Table 5.2. When we compare the quantitative measures of the proposed approach with the other methods, we can see that the proposed method shows better performance for the $Q4$, Q_{AVG}, ERGAS and SCC indicating that the spatial as well as spectral

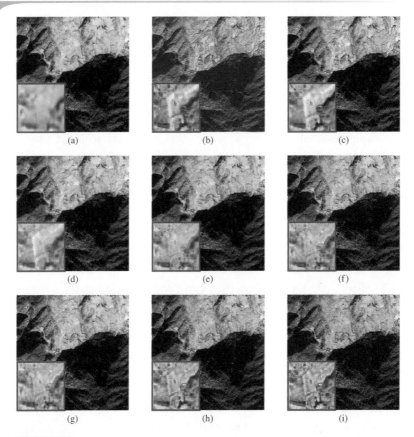

(a) (b) (c)

(d) (e) (f)

(g) (h) (i)

Figure 5.7 Results of Pan-sharpening on un-degraded (original) of dataset Ikonos-2 satellite consisting of an urban area shown as color composites of bands 4, 3 and 1 ($q = 4$). Pan-sharpened images obtained using (a) EXP, (b) GIHS, (c) GSA, (d) PRACS, (e) AWLP, (f) MTF–GLP, (g) MTF–GLP–CBD, (h) Aly and Sharma, (i) proposed approach. The magnified image of a small square region with a red border shown in (i) is displayed at the bottom left corner of all the images. (Courtesy: www.glcf.umd.edu)

features are better preserved in the proposed method. Although the value of SAM is better for the fusion method proposed by Aly and Sharma [22] when compared to our approach, the difference between them is not significant. Since the original Pan-sharpened image is unavailable in the experiment on un-degraded data, the performance in this case is tested in terms of the QNR measure and the same is also shown in Table 5.2. Here, spatial distortion (D_s) and QNR are better for the AWLP fusion method. However, visual comparison of the results of the AWLP method with the results of the proposed method shows that the proposed method performs better for un-degraded datasets. The spectral distortion (D_λ) is better for the proposed Pan-sharpening method. One can conclude from the experiments on degraded and un-degraded images of the Ikonos-2 satellite that the preservation of the spatial and spectral details in the proposed method is better when compared to other approaches.

5.6.3 Experimental results on degraded and un-degraded Quickbird datasets

In this section, we describe the results obtained using the degraded and original datasets of the Quickbird satellite. These images were downloaded from http://www.glcf.umd.edu/data/quickbird/sundarbans.shtml. Table 5.1 lists the details of the data captured using this satellite. Similar to the previous experiment on the Ikonos-2 satellite, the results of the degraded and un-degraded datasets for Quickbird satellite are displayed in Fig. 5.8 and Fig. 5.9, respectively. Here, experiments are conducted on the dataset consisting of a semi-urban area of Sundarban, India, and results are displayed using the color composition of bands 3, 2 and 1. Use of different color composition than the Ikonos-2 helps us in testing the performance of our approach over various spectral bands. The interpolated MS images for the degraded and original datasets are displayed in Fig. 5.8(a) and Fig. 5.9(a), respectively. In Fig. 5.8(b–h), we display the Pan-sharpening results using GIHS, GSA, PRACS, AWLP, MTF–GLP, MTF–GLP–CBD and Aly and Sharma approaches on the degraded dataset. Similarly, results of these for the un-degraded dataset are shown in Fig. 5.9(b–h). Finally, in Fig. 5.8(i) and Fig. 5.9(i), we display the Pan-sharpening results for the proposed method. The quantitative evaluation corresponding to these experiments is listed in Table 5.3. In each of these results displayed in Fig. 5.8 and Fig. 5.9, we also display the zoomed-in version of a small square area on the bottom left corner. These zoomed portions correspond to the roof of a stadium shown in Fig. 5.8(j) and the top view of a house and nearby areas as indicated in Fig. 5.9(i).

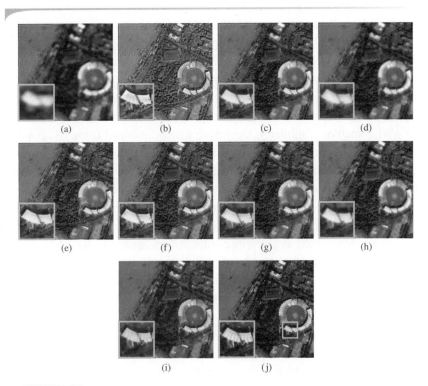

Figure 5.8   Results of Pan-sharpening on degraded dataset of Quickbird satellite consisting of a semi-urban area shown as color composites of bands 3, 2 and 1 ($q = 4$). Pan-sharpened images obtained using (a) EXP, (b) GIHS, (c) GSA, (d) PRACS, (e) AWLP, (f) MTF–GLP, (g) MTF–GLP–CBD, (h) Aly and Sharma, (i) proposed approach. (j) Original MS image. The magnified region of a small square region shown with a green border in (j) is displayed at the bottom left corner of all the images. (Courtesy: www.glcf.umd.edu)

Looking at the results of the degraded dataset in Fig. 5.8, one can make the following observations. The GIHS method fails in preserving the spectral contents (see Fig. 5.8[b]). The result due to the GSA technique, which is displayed in Fig. 5.8(c), improves the color details but spatial distortion is clearly seen in the magnified region. The PRACS method fails in preserving spatial and spectral details as displayed in Fig. 5.8(d). The result of the AWLP method which is shown in Fig. 5.8(e) exhibits less color and spatial distortions. However, by comparing the zoomed-in versions of the results of AWLP and the proposed method displayed in Fig. 5.8(e) and Fig. 5.8(i), respectively, one can clearly see that the proposed method performs better in preserving spectral features and edge details when compared to that of the AWLP method. Similarly, the fusion results obtained using MTF–GLP, MTF–GLP–CBD and Aly and Sharma approaches show improvement in the color and edge details when compared with the result of the AWLP method. However, one can see that the preservation of high frequency details using these methods is poor when compared to that of the proposed method. By comparing the zoomed-in images of those results, we may conclude that spectral attributes such as the white color stripes appear distorted in all the results when compared to the result of the proposed method. Moreover, the proposed approach has better preservation of spatial features such as the different segments in the roof area of the stadium when compared to the other approaches.

Similar to the degraded dataset, the potential of the proposed method is also evaluated by comparing it with the results of other approaches using un-degraded images which is shown in Fig. 5.9. Looking at the magnified regions of the various approaches, we can say that the Pan-sharpened images of the GIHS method and PRACS technique displayed in Fig. 5.9(b) and Fig. 5.9(d), respectively, have comparatively higher spatial distortions. The results of GSA, AWLP, MTF–GLP, MTF–GLP–CBD and Aly and Sharma methods have better preservation of spectral and spatial information when compared to the results of the GIHS and PRACS approaches. Among these many approaches, Aly and Sharma [22] fusion method perform better. However, on comparing the magnified images of Aly and Sharma [22] fusion approach and the proposed methods displayed in Fig. 5.9(h) and Fig. 5.9(i), respectively, one can see that the top portion of the house and its nearby

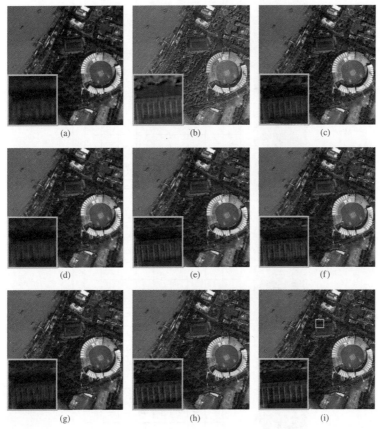

Figure 5.9 Results of Pan-sharpening on un-degraded dataset of Quickbird satellite consisting of a semi-urban area shown as color composites of bands 3, 2 and 1 ($q = 4$). Pan-sharpened images obtained using (a) EXP, (b) GIHS, (c) GSA, (d) PRACS, (e) AWLP, (f) MTF–GLP, (g) MTF–GLP–CBD, (h) Aly and Sharma, (i) proposed approach. The magnified image of a small square region with a green border shown in (i) is displayed at the bottom left corner of all the images. (Courtesy: www.glcf.umd.edu)

Table 5.3 Quantitative measures for Quickbird imagery shown in Fig. 5.8 and Fig. 5.9. Here, a boldface value indicates that the value is better amongst the other methods. The numbers in the brackets indicate the ideal values

Dataset	Measure	GIHS	GSA	PRACS	AWLP	MTF-GLP	MTF-GLP-CBD	Aly and Sharma	Proposed
Degraded (Fig. 5.8)	$Q4$ (1)	0.4803	0.6744	0.7167	0.6663	0.6624	0.6947	**0.8281**	0.8191
	Q_{AVG} (1)	0.5609	0.7018	0.7457	0.7007	0.6953	0.7236	0.8303	**0.8761**
	SAM (0)	3.6361	3.3657	3.2216	3.1313	3.2645	4.4904	**2.3569**	3.8954
	ERGAS (0)	3.3093	3.2604	2.9537	3.0679	2.9933	3.0719	**2.0283**	3.0381
	SCC (1)	0.7281	0.7478	0.7644	0.7484	0.7662	0.7573	0.8948	**0.9060**
Un-degraded (Fig. 5.9)	D_S (0)	0.3802	0.2797	0.1541	0.1865	0.1898	**0.1236**	0.2853	0.2234
	D_λ (0)	0.1401	0.0796	**0.0189**	0.0861	0.1041	0.0549	0.0886	0.0495
	QNR (1)	0.5330	0.6629	**0.8299**	0.7434	0.7259	0.8283	0.6513	0.7381

areas are well separated in the result of the proposed method (see Fig. 5.9(i)). Similar to the degraded experiment, here also we can conclude that the proposed method has better perceptual performance when compared to the other approaches. The Pan-sharpened result of the proposed method has less color distortion with significant improvement in edge features.

The quantitative comparison shown in Table 5.3 indicates that the proposed approach performs better in terms of quantitative measures as well, showing better values for the measures such as Q_{AVG} and SCC. The measures such as Q4, SAM and ERGAS are better for the Pan-sharpening method proposed by Aly and Sharma [22]. It may be of interest to stress here that quantitative measures used in evaluating fusion fidelity may not always reflect the true signal quality. This is because they are not derived by taking into effect the parameters that consider the visual perception [249]. The quantitative comparison for the un-degraded dataset shows that PRACS fusion method performs better in terms of D_λ and QNR. Moreover, spatial distortion (D_s) is lowest for the MTF–GLP–CBD fusion method. However, we can clearly see that visually the results of the degraded as well as the un-degraded images look better for the results obtained using the proposed Pan-sharpening approach. One may arrive at the following conclusions from the displayed results and the quantitative assessment. Due to the Gabor filter which extracts the bandpass details present at different regions, the proposed method exhibits better preservation of spatial features. Estimation of initial HR approximation using self-similarity and the sparse representation theory improves the performance of the proposed method in obtaining the accurate degradation matrix between the LR and HR images and this in effect leads to a better final estimate.

5.6.4   Experimental results on degraded and un-degraded Worldview-2 datasets

Finally, we explain the results on the degraded and un-degraded images of Worldview-2 satellite. This satellite provides MS and Pan images with the highest spatial resolution among the other satellites as indicated in Table 5.1, which also shows the other details of the data captured using this satellite. This dataset was downloaded from http:// www.digitalglobe.com/. Similar to the earlier experimentations, here also we compared the results of various state-of-the-art Pan-sharpening techniques with that obtained using the proposed method and the results are shown as color composites for bands 5, 3 and 1 in Fig. 5.10 and Fig. 5.11, respectively. Since the parameters used on Worldview-2 dataset by Aly and Sharma [22] were unavailable, we have not included the results of this approach. Instead, we include the results obtained using the Pan-sharpening method proposed by Lee and Lee [140], which was obtained using GLP–MTF matched filter [12] and multiplicative injection model. This method is referred to as the MTF–GLP–CBD–PP method and the results of the same are displayed in Fig. 5.10(h) and Fig. 5.11(h) for degraded and un-degraded datasets, respectively. A magnified region is also displayed in all these images as done in the experiments on Ikonos-2 and Quickbird images. The quantitative measures of these results are listed in Table 5.4.

Looking at the results of the GIHS approach displayed in Fig. 5.10(b) and Fig. 5.11(b) for degraded and un-degraded datasets, we observe spatial and spectral distortions in these results. Similarly, the Pan-sharpening results of the PRACS method (see Fig. 5.10[d] and Fig. 5.11[d]) also lack in preserving the color details. Comparing the results of GSA and AWLP methods for the degraded dataset which are displayed in Fig. 5.10(c) and Fig. 5.10(e), respectively, we may say that the GSA method has better spatial features with lesser spectral distortions when compared to the result of the AWLP method. This observation is also true for the un-degraded dataset which is evident by comparing their results displayed in Fig. 5.11(c, e). However, comparing the result of the GSA method shown in Fig. 5.10(c) with that of the proposed method which is displayed in Fig. 5.10(i), we notice that in the proposed method, various regions in the urban area have textures comparable to the original MS image displayed in Fig. 5.10(j). The same conclusion holds for the results of the un-degraded dataset displayed in Fig. 5.11(c, i). Similar to the earlier experiments, the results of the MTF–GLP, MTF–GLP–CBD and MTF–GLP–CBD–PP methods, which are displayed in Fig. 5.10(f, g, h) and Fig. 5.11(f, g, h) for degraded and un-degraded datasets, respectively perform better when compared to the results of the GSA method. However, one can notice that the results of the proposed method (Fig. 5.10(i) and Fig. 5.11(i)) show significant improvement in spatial details with reduced color distortion when compared to the results of other fusion methods (Fig. 5.10[f, g, h] and Fig. 5.11[f, g, h]).

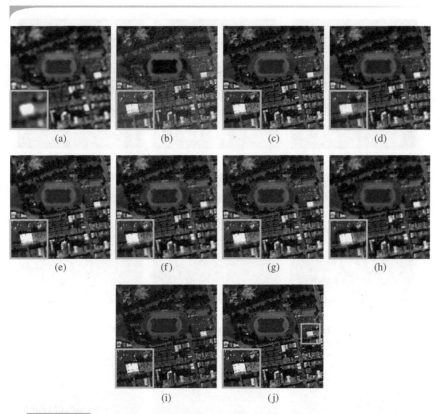

(a) (b) (c) (d)

(e) (f) (g) (h)

(i) (j)

Figure 5.10 Results of Pan-sharpening on the degraded dataset of Worldview-2 satellite consisting of an urban area shown as color of band compositions 5, 3 and 1 ($q = 4$). Pan-sharpened images obtained using (a) EXP, (b) GIHS, (c) GSA, (d) PRACS, (e) AWLP, (f) MTF–GLP, (g) MTF–GLP–CBD, (h) MTF–GLP–HPM–PP, (i) proposed approach. (j) Original MS image. The magnified region of a small square region shown with a green border in (j) is displayed at the bottom left corner of all the images. (Courtesy: www.digitalglobe.com)

In the results of using degraded datasets, we highlighted few objects consisting of buildings, roads etc, by magnifying that region. Comparing the zoomed-in regions of all the results, we can conclude that the edge features of

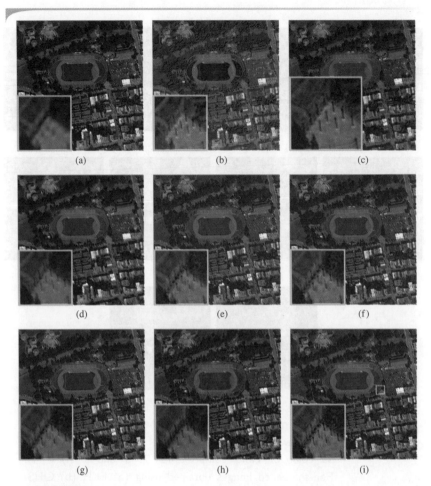

Figure 5.11 Results of Pan-sharpening on un-degraded dataset of Worldview-2 satellite consisting of an urban area shown as color composites of bands 5, 3 and 1 ($q = 4$). Pan-sharpened images obtained using (a) EXP, (b) GIHS, (c) GSA, (d) PRACS, (e) AWLP, (f) MTF–GLP, (g) MTF–GLP–CBD, (h) MTF–GLP–HPM–PP, (i) proposed approach. The magnified image of a small square region with a green border shown in (i) is displayed at the bottom right corner of all the images. (Courtesy: www.digitalglobe.com)

Table 5.4 Quantitative measures for Worldview-2 imagery shown in Fig. 5.10 and Fig. 5.11. Here, a boldface value indicates that the value is better amongst the other methods. The numbers in the brackets indicate the ideal values

Dataset	Measure	GIHS	GSA	PRACS	AWLP	MTF-GLP	MTF-GLP-CBD	MTF-GLP-HPM-PP	Proposed
Degraded (Fig. 5.10)	$Q8(1)$	0.6559	0.7319	0.7333	0.7527	0.7374	0.7515	0.7461	**0.8061**
	$Q_{AVG}(1)$	0.6585	0.7211	0.7195	0.7420	0.7423	0.7515	0.7309	**0.8578**
	SAM(0)	9.2524	8.7174	8.8694	8.4876	8.7881	8.6056	8.7222	**7.1849**
	ERGAS(0)	8.5832	8.4724	7.9248	7.9117	7.9805	7.9682	8.1339	**6.9820**
	SCC(1)	0.5375	0.5347	**0.5649**	0.5638	0.5572	0.5592	0.5636	0.5489
Un-degraded (Fig. 5.11)	$D_S(0)$	0.2476	0.2980	0.1821	0.1315	0.1383	**0.1096**	0.1657	0.1450
	$D_\lambda(0)$	0.0580	0.0865	**0.0202**	0.0520	0.0575	0.0439	0.0935	0.0942
	QNR(1)	0.7087	0.6413	0.8014	0.8234	0.8121	**0.8513**	0.7563	0.7744

buildings and roads are better preserved in the result of the proposed method (see Fig. 5.10[i]) when compared to the results of all other state-of-the-art methods. Similarly, from the results of the un-degraded dataset depicted in Fig. 5.11, we observe that the proposed method shows significant improvement when compared to the other Pan-sharpening techniques. The quantitative assessment for these results listed in Table 5.4 shows that the performance of the proposed method for the degraded dataset is better in terms of every measure except SCC which is better for the PRACS method. However, visual comparison of the results of PRACS and the proposed methods shows that the proposed method performs better in preserving both spatial as well as color details. For the case of un-degraded datasets, the spatial distortion (D_s) and QNR are smaller for the MTF–GLP–CBD method when compared to all the other methods. Moreover, the spectral distortion (D_λ) is better for the PRACS Pan-sharpening approach. However, it is important to note that the results of the proposed Pan-sharpening method have better preservation of spatial and color details when compared to all other fusion methods. Looking at the displayed results and the quantitative measures obtained using the dataset of the three satellites, one may conclude that the Pan-sharpened image obtained using the proposed method results in better preservation of edge features, object shapes and colors in the scene.

5.6.5 Comparison of fusion results with CS and TV based approaches

In order to compare the fusion results obtained using the proposed Pan-sharpening method with compressive sensing (CS) and total variation (TV) based techniques, we conducted an additional experiment on the degraded and un-degraded datasets of Ikonos-2 satellite images. We downloaded these images from http://www.isprs.org/data/ikonos_hobart/ default.aspx; they consisted of images of an urban area in Mount Wellington nearer to Hobart, Tasmania. The Pan-sharpening results obtained using different CS [283, 143] and NLTV [68] based approaches including the proposed method are displayed in Fig. 5.12 and Fig. 5.13 for degraded and un-degraded images using color composition of 4, 3 and 2 bands. The interpolated version of the MS image and the original MS images are displayed in Fig. 5.12(a) and Fig. 5.13(a), respectively. Similarly, degraded and original Pan images are depicted in Fig. 5.12(b) and Fig. 5.13(b), respectively. Pan-sharpened images obtained using CS based methods [283,143] for the degraded datasets are displayed in Fig. 5.12(c, d) and their results obtained using un-degraded datasets are displayed in Fig. 5.13(c, d), respectively. In Fig. 5.12(e) and Fig. 5.13(e), we depict the results of the NLTV based fusion method [68] for degraded and un-degraded datasets, respectively. In Fig. 5.12(f, g) and Fig. 5.13(f, g), we display the initial estimate and final Pan-sharpened results of the proposed method for degraded and un-degraded datasets. Finally, in Fig. 5.12(h), we display the original MS image. Similar to earlier experiments, here also, we display the zoomed-in versions of a small area for better visualization.

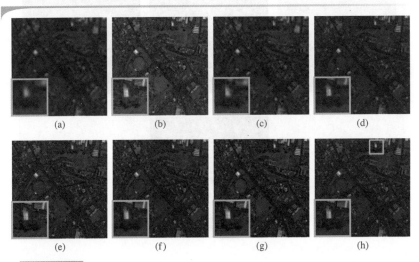

Figure 5.12   Results of Pan-sharpening on degraded dataset of Ikonos-2 satellite consisting of an urban area shown as color composites of bands 4, 3 and 2 ($q = 4$). (a) LR MS image of size 64×64 upsampled to the size of the Pan image. (b) Pan image of size 256×256. Pan-sharpened images obtained using (c) sparseFI [283], (d) [143], (e) NLTV [68]. (f) Initial estimate image using self-similarity and sparse representation theory and (g) final Pan-sharpened image obtained using proposed approach. (h) Original MS image. The magnified image of a small square region with a green border shown in (h) is displayed at the bottom left corner of all the images. (Courtesy: www.isprs.org)

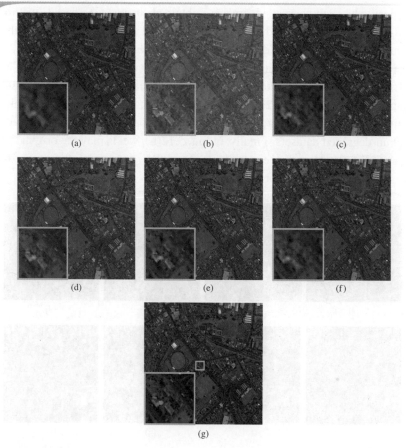

Figure 5.13 Results of Pan-sharpening on un-degraded (original) dataset of Ikonos-2 satellite consisting of an urban area shown as color composites of bands 4, 3 and 2 ($q = 4$). (a) Original MS image of size 256 × 256 upsampled to the size of the Pan image. (b) Original Pan image of size 1024 × 1024. Pan-sharpened images obtained using (c) sparseFI [283], (d) [143], (e) NLTV [68]. (f) Initial estimate image using self-similarity and sparse representation theory and (g) final Pan-sharpened image obtained using proposed approach. The magnified image of a small square region with a green border shown in (g) is displayed at the bottom left corner of all the images. (Courtesy: www.isprs.org)

One can summarize the following observations by comparing the different Pan-sharpening results displayed in Fig. 5.12 and Fig. 5.13. The results based on the CS theory which are displayed in Fig. 5.12(c, d) and Fig. 5.13(c, d) do not perform well as far as the preservation of the spatial details are concerned. They also show color saturation. This effect can be clearly seen in the magnified regions. The fusion results obtained using edge-preserving prior such as NLTV [68], which are displayed in Fig. 5.12(e) and Fig. 5.13(e) lack spatial and spectral details. However, we can see that the preservation of spatial features and color information are better in the fused images obtained using the proposed fusion approach (see Fig. 5.12[g] and Fig. 5.13[g]) when compared to the fusion results obtained using CS and NLTV based Pan-sharpening techniques (see Fig. 5.12[c, d, e] and Fig. 5.13[c, d, e]). Furthermore, we can see that spatial details are incorporated during regularization via Gabor prior in the initial estimate images which are displayed in Fig. 5.12(f) and Fig. 5.13(f). One can conclude that fusion results obtained using self-similarity and sparse representation theory are better when compared to the same with the CS and NLTV based Pan-sharpening approaches.

Table 5.5 Quantitative measures for fusion results shown in Fig. 5.12 and Fig. 5.13. Here, a boldface value indicates that the value is better amongst the other methods. The numbers in the brackets indicate the ideal values

Dataset	Measure	sparseFI [283]	Approach in [143]	NLTV [68]	Proposed
Degraded	Q8(1)	0.6811	0.6023	0.6940	**0.7182**
(Fig. 5.12)	Q_{AVG} (1)	0.6909	0.5843	0.7581	**0.8042**
	SAM^0(0)	5.9351	7.1801	5.8781.	**5.5847**
	ERGAS(0)	6.3824	4.9275	4.2812	**4.0861**
	SCC(1)	0.5889	0.5940	**0.6591**	0.6412
Un-degraded	D_S(0)	0.3674	0.1783	0.1389	**0.1210**
(Fig. 5.13)	D_λ(0)	0.1284	0.0773	0.0752	**0.0710**
	QNR(1)	0.5512	0.7580	0.7963	**0.8165**

Similar to earlier experimentation, we have also carried out quantitative analysis for this experiment which is depicted in Table 5.5. One can see that the proposed Pan-sharpening approach performs better for all the measures for both degraded and un-degraded datasets except for SCC where the fusion approach based on NLTV performs better among the other approaches. However, perceptually, the proposed approach performs better than the NLTV approach.

5.6.6   Computation complexity

The proposed approach and all the other Pan-sharpening methods have been implemented using Matlab 7.6 installed on a system with 2.4 GHz, 4 GB RAM, Intel $i3$ processor. The average computation time for each method is listed in Table 5.6. The following observations can be made by looking at the times given in Table 5.6. From the table, we see that the proposed approach takes higher execution time when compared to the other approaches including the approach proposed by Aly and Sharma [22]. This increase in computation time is due to the additional time required for the estimation of an initial HR approximation and also due to the time needed for performing regularization using iterative optimization techniques. Other fusion methods are not iterative except the method proposed by Aly and Sharma [22] which requires the number of parameters to be estimated as well as few parameters to be tuned for obtaining better results which may lead to increase in computational complexity. It is worthwhile to mention here that although the computational time for the proposed approach is higher when compared to other approaches, it is also lower when compared to the CS based fusion algorithms proposed by Li and Yang [143] and Harikumar et al. [105], which take additional time for constructing the dictionary. Since Pan-sharpening is an ill-posed problem, it is advantageous to use a degradation model in order to obtain a better solution, which is done in the proposed method by estimating the degradation between LR and HR MS images. Regularization using a new prior based on Gabor filtering adds to the improvement in the solution. Although the time complexity of the proposed approach is higher when compared to non-iterative approaches, it has lesser distortions in both spatial and spectral contents. One can speed up the processing time of the proposed method by implementing the optimized code on a graphical processing unit (GPU).

Table 5.6   Average computation time involved in different Pan-sharpening approaches

Experiment	Average computation time to obtain Pan-sharpened image (in seconds)							
	GIHS	GSA	PRACS	AWLP	MTF-GLP	MTF-GLP-CBD	Aly and Sharma	Proposed
Degraded dataset	0.03	0.38	0.48	0.29	0.29	0.33	12.20	159.29

5.7   Conclusion

We have proposed a novel Pan-sharpening method using the concept of self-similarity and Gabor prior. In this chapter, we cast the multi-resolution fusion or Pan-sharpening problem in a restoration framework and obtained the final solution by regularizing the cost function. A new Gabor prior is proposed by extracting the bandpass features from the Pan image and using them for Pan-sharpening. The final cost function is optimized using simple gradient based optimization technique. The potential of the proposed fusion method has been verified by conducting experiments on both degraded and un-degraded images captured by different satellites such as Ikonos-2, Quickbird and Worldview-2. Quantitative evaluation of our results involved the use of traditional as well as new quality indices. From the Pan-sharpened images and the quantitative measures, one can conclude that the proposed method has better preservation of color and edge information when compared to the other techniques.

6

Image Fusion
Application to •
Super-resolution of
Natural Images

Increasing the spatial resolution of a given test image is of interest to the image processing community since the enhanced resolution of the image has better details when compared to the corresponding low resolution image. Super-resolution (SR) is an algorithmic approach in which a high spatial resolution image is obtained by using single/multiple low resolution observations or by using a database of LR–HR pairs. The linear image formation model discussed for image fusion in Chapter 4 is extended here to obtain an SR image for a given LR test observation. In the image fusion problem, the available Pan image was used in obtaining a high resolution fused image. Similar to the fusion problem, SR is also concerned with the enhancement of spatial resolution. However, we do not have a high resolution image such as a Pan image as an additional observation. Hence, we make use of a database of LR–HR pairs in order to obtain the SR for the given LR observation. Here, we use contourlet based learning to obtain the initial SR estimate which is then used in obtaining the degradation as well as the MRF parameter. Similar to the fusion problem discussed in Chapter 4, an MAP–MRF framework is used to obtain the final SR image. Note that we are not using the self-learning and sparse representation based approach proposed in Chapter 5 to obtain the fused image since the objective of this chapter is to illustrate a new approach for SR using the data model used in fusion.

6.1 Related Work

The low cost and ease of operation have significantly contributed to the growing popularity of digital imaging systems. Low cost cameras are fitted with low precision optics and lesser density detectors. Images captured using such a camera suffer from the drawback of reduced spatial resolution compared to traditional film cameras. Images captured using a camera fitted with high precision optics and image sensors comprising high density detectors provide better details that are essential in many imaging applications such as medical imaging, remote sensing and surveillance. However, the cost of such a camera is prohibitively high and obtaining a high resolution image is an important concern in many commercial applications requiring HR imaging. Images captured using a low cost camera represent the under-sampled images of a scene containing aliasing, blur and noise. Therefore algorithmic approaches towards increasing the spatial resolution are required for low cost imaging applications.

Super-resolution (SR) refers to an algorithmic approach to construct HR image by using multiple LR observations or a single LR observation. SR approaches are mainly classified into two classes: *reconstruction based* and *learning based*. In the *reconstruction based* approach, multiple LR images of the same scene are captured by the camera and the additional information available in each of these images is used for constructing the SR image [228, 75, 194]. In the *learning based* approach, for a given single LR observation, a training database of images is used to learn the details and obtain the corresponding SR image. These algorithms use a scheme to capture the high-frequency details by learning the required transformation features using a set of LR and HR training images. The input LR image is split into patches and for each patch from the input image, either one best-matched patch or a set of the best-matched LR patches is selected from the training set. The corresponding HR patches are used to reconstruct the output HR image [80, 44, 223, 117, 222, 42, 247, 246, 129, 177, 142, 257, 225, 175, 260, 118, 189, 29, 285, 31, 262, 127, 95, 62, 134].

In most learning based approaches, the training database consists of LR training images obtained by down-sampling the HR training images. Moreover, they do not attempt to estimate the image degradation and prior parameters from the available database. Similar to the learning based approach, many researchers in [261, 63, 224, 73, 285, 184, 96] have solved the SR problem with sparse representation. They use the sparse representation for patches of LR and HR image pair and learn the dictionary. The final solution is obtained by regularizing the cost function with a sparsity prior. Glasner et al. [89] have proposed a technique that takes advantage of the power of both the types of SR approach. They obtained the SR image from as little as a single low-resolution image without any additional external information. Their approach assumes significant redundancy within a single image and it requires accurate sub-pixels which is a difficult and computationally taxing task.

There are several SR approaches which use the image formation model and obtain the solution by formulating it as an ill-posed inverse problem. Many of them exploit the variational regularization framework. The approach of total variation (TV) was initially introduced for the regularization of inverse problems by Rudin et al. [201] for solving the denoising problem. Due to its ability to preserve sharp discontinuities such as edges, it has gained greater popularity in applications such as image restoration, denoising, inpainting, etc. The super-resolution approach based on the variational framework was first attempted by Guichard and Malgouyres [102]. Other SR methods based on TV regularization have also been reported in [160, 21, 41]. Malgouyres and Guichard [160] used the TV regularization for zooming of 1-D and 2-D signals. Similarly, Aly and Dubois [21] used an image formation model with a TV regularizer to obtain the up-sampling of the LR test image. They used level-sets motion optimization method to obtain the final solution. The super-resolution of text images is described by Capel and Zisserman [139] who show the effectiveness of a TV prior in comparison with a Huber prior. Furthermore, TV regularization is also applied to obtain the super-resolution of video signals by many researchers [171, 75, 74]. Moreover, the TV prior is extended to the non local TV (NLTV) [158, 87] method. An SR approach based on the NLTV was proposed by Zeng and Lu [270]. Here, the final cost function consists of two terms: the first term forces the SR image to be consistent with the LR observation while the second corresponds to a non-local regularization term which acts as a neighborhood filter on the final SR image. Although TV and NLTV regularization may give better SR results, they suffer from high computational complexity and implementations issues [46].

In this chapter, we propose a technique for SR based on degradation estimation and regularization framework. We use contourlet transform to learn the edge details and obtain an initial HR estimate. The final solution is obtained by using the regularization framework in which the SR image is modelled as a homogeneous MRF to incorporate prior knowledge into the solution. The model parameter is estimated using the initial estimate of the SR image. The block diagram of the proposed SR work is displayed in Fig. 6.1. Although, the proposed method is built based on the approach presented by Upla et al. [235], it differs considerably from the same and has advantages over it. In Upla et al.'s work [235], decimation matrix is estimated by assuming blur as an identity matrix. However, a more practical model for LR image formation should include the degradation caused due to aliasing as well as blurring. Therefore, we estimate a degradation matrix that takes care of both the aliasing and blurring and use it for super-resolving. This results in a more accurate image formation model and, hence, leads to a better SR solution. In addition to this, in Upla et al.'s work [235], the given LR test image is modelled as an MRF. However, since the MRF parameters do not

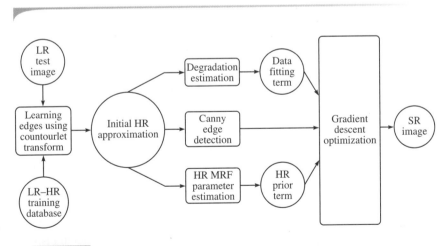

Figure 6.1   Proposed SR approach.

infuse across the scales, one has to estimate these parameters separately for LR observation as well. We know that for a given SR image, there may be many possible LR observations based on the image formation process. Hence, modelling the available LR observation as an MRF and using the estimated MRF parameter may fail to better characterize the SR image. Due to this, in this work we avoid regularization using the given LR observation. Inclusion of this step also adds to additional computations in Upla et al.'s work [235], which is avoided in the present work. Our results are compared with a number of state-of-the art methods in order to show the effectiveness of the proposed SR approach.

The advantages of the proposed method in comparison with other SR approaches are as follows:

- The proposed approach uses a training database of LR and HR images which are captured by a real camera.

- Our approach estimates degradation using the available LR test and initial estimate images. Since the degradation matrix is estimated from the given data itself, the approach yields an accurate estimation of the SR image.

- Use of homogeneous MRF prior offers a computational advantage. Although the prior is homogeneous MRF, the method takes care of preserving-edge pixels.

- As done in Chapter 4, the optimization is only carried out on non-edge pixels. Thus, it avoids oversmoothing of edge regions.

6.2 Estimation of Close Approximation of the SR Image

In order to recover missing details of the HR image, we exploit the spatial relationship between LR and HR images using a training database consisting of images acquired with different resolution settings of a real camera. Since HR and LR images in the training database are not generated synthetically, they exhibit the true spatial relationship across the scales. In our work, we obtain the initial estimate to an SR image using contourlet transform (CT). We learn the high frequency information using the CT domain. A detailed description of contourlet transform is presented in Section 4.3. Our

SR approach yields a better estimate when compared to other approaches since the spatial relationship between LR and HR images is obtained by making use of LR–HR training pairs captured using a real camera.

The primary goal of our approach is to recover the missing details of the super-resolved image. One can obtain global characteristics such as high frequency details and the transformation between LR–HR. To do this, one has to capture the high frequency details representing the edges in different directions along with the smooth contours. This motivates us to use a database and CT which captures the details in the dominant directions to get edge-preserving SR. It may be of interest to mention here that we did not use LR–HR pairs in Chapter 4 for obtaining the initial estimate of the fused image. This is because, in that case the high resolution Pan image was already available with us and we made use of the same in order to extract the high frequency details. The procedure for learning an initial HR estimate for a resolution factor (decimation factor) of $q = 2$ is as follows. Refer to Fig. 6.2(a) and Fig. 6.2(c) that illustrate the two level contourlet decomposition of the LR observation and the LR training images, respectively. Figure 6.2(b) and Fig. 6.2(d) display the three level contourlet decomposition of the SR image and the HR training images, respectively. Note that we use the LR test image while learning the initial SR estimate. The sub-bands 0–VIII represent coarser levels and the sub-bands IX–XVI represent the finer levels. Each coefficient in sub-bands 0 is related to one coefficient in each of the sub-bands I–IV and four coefficients in 2×2 blocks in each of the sub-bands V–VIII. The coefficients in sub-bands IX–XVI represent the missing details of the super-resolved image which are learned using the proposed learning approach. Our task is to learn the transform coefficients in the sub-bands IX–XVI (shaded gray) shown in Fig. 6.2(b).

We obtain a block of 2×4 contourlet coefficients in each of the sub-bands IX, X, XI, XII and 4×2 contourlet coefficients in each of the sub-bands XIII, XIV, XV and XVI for each coefficient in the sub-bands I–IV and the corresponding 2×2 blocks in the sub-bands V–VIII. Thus, we learn a total of 64 coefficients for each coefficient in sub-bands 0. Considering the sub-bands I–VIII of the LR image, let $c(i, j)$ be the contourlet coefficient at a location (i, j), where $0 \leq i, j < M/4$ in sub-band I. We learn unknown coefficients $\{c_{IX}(k, l)\}_{k=2i, l=4j}^{k=2i+1, l=4j+3}$, $\{c_{X}(k, l)\}_{k=2i, l=4j}^{k=2i+1, l=4j+3}$, $\{c_{XI}(k, l)\}_{k=2i, l=4j}^{k=2i+1, l=4j+3}$, and $\{c_{XII}(k, l)\}_{k=2i, l=4j}^{k=2i+1, l=4j+3}$ of the observed image. Similarly, we also learn unknown coefficients $\{c_{\mathrm{XIII}}(k,l)\}_{k=4i,l=2j}^{k=4i+3,l=2j+1}$, $\{c_{\mathrm{XIV}}(k,l)\}_{k=4i,l=2j}^{k=4i+3,l=2j+1}$, $\{c_{\mathrm{XV}}(k,l)\}_{k=4i,l=2j}^{k=4i+3,l=2j+1}$, and $\{c_{\mathrm{XVI}}(k,l)\}_{k=4i,l=2j}^{k=4i+3,l=2j+1}$.

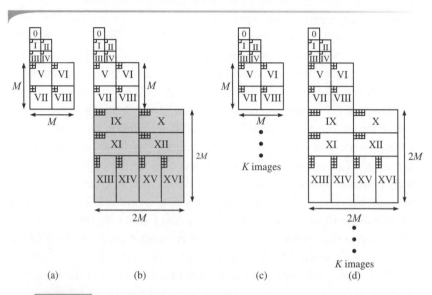

(a)   (b)   (c)   (d)

Figure 6.2   Computation of initial estimate using contourlet decompositions. (a) Two level decomposition of the observation. (b) Three level decomposition of the super-resolved image. The coefficients in the shaded sub-bands are to be computed. (c) Two level decomposition of LR training images in the database. (d) Three level decomposition of HR training images in the database. LR images are of size $M \times M$ and HR images are of size $2M \times 2M$.

We perform a search in the corresponding coarser levels of all the LR training images at all pixel locations for the best match in terms of minimum absolute difference (MAD) and copy the corresponding, contourlet block of size 2×4 in sub-bands IX–XII and that of size 4×2 in sub-bands XIII–XVI in the test image. The criteria for best match is:

$$\hat{m}(\hat{i},\hat{j}) = \underset{m,s,t}{\arg\min} \Big[\, |\, c_I(i,j) - c_I^{(m)}(s,t)\, |$$

$$+ \quad |\, c_{II}(i,j) - c_{II}^{(m)}(s,t)\, |$$

$$+ \quad |\, c_{III}(i,j) - c_{III}^{(m)}(s,t)\, |$$

$$+ \quad |\, c_{IV}(i,j) - c_{IV}^{(m)}(s,t)\, |$$

$$+ \quad S_V + S_{VI} + S_{VII} + S_{VIII} \Big],$$

where,

$$S_V = \sum_{\substack{S=2s \\ I=2i}}^{\substack{I=2i+1 \\ S=2s+1}} \sum_{\substack{T=2t \\ J=2j}}^{\substack{J=2j+1 \\ T=2t+1}} \Big| c_V(I,J) - c_V^{(m)}(S,T) \Big|.$$

Similarly, S_{VI}, S_{VII} and S_{VIII} are sums corresponding to sub-bands VI, VII, and VIII, respectively, and for K, the number of image pairs in the database $m = 1, 2, \ldots, K$. Here $c_l^{(m)}$ denotes the contourlet coefficient for the mth training image at the lth sub-band and $\hat{m}(\hat{i},\hat{j})$ denotes the $(\hat{i},\hat{j})$ location for the $\hat{m}^{\text{th}}$ training image that best matches the test image at (i,j) location. We pick the best match HR contourlet coefficients in sub-bands IX–XVI of corresponding HR training image and place them in the sub-bands IX–XVI of the observed image. In sub-bands IX–XII, we have

$$\{c_{IX}(k,l)\}_{k=2i,l=4j}^{k=2i+1,l=4j+3} \quad := \quad \{c_{IX}^{(\hat{m})}(k,l)\}_{k=2\hat{i},l=4\hat{j}}^{k=2\hat{i}+1,l=4\hat{j}+3}$$

$$\{c_{X}(k,l)\}_{k=2i,l=4j}^{k=2i+1,l=4j+3} \quad := \quad \{c_{X}^{(\hat{m})}(k,l)\}_{k=2\hat{i},l=4\hat{j}}^{k=2\hat{i}+1,l=4\hat{j}+3}$$

$$\{c_{XI}(k,l)\}_{k=2i,l=4j}^{k=2i+1,l=4j+3} \quad := \quad \{c_{XI}^{(\hat{m})}(k,l)\}_{k=2\hat{i},l=4\hat{j}}^{k=2\hat{i}+1,l=4\hat{j}+3}$$

$$\{c_{XII}(k,l)\}_{k=2i,l=4j}^{k=2i+1,l=4j+3} \quad := \quad \{c_{XII}^{(\hat{m})}(k,l)\}_{k=2\hat{i},l=4\hat{j}}^{k=2\hat{i}+1,l=4\hat{j}+3}$$

$$(6.1)$$

and in sub-bands XIII–XVI, we have

$$\{c_{\text{XIII}}(k,l)\}_{k=4i,l=2j}^{k=4i+3,l=2j+1} \quad := \quad \{c_{\text{XIII}}^{(\hat{m})}(k,l)\}_{k=4\hat{i},l=2\hat{j}}^{k=4\hat{i}+3,l=2\hat{j}+1}$$

$$\{c_{\text{XIV}}(k,l)\}_{k=4i,l=2j}^{k=4i+3,l=2j+1} \quad := \quad \{c_{\text{XIV}}^{(\hat{m})}(k,l)\}_{k=4\hat{i},l=2\hat{j}}^{k=4\hat{i}+3,l=2\hat{j}+1}$$

$$\{c_{\text{XV}}(k,l)\}_{k=4i,l=2j}^{k=4i+3,l=2j+1} \quad := \quad \{c_{\text{XV}}^{(\hat{m})}(k,l)\}_{k=4\hat{i},l=2\hat{j}}^{k=4\hat{i}+3,l=2\hat{j}+1}$$

$$\{c_{\text{XVI}}(k,l)\}_{k=4i,l=2j}^{k=4i+3,l=2j+1} \quad := \quad \{c_{\text{XVI}}^{(\hat{m})}(k,l)\}_{k=4\hat{i},l=2\hat{j}}^{k=4\hat{i}+3,l=2\hat{j}+1}.$$

$$(6.2)$$

Once the unknown CT coefficients are estimated, we take the inverse CT to obtain the close approximations to SR image. The same procedure can be applied iteratively to learn the finer details at higher resolution factors. For $q = 4$, the training database consists of pairs of $2M \times 2M$ and $4M \times 4M$ images. Once the close approximation is available, we extract the edges from it using Canny edge detector.

6.3   Refining SR Using MAP–MRF Framework

Learning based SR algorithms attempt to estimate the unknown pixel values corresponding to high resolution from a single low resolution observation. Once the initial estimate is known, the final solution is computed using MAP formulation and introducing additional constraints in the form of prior information. In order to solve this problem using the MAP framework, we need to model the down sampling process and the blurring introduced while capturing the image. The model is given as [81],

$$\mathbf{y} = A\mathbf{z} + \eta. \tag{6.3}$$

Here, $\mathbf{y}$ and $\mathbf{z}$ are the lexicographically ordered LR and SR vectors of size $M^2 \times 1$ and $q^2 M^2 \times 1$, respectively. Mean and variance of the independent and identically distributed (i.i.d.) noise vector η of size $M^2 \times 1$ are 0 and σ_η^2, respectively.

Our problem is to estimate the SR image $\mathbf{z}$ given $\mathbf{y}$. MAP formulation requires additional constraint in the form of a prior to regularize the solution. For this, one has to know A but here it is unknown as we do not have the SR image. Since, we already know the initial HR estimate of the SR image, we use it to compute A. It may be given as

$$A = DH. \tag{6.4}$$

Here, D is the downsampling (decimation) matrix that has a size $M^2 \times q^2 M^2$ and H is the blur matrix of size $q^2 M^2 \times q^2 M^2$. We assume that the blur matrix is space invariant. While solving the SR problem, H is usually considered as an identity matrix [235]. However, in this work, a non-identity blur matrix as used in Chapter 4 is assumed. It is important to note that this D matrix models the distortion introduced due to aliasing as a result of undersampling of the LR test image. Considering a space invariant blur, the blur matrix H as given in equation (4.8) is repeated here as

$$H = \begin{pmatrix} H_0 & H_{qM^2-1} & H_{qM^2-2} \cdots & H_1 \\ H_1 & H_0 & H_{qM^2-1} \cdots & H_2 \\ \cdot & \cdot & \cdots & \cdot \\ H_{qM^2-1} & H_{qM^2-2} & H_{qM^2-3} \cdots & H_0 \end{pmatrix}, \tag{6.5}$$

where each H_j is given by

$$H_j = \begin{pmatrix} h_{j,0} & h_{j,q-1} & h_{j,q-2} \cdots & h_{j,1} \\ h_{j,1} & h_{j,0} & h_{j,q-1} \cdots & h_{j,2} \\ \cdot & \cdot & \cdot & \cdots & \cdot \\ h_{j,q-1} & h_{j,q-2} & h_{j,q-3} \cdots & h_{j,0} \end{pmatrix} \tag{6.6}$$

with $\{h_{.,.}\}$ representing the value of the point spread function (PSF) for blur. Note that H is a block circulant matrix when the blur is space invariant. The product of D and H yields A matrix which is given by

$$A = \begin{pmatrix} A_1 & A_2 & \cdots & A_{q^2M^2-1} & A_{q^2M^2} \\ A_{q^2M^2-q+1} & \cdots & A_1 & A_2 \cdots & A_{q^2M^2-q} \\ \cdot & \cdot & \cdot & \cdot & \cdot \\ \cdots & \cdots & \cdots A_1 & \cdots & \cdots \end{pmatrix}. \tag{6.7}$$

We obtain the entries in equation (6.7) using the LR observation image and the initial estimate image. Since A has more number of columns than rows, it is estimated using a minimum norm approach. We estimate A using the method followed by Katsikis and Pappars [125] using the least squares approach already discussed in Chapter 4.

6.4   MRF Prior and SR Regularization

SR problem can be solved using regularization with a suitable prior. MRF is widely accepted as a prior due to its capability to capture local dependencies. In our approach, the SR image is modelled as MRF. The energy function considering MRF prior can be expressed as

$$\sum_{c \in C} V_c(\mathbf{z}) = \gamma \sum_{k=1}^{qM} \sum_{l=1}^{qM} \left[(Z_{k,l} - Z_{k,l-1})^2 + (Z_{k,l} - Z_{k-1,l})^2 \right], \tag{6.8}$$

where $V_c(\mathbf{z})$ represents the clique potential and γ is the MRF parameter which represents weightage for the smoothness term in $\mathbf{z}$. Here, C represents the set of all cliques.

The prior parameter γ is unknown and if not estimated, increases the computational burden as it has to be chosen on a trial and error basis during the regularization process. However, we avoid this burden by estimating it using the initial HR approximation. We use the maximum pseudo likelihood [145] for estimating γ. The final cost function consisting of a data fitting term and a prior term can now be expressed as

$$\hat{\mathbf{z}} = \underset{z}{\arg \min} \left[\frac{\| \mathbf{y} - A\mathbf{z} \|^2}{2\sigma_\eta^2} + \sum_{c \in C} V_c(\mathbf{z}) \right]. \tag{6.9}$$

This cost function can be minimized using computationally efficient gradient descent optimization technique. It makes our approach fast when compared to other edge-preserving SR techniques. We reiterate here that the minimization is carried out on non-edge regions only. The minimization leads to the final SR image.

Note that our method uses a Canny edge detector instead of edge-preserving in order to reduce computational complexities. As discussed in chapter 4, a Huber-MRF is an edge-preserving prior and it is convex. Hence, it could be a good choice for edge preservation which allows us to minimize the cost function by using gradient descent technique [207].

However, the performance of this prior is highly dependent on selection of the threshold used in defining the prior. Moreover, the use of a single threshold cannot take care of preserving the edges having different gradients present in the image. The estimation of this threshold is a very challenging task and it is image dependant.

Although, TV and NLTV regularizations may give better SR results, they suffer from high computational complexity [46] and implementations issues. Due to these reasons, we have resorted to a very simple approach of edge-preserving SR.

6.4.1 Optimization process

Here, we describe the gradient descent optimization technique. The gradient of the cost function given in equation (6.9) is obtained by differentiating it with respect to $\mathbf{z}$ as

$$\nabla E(\mathbf{z}) = -2A^T(\mathbf{y} - A\mathbf{z})/2\sigma_\eta^2 + 2\gamma\hat{\mathbf{g}}. \tag{6.10}$$

Here, the first term corresponds to differentiation of the data term, while $\hat{\mathbf{g}}$ vector is computed after differentiating $\sum_{c \in C} V_c(\mathbf{z})$ at every location. The differentiation with respect to $Z(k,l)$ of the second term at a (k,l) location is given by

$$\hat{G}(k,l) = 2[4Z_{(k,l)} - Z_{(k,l-1)} - Z_{(k,l+1)} - Z_{(k-1,l)} - Z_{(k+1,l)}]. \tag{6.11}$$

Note that $\nabla E(\mathbf{z})$ is a vector of size $q^2 M^2 \times 1$. The complete gradient descent optimization process is depicted in algorithm 6.1. The parameter α controls the rate of convergence in gradient descent algorithm. A smaller value of α will lead to slower convergence and for a larger value, the algorithm may not converge. In order to ensure convergence, we use a varying step size α^n with n representing the iteration number and the same is estimated as in [207];

$$\alpha^n = \frac{[\nabla E(\mathbf{z}^n)]^T \nabla E(\mathbf{z}^n)}{[\nabla E(\mathbf{z}^n)]^T (A^T A / 2\sigma_\eta^2 + \gamma \nabla^2 \hat{\mathbf{g}}) \nabla E(\mathbf{z}^n)}. \tag{6.12}$$

The speed of convergence also depends on the initial estimate fed to the optimization process. Use of the available initial estimate as an initial solution helps to speed-up the convergence. In order to preserve the edges in the final solution, we detect the edges from the initial estimate with the help of the Canny edge detector as mentioned earlier and we do not perform optimization on those edge pixels.

Algorithm 6.1: Gradient descent technique

Data: LR MS image ($\mathbf{y}$), initial estimate obtained using CT ($\mathbf{z}^0$),
           degradation matrix (A) and γ

Result: SR image ($\hat{\mathbf{z}}$)

for LR test image $\mathbf{y}$ **do**
    Set $n = 0$;
    repeat
        Find gradient with respect to $\mathbf{z}^n$ of cost function given in equation (6.9) using equation (6.10);
        estimate the step size α^n using equation (6.12);
        Perform $\mathbf{z}^{n+1} = \mathbf{z}^n - \alpha^n (\nabla E(\mathbf{z}^n))$, where α^n is the step size of nth iteration;
        $n = n + 1$;
    until $\dfrac{\|z^m - z^{n-1}\|^2}{\|z^{n-1}\|^2} \leq 10^{-06}$;
    Set $\hat{\mathbf{z}} = \mathbf{z}^{n-1}$;

6.5   Experimental Demonstrations

In this section, we compare the performance of our approach with the existing techniques considering gray scale as well as color images. All the experiments are conducted on images acquired using a real camera. Size of the test and the reconstructed images are 64×64 and 256×256, respectively. The training database consists images of 750 scenes. It includes indoor as well as outdoor scenes covering abundant textured regions. For each scene, there are 3 images of size 64×64, 128×128 and 256×256. Thus, we have a total of $3 \times 750 = 2250$ images. Randomly selected training image pairs are shown in Fig. 6.3. It may be noted that construction of this database was offline and a one time operation. We used peak signal-to-noise ratio (PSNR), edge stability mean squared error (ESMSE) [179] and feature similarity (FSIM) [272] as quantitative measures to assess the quality of the reconstructed images. In addition to this, we also carried out visual assessment in order to compare our results with other methods. For testing the performance of our approach using various quantitative measures, we used a couple of LR training images as the test images. We removed the HR images of these test images from the database during our experimentations.

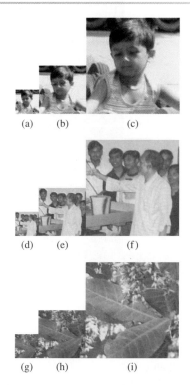

(a)   (b)   (c)

(d)   (e)   (f)

(g)   (h)   (i)

Figure 6.3   Randomly selected LR–HR training images from the database. (a, d, g) LR images of size 64 × 64 pixels (× 1); (b, e, h) HR images of size 128 × 128 pixels (× 2) and (c, f, i) HR images of size 256 × 256 pixels (× 4).

6.5.1   SR results on gray scale images

Figure 6.4(a, c, e) display three gray scale LR observation images 'Ganesha', 'Label' and 'Lambodar' each of size 64 × 64. The original images of these test images are depicted in Fig. 6.4(b, d, f), respectively. The qualitative

(a)   (b)
'Ganesha'

(c)   (d)
'Label'

(e)   (f)
'Lambodar'

Figure 6.4   Test and original gray scale images of size 64 × 64 and
256 × 256, respectively. (a, b) 'Ganesha' (c, d) 'Label'
(e, f) 'Lambodar'.

comparison of our approach with the others for $q = 4$ is shown in Figs. 6.5–6.7
for gray scale images. Figures 6.5(a)–6.7(a) display the images reconstructed
using the SR approach proposed by Upla et al. [235]. In this approach,
the authors used the decimation matrix instead of the degradation matrix
with no inclusion of blur effect as done here. Moreover, they used an
LR MRF prior in the final cost function in addition to the HR prior.
Super-resolved images reconstructed using the method proposed by Gajjar
and Joshi [81] are shown in Figs. 6.5(b)–6.7(b). In Figs. 6.5(c, d)–6.7(c, d),
we display the super-resolved images obtained using approaches by Peleg
and Elad, and Mallat and Yu [184, 161], respectively. Images displayed in
Figs. 6.5(e)–6.7(e) are the results of the method proposed by Dong et al. [63].

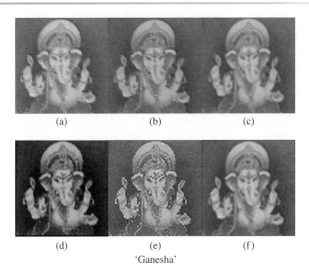

(a)   (b)   (c)

(d)   (e)   (f)

'Ganesha'

Figure 6.5 Comparison of super-resolution approaches for gray scale image 'Ganesha' ($q = 4$). Super-resolved images obtained using (a) approach by Upla et al. [235], (b) wavelet based learning approach [81], (c) approach by Peleg and Elad [184], (d) approach by Mallat and Yu [161], (e) approach by Dong et al. [63] and (f) the proposed approach.

The super-resolved images obtained using our approach are shown in Figs. 6.5(f)–6.7(f).

One can observe that in Fig. 6.5(a–d), the area near the eyes and ears of 'Ganesha' are not sharp. There is an excess amount of contrast in the image displayed in Fig. 6.5(e). Comparison of the images show better details in the super-resolved images using our approach. It can be seen that the edges are restored quite well and the artefacts are minimized in the images reconstructed using the proposed method. The ears and eyes are clearly seen in the 'Ganesha' image. The 'Label' image looks noisy and unpleasant with the use of Dong et al. approach; however one can clearly see the improved edges of the text portions in the proposed approach. Similar improvement can be seen in the 'Lambodar' image too. The reason why edges are improved

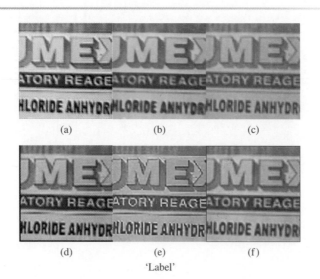

(a)   (b)   (c)

(d)   (e)   (f)
'Label'

Figure 6.6   Comparison of super-resolution approaches for gray scale image 'Label' ($q = 4$). Super-resolved images obtained using (a) approach by Upla et al. [235], (b) wavelet based learning approach [81], (c) approach by Peleg and Elad [184], (d) approach by Mallat and Yu [161], (e) approach by Dong et al. [63] and (f) the proposed approach.

in the images obtained by the proposed approach when compared to that used by Gajjar and Joshi [81] is due to the ability of the CT to capture edges in arbitrary directions over the wavelet transform. Moreover, by comparing the SR results obtained using the proposed approach with that given by Upla et al. [235], one may note that use of the degradation matrix in the proposed approach results in a more accurate image formation model which results in better SR images of the proposed SR approach when compared to that with the approach proposed by Upla et al. [235]. Furthermore, the use of LR test image modelling in the SR approach proposed by Upla et al. [235] does not improve the quality of SR images when compared to the same with the SR images obtained using the proposed SR technique.

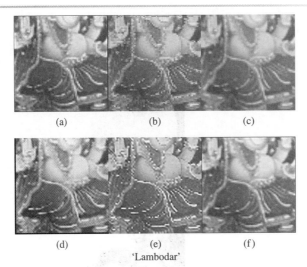

(a)   (b)   (c)

(d)   (e)   (f)

'Lambodar'

Figure 6.7   Comparison of super-resolution approaches for gray scale image 'Lambodar' ($q = 4$). Super-resolved images obtained using (a) approach by Upla et al. [235], (b) wavelet based learning approach [81], (c) approach by Peleg and Elad [184], (d) approach by Mallat and Yu [161], (e) approach by Dong et al. [63] and (f) the proposed approach.

6.5.2   SR results on color images

In this section, we show experimental results for color images. We conducted the experiments on color images in the YC_bC_r color space. Since human eyes are highly sensitive to luminance component, we applied the SR to the luminance component only. Chrominance components are expanded by a simple interpolation technique. Figure 6.8(a, c, e) shows three color test images 'Baby', 'Boy', and 'Nature'; their original images are displayed in Fig. 6.8(b, d, f). Figures 6.9(a)–6.11(a) display images super-resolved using SR technique proposed by Upla et al. [235]. Images reconstructed using the method by Gajjar and Joshi [81] are displayed in Figs. 6.9(b)–6.11(b). In Figs. 6.9(c, d)–6.11(c, d), we show the SR images obtained using the methods proposed by Peleg and Elad, and Mallat and Yu [184, 161], respectively. The SR images in Figs. 6.9(e)–6.11(e) are the results obtained using the Dong et al. [63] approach. The images reconstructed using the proposed approach are shown in Figs. 6.9(f)–6.11(f). For better visual inspection, we have displayed zoomed-in versions of the marked rectangular regions in the SR images. Here, one can see that the hair on the eye and the nostrils in the 'Baby'

(a)   (b)
'Baby'

(c)   (d)
'Boy'

(e)   (f)
'Nature'

Figure 6.8   Test and original color images of size 64 × 64 and 256 × 256, respectively. (a, b) 'Baby' (c, d) 'Boy' (e, f) 'Nature'.

image super-resolved using the proposed approach look better and sharper than those in images obtained using other methods. Similar improvement can be seen in the 'Boy' image in which the iris portion of the eye can be better distinguished from the surrounding portion. One may see improvement in the 'Nature' image too, as visible in the zoomed region in which the blockiness seen in the Dong et al. approach [63] is clearly reduced. It can be seen

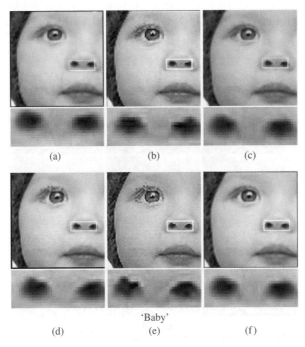

'Baby'

(a)   (b)   (c)

(d)   (e)   (f)

Figure 6.9   Color image super-resolution results for 'Baby' image ($q = 4$). Super-resolved images obtained using (a) approach by Upla et al. [235], (b) wavelet based learning approach [81], (c) method by Peleg and Elad [184], (d) approach by Mallat and Yu [161], (e) method by Dong et al. [63] and (f) the proposed approach.

from Figs. 6.9–6.11 that the proposed method better preserves the texture and details for color images as well, thus outperforming the other methods. It can also be observed from Figs. 6.9–6.11 that although the method proposed by Dong et al. [63] preserves the edge details in the SR image, it looks noisy, exhibiting unpleasant appearance. The quantitative comparisons using PSNR, ESMSE and FSIM are shown in Table 6.1. We point out here that the values of FSIM obtained using the proposed technique are comparable to that of Dong et al. algorithm and are better than the other approaches [235, 81]. It can be concluded that, in addition to the perceptual enhancement there is also a considerable improvement in PSNR, ESMSE and FSIM for our method.

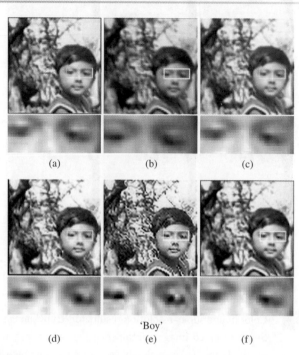

(a)   (b)   (c)

'Boy'

(d)   (e)   (f)

Figure 6.10   Color image super-resolution results for 'Boy' image ($q = 4$). Super-resolved images obtained using (a) approach by Upla et al. [235], (b) wavelet based learning approach [81], (c) method by Peleg and Elad [184], (d) approach by Mallat and Yu [161], (e) method by Dong et al. [63] and (f) the proposed approach.

'Nature'

(a) (b) (c)

(d) (e) (f)

Figure 6.11 Color image super-resolution results for 'Nature' image ($q =$ 4). Super-resolved images obtained using (a) approach by Upla et al. [235], (b) wavelet based learning approach [81], (c) method by Peleg and Elad [184], (d) approach by Mallat and Yu [161], (e) method by Dong et al. [63] and (f) the proposed approach.

Table 6.1 Performance comparison of SR using PSNR, ESMSE and FSIM. The values in boldface indicate better performance

Image	Approach in [235]	Gajjar and Joshi approach [81]	Approach in [184]	Approach in [161]	Dong et al. approach	Proposed approach
			PSNR (in dB)			
'Ganesha'	24.42	21.49	24.16	21.40	23.53	**25.09**
'Label'	18.29	18.75	22.61	17.67	21.11	**23.54**
'Lambodar'	21.23	20.05	22.09	19.30	21.28	**23.50**
'Baby'	28.13	26.13	30.14	25.81	29.15	**32.53**
'Boy'	21.05	15.07	23.62	18.51	20.14	**24.40**
'Nature'	20.55	18.40	23.33	19.15	21.04	**24.52**
			ESMSE			
'Ganesha'	8.96	9.97	6.85	10.01	6.21	**5.84**
'Label'	7.11	14.58	7.88	14.41	7.39	**5.95**
'Lambodar'	8.97	8.71	8.45	8.44	5.94	**5.58**
'Baby'	7.89	7.61	6.19	7.45	6.18	**4.98**
'Boy'	8.94	10.84	5.76	10.91	6.18	**4.46**
'Nature'	8.84	11.19	7.08	11.57	6.60	**5.88**
			FSIM			
'Ganesha'	0.7862	0.7356	0.7895	0.7311	0.7826	**0.8060**
'Label'	0.7765	0.7445	0.7725	0.6629	0.7925	**0.7944**
'Lambodar'	0.72962	0.6848	0.7490	0.6877	0.7177	**0.7537**
'Baby'	0.8926	0.8576	0.9075	0.8671	0.9102	**0.9247**
'Boy'	0.7822	0.5307	0.7800	0.5323	0.7354	**0.7983**
'Nature'	0.7422	0.5763	0.7498	0.5707	0.7084	**0.7548**

6.6 Conclusion

In this chapter, we have investigated an approach to super-resolve an image based on degradation estimation and MRF prior. The edge details are learnt in the form of contourlet transform coefficients that represent edges. Our method uses computationally efficient optimization method for edge preservation. The regularization framework and use of the Canny edge detector result in the SR image that has edges preserved in different directions.

Chapter 7

Conclusion and Directions for Future Research

7.1 Conclusion

Remote sensing satellites capture data in the form of images which are processed and utilized in various applications such as land area classification, map updating, weather forecast, urban planning, etc. However, due to the constraints on the hardware of the sensors and the available transmission bandwidth of the transponder, many commercial satellites provide earth information by capturing images which have complementary characteristics. In this book, we have addressed the problem of multi-resolution image fusion or Pan-sharpening. Here, the low spatial resolution MS image and high spatial resolution Pan image are combined to obtain a single fused image which has both high spatial and spectral resolutions. We seek a fused image which has spectral resolution of the MS image and the spatial resolution of the Pan image. Although the MS and Pan images capture the same geographical area, the complementary nature of these images in terms of the spatial and spectral resolutions gives rise to variation in the two images. Because of this, when we fuse the given images by using direct pixel intensity values, the resultant fused data suffers from spatial as well as spectral distortions. Another important issue in the problem of multi-resolution image fusion is the registration of MS and Pan images. Accurate registration is a difficult task and in this book, we have not addressed it; instead we have used registered data. Here, we present the conclusions which are drawn based on the different proposed methods for Pan-sharpening/ image fusion.

We began our work by proposing two new fusion techniques based on the edge-preserving filters. The Pan image has high frequency details that can be extracted with the help of edge-preserving filter. These extracted details are injected into the upsampled MS image. In our work, we used two edge-preserving filters, namely, the guided filter and difference of Gaussians (DoGs) in order to extract the required details present in the Pan image. The extension of the guided filter in multistages is introduced which effectively extracts the details from Pan and MS images. Similarly, the concept of DoGs is also used to extract the high frequency features from the Pan image. The potential of the proposed methods were evaluated by conducting the experiments on the original as well as the degraded datasets captured using various satellites. The results were compared with state-of-the art methods. In addition to the qualitative evaluation, we have also checked the quantitative performance of the proposed approaches by calculating traditional measures as well as a new measure called quality with no reference (QNR).

The main drawback of the edge preservation based fusion techniques, including many of those proposed in the literature, is the use of upsampling of the MS image and performing fusion without using regularization. The use of upsampling on the test image introduces distortion in the fused image due to aliasing. Hence, our next two approaches avoid using interpolated image directly; these methods are based on using a model for image formation. Here, the given low resolution MS image is modelled as an aliased, blurred and noisy version of the unknown high resolution MS image, that is, it represents the degraded version of the fused image. Since this is an ill-posed problem, it requires suitable regularization in order to obtain a better solution.

In the first model based approach, we obtain an initial HR approximation (initial estimate) with the help of directional transforms such as sub-sampled and non sub-sampled contourlet transforms (CT/NSCT). Use of these transforms is preferred due to their desirable properties such as anisotropy, directionality, etc. Since the edge features in an image occur with different directions and also along smooth contours, the limited directional transform such as wavelet fails to capture those features. Using CT and NSCT transforms, the high frequency details present in the Pan image are extracted in the transform domain to obtain the initial HR approximation separately for each transform. The estimated initial estimate was used in obtaining the transformation between LR and HR MS images by estimating the degradation matrix. A MAP–MRF regularization framework was used to obtain the final solution where we model the unknown high resolution MS image as an MRF. Here, the initial estimate was also used in estimating the MRF parameter which avoids the use of an empirically chosen parameter as done in many of the MRF based techniques. The final cost function being convex, a simple gradient based optimization was used to minimize the same. The edges in the final fused image were preserved by extracting the edges of the initial estimate using the Canny edge operator and hence, the optimization was restricted to the non-edge pixels only. The proposed method preserves fine details present in different directions with minimum spectral distortion. The experimental results demonstrate that the proposed technique yields a better solution when compared to those obtained using the recent state-of-the-art approaches.

Our next model based fusion approach uses the concept of self-similarity and sparse representation theory. The motivation behind using the self-similarity is the redundant details present at different resolutions of an image. Here, the initial estimate was obtained with the help of self-similarity and sparse representation theory. It is important to note that in this case, only the LR MS image was used in obtaining the initial approximation. This resulted in accurate estimation of the degradation matrix since we avoided the use of low spectral resolution Pan images. The degradation matrix was estimated on the LR–HR patch pairs instead of the entire image. Finally, the Pan-sharpening problem was cast as a restoration framework and once again the final solution was obtained by using regularization. A new prior which we called Gabor prior was proposed in order to extract the high frequency details from the Pan image. The final cost function was minimized using the gradient descent optimization. To show the effectiveness of the proposed approach, we conducted experiments on the datasets acquired from different satellites and the results were compared with other state-of-the-art methods. From the results and the quantitative measures, we conclude that the proposed method gives Pan-sharpened images with better preservation of color and edge regions when compared to the state-of-the art methods.

The proposed framework for fusion of remotely sensed images was then extended for the super-resolution of natural images. In this case, since the high resolution image such as Pan is unavailable, one has to resort to a different approach in order to enhance the spatial resolution of the given low resolution observation. We used an offline operation in which an LR–HR set of image pairs of the same scene were used to obtain the initial estimate of the SR image. The high frequency details in the initial SR approximation were obtained using contourlet transform. Here also the final super-resolved image was obtained using regularization in which we used MRF prior on HR image. The MRF parameter was estimated using the initial approximation to SR. The efficacy of the proposed SR approach was tested by conducting experiments on the gray scale as well as color images. The results were compared with other state-of-the-art SR approaches. Based on the results and measures, we conclude that our approach used in multi-resolution fusion can be applied on natural images for super-resolving them.

Before we end the conclusion, it may be of interest to mention the following points regarding the use of the initial estimate in our works. We assumed that the initial estimate represents a close approximation to the final fused image. Note that, though it can be considered as close to the fused image, one cannot accept it as the final solution. This is because the problem of fusion is ill-posed and the solution space of the initial estimate without regularization is larger when compared to that obtained after regularization. However, one may still consider the initial estimate to represent global characteristics such as edge details, spatial dependencies, etc., of the final solution. In addition to this, we often require an accurate estimate of the input–output relationship where the output is often not known. In such situations, it is reasonable to derive an initial estimate of the output from the given data and use the same for finding the transformation. Due to these reasons, we derived an initial estimate and used it for obtaining an improved solution. To this end, one may argue that recent machine learning based approaches using deep networks can be used in obtaining the mapping between the input and the output. However, the algorithms based on deep learning are computationally expensive. They do not guarantee convergence and the network structures used in learning the mapping is often ad hoc.

7.2 Future Research Work

In multi-resolution image fusion, the data captured, in the form of MS and Pan images, by the satellites is used to obtain a single fused image with high spatial and spectral resolutions. Most fusion techniques suffer from drawbacks such as poor preservation of spectral details, insufficient injection of spatial details, registration error, and computational complexity. In this book, we have addressed the fusion problem using the model based approach and also using the methods based on details injection into the MS image. In the model based approach, we modelled the given LR MS image as degraded version of the unknown fused MS image. Since this is an ill-posed inverse problem, regularization is required to obtain a better fused image. We modelled the true MS image as an MRF and used the smoothness prior in the final cost function. In addition to the MRF prior, we also used the Gabor prior in order to obtain the high frequency details from the Pan image. However, there is still scope for improving the quality of the final fused image. In this section, we shall list the future directions for the work described in this book.

- One of the limitations of many fusion techniques, including the proposed approach, is the requirement of registration of the given MS and Pan images. Since the MS and Pan images are captured by two different sensors, there are always chances of registration error. Moreover, due to the motion of the satellite in its orbital path, a slight time difference in capturing the MS and Pan data leads to acquiring images of different geographical area; this results in registration error. In the proposed fusion methods, we assumed that the given MS and Pan data were co-registered. However, it is always an interest within the fusion community to overcome this limitation. One can extend the fusion work proposed in this book in order to overcome this limitation.

- In this book, we have proposed two Pan-sharpening techniques in which the extracted details from the Pan image using the different edge-preserving filters are injected into the upsampled MS image with an appropriate scaling factor. This scale factor accounts for the proportionate detail injection of the Pan image which was calculated using the intensity values of the MS images. Literature on satellite imaging indicates that there is a considerable difference between the spectral response of the MS and Pan sensors. For example, in the dataset of Ikonos-2 satellite, the spectral response of the Pan sensor covers the NIR spectral band completely. However, the blue spectral band is not complete under the spectral response of the Pan sensor. Moreover, the spectral response function of the Pan sensor goes beyond the range of the blue band. This difference in spectral characteristic of the two sensors, that is, the MS and Pan affects the fused data in terms of spectral or spatial distortions. One can add this observation of the spectral response of the two different sensors in order to calculate the scaling factor. The scaling factor based on the spectral response can inject accurate details into the MS image and it leads to a better fused image. Apart from this, the interpolation in the MS image leads to aliasing effect. It would be of interest to look into this as well while injecting the details into the MS image.

• In the proposed model based fusion approach, we estimated the degradation that occurs due to the downsampling and blur in the MS image. In order to do this we require the original fused MS image. In such situations, we use a close approximation to the final fused (initial HR approximation). In order to get the accurate values of the degradation matrix coefficients, we require the initial HR approximation as close as possible to the true high resolution MS image. Because of the different desirable properties of the directional transforms such as CT and NSCT, we used them in our work to obtain the initial HR approximation of the final fused image. These transforms decompose the images using the bases that yield edges along the smooth contour as well. We decompose the MS and Pan images using CT and NSCT with a limited number of levels. It would be of interest to increase the number of decomposition levels making them adaptive to the details present in the image without considerably increasing the time complexity. One can use adaptive directional transforms to fulfil this objective. Use of adaptive directional transform may increase the complexity of the method. However, it can be reduced by using present day modern high computing processors such as a graphical processing unit.

• While using the regularization framework, we have modelled the unknown fused MS image as an MRF; the smoothness constraint was used as the prior term in the final cost function. We used a Canny edge detector in order to preserve the edges into the final fused image. This gave us the advantages of reduced complexity with edge preservation without using discontinuity preserving priors in the final cost function. However, one can use the edge-preserving prior such as MRF with line fields to preserve the edges in the final fused image. The resulting cost function may lead to a non-convex function which cannot be minimized by computationally efficient gradient based optimization techniques. But one may try using graph cuts in order to minimize such non-convex cost functions. Such an optimization technique is computationally less complex and yields a solution closer to the optimum.

- The linear image formation model for LR MS image has been used in the proposed model based approach. This model gives simplicity in the form of a mathematical tractability in order to find the solution. In the proposed method, we estimated the degradation between the LR MS and the fused images using a linear image formation model. The degradation consists of the decimation along with blur. In order to add the blur as a non-identity matrix, we used the space invariant blur that results in a simpler structure for the final degradation matrix. A better solution of the final fused image can be obtained by using the space variant blur instead of the space invariant. The patchwise use of the space variant blur matrix may serve as a more accurate model for the image formation and the same can be used to obtain the final fused image in order to get better fusion.

- We use a model based approach to obtain a final fused image where the initial estimate has been obtained with both MS and Pan images or only with MS image. In both the cases, we use the linear image formation model to obtain the final fused image. However, it is interesting to model the image formation chain including the relations between MS bands, Pan, and an ideal HR MS image using Bayesian inference. These could be applied to extract the optimal matrices while marginalising over the unknown HR MS image, yielding an iterative, but more rigorous approach.

Bibliography

[1] Anonymous. 1986; revised January 1991. *Guide des Utilisateurs des Donnes SPOT.* 3 volumes Toulouse, France: CNES and SPOT.

[2] International Society for Photogrammetry and Remote Sensing. Last modified September 2012. Available at http://www.isprs.org/data/ikonos hobart/default.aspx.

[3] DigitalGlobe. 'Product Samples'. Last modified September 2012. Available at http://www.digitalglobe.com/product-samples.

[4] DigitalGlobe. Last modified May 2013. Available at http://www.digitalglobe.com/downloads/microsites/dfc/optical/WV2 9Oct2011.zip.

[5] Global Land Cover Facility. 'Quickbird: Sundarbans'. Last modified February 2014. Available at http://www.glcf.umd.edu/data/quickbird/ sundarbans.html.

[6] Aanaes, H., J. R. Sveinsson, A. A. Nielsen, T. Bovith, and J. A. Benediktsson. 2008. 'Model Based Satellite Image Fusion'. *IEEE Transactions on Geosciences and Remote Sensing* 46 (5): 1336–1346.

[7] Aiazzi, Bruno, L. Alparone, Stefano Baronti, and R. Carl. 1996. 'A Pyramid Approach to Fusion of Landsat TM and SPOT-PAN Data to Yield Multispectral High-Resolution Images for Environmental Archaeology'. In *Remote Sensing for Geography, Geology, Land Planning and Cultural Heritage*, volume 2960 of *Proceedings of SPIE*, EUROPTO Series, 153–162.

[8] Aiazzi, Bruno, L. Alparone, Stefano Baronti, V. Cappellini, R. Carl, and L. Mortelli. 1997. 'A Laplacian Pyramid with Rational Scale Factor for Multisensor Image Data Fusion. In *Proceedings of the International Conference on Sampling Theory and Applications—SampTA, 97*, 55–60.

[9] Aiazzi, Bruno, L. Alparone, Stefano Baronti, and I. Pippi. 1999a. 'Fusion of 18mMOMS- 2P and 30 m Landsat TM Multispectral Data by the Generalized Laplacian Pyramid'. In *Proceedings of ISPRS International Archives of the Photogrammetry, Remote Sensing and Spatial Information Sciences*, 116–122.

[10] Aiazzi, Bruno, L. Alparone, A. Barducci, Stefano Baronti, and I. Pippi. 1999b. 'Multispectral Fusion of Multisensor Image Data by the Generalized Laplacian Pyramid. In *Proceedings of the International Geoscience and Remote Sensing Symposium*, 1183–1185.

[11] Aiazzi, Bruno, L. Alparone, Stefano Baronti, and A. Garzelli. 2002. 'Context Driven Fusion of High Spatial and Spectral Resolution Images Based on Oversampled Multiresolution Analysis'. *IEEE Transactions on Geosciences and Remote Sensing* 40 (10): 2300–2312.

[12] Aiazzi, Bruno, L. Alparone, S. Baronti, A. Garzelli, and Massimo Selva. 2006. MTF Tailored Multiscale Fusion of High-Resolution MS and Pan Imagery. *Photogrammetric Engineering and Remote Sensing* 72 (5): 591–596.

[13] Aiazzi, Bruno, Stefano Baronti, and Massimo Selva. 2007. 'Improving Component Substitution Pansharpening through Multivariate Regression of MS + Pan Data. *IEEE Transactions on Geosciences and Remote Sensing* 45 (10): 3230–3239.

[14] Aiazzi, Bruno, Stefano Baronti, Massimo Selva, and Luciano Alparone. 2013. 'Bi-cubic Interpolation for Shift-Free Pan-Sharpening'. *ISPRS Journal of Photogrammetry and Remote Sensing* 86: 65–76.

[15] Akhtar, Naveed, Faisal Shafait, and Ajmal Mian. 2014. 'Sparse Spatio-Spectral Representation for Hyperspectral Image Super-Resolution'. In *Proceedings of the European Conference on Computer Vision*, 63–78.

[16] Akhtar, Naveed, Faisal Shafait, and Ajmal Mian. 2015. 'Bayesian Sparse Representation for Hyperspectral Image Super Resolution'. In *Proceedings of the IEEE Conference on Computer Vision and Pattern Recognition*, 3631–3640.

[17] Alparone, Luciano, Stefano Baronti, Andrea Garzelli, and F. Nencini. 2004. 'A Global Quality Measurement of Pan-Sharpened Multi-Spectral Imagery'. *IEEE Transactions on Geosciences and Remote Sensing* 1 (4): 313–317.

[18] Alparone, Luciano, L. Wald, J. Chanussot, C. Thomas, P. Gamba, and L. M. Bruce. 2007. 'Comparison of Pan-sharpening Algorithms: Outcome of the 2006 GRS-S Data Fusion Contest'. *IEEE Transactions on Geosciences and Remote Sensing* 10 (45): 3012–3021.

[19] Alparone, Luciano, Bruno Aiazzi, Stefano Baronti, Andrea Garzelli, F. Nencini, and M. Selva. 2008. 'Multispectral and Panchromatic Data Fusion Assessment Without Reference'. *Photogrammetric Engineering and Remote Sensing* 74 (2): 193–200.

[20] Alparone, Luciano, Bruno Aiazzi, Stefano Baronti, and Andrea Garzelli. 2015. *Remote Sensing Image Fusion*. Florida, USA: CRC Press.

[21] Aly, Hussein. A., and Dubois, E. 2005. 'Image Up-Sampling Using Total-Variation Regularization with a New Observation Model'. *IEEE Transactions on Image Processing* 14 (10): 1647–1659.

[22] Aly, Hussein A., and Gaurav Sharma. 2014. 'A Regularized Model-Based Optimization Framework for Pan-Sharpening'. *IEEE Transactions on Image Processing* 23 (6): 2596–2608.

[23] Anon. 1993. *Design and Development of Airborne Imaging Spectrometer*. SAC/EOSDG/AIS/09/93. Ahmedabad, India: Space Applications Centre. Technical Report.

[24] Arya, Sunil, and David M. Mount. 1993. 'Approximate Nearest Neighbor Queries in Fixed Dimensions'. In *Proceedings of the Fourth Annual ACM-SIAM Symposium on Discrete Algorithms*, 271–280.

[25] Ballester, C., V. Casellesa, L. Igual, and J. Verdera. 2006. 'Process for Enhancing the Spatial Resolution of Multispectral Imagery Using Pan-Sharpening'. *International Journal of Computer Vision* 69 (1): 43–58.

[26] Bamberger, H. R., and M. J. T. Smith. 1992. 'A Filter Bank for the Directional Decomposition of Images: Theory and Design'. *IEEE Transactions on Signal Processing* 40 (4): 882–893.

[27] Barnsley, M. J., J. J. Settle, M. A. Cutter, D. R. Lobb, and F. Teston. 2004. 'The PROBA/CHRIS Mission: A Low-Cost SmallSat for Hyperspectral Multiangle Observations of the Earth Surface and Atmosphere. *IEEE Transactions on Geoscience and Remote Sensing* 42 (7): 1512–1520.

[28] Baronti, Stefano, Bruno Aiazzi, Massimo Selva, Andrea Garzelli, and Luciano Alparone. 2011. 'A Theoretical Analysis of the Effects of Aliasing and Misregistration on Pan-sharpened Imagery'. *IEEE Journal of Selected Topics in Applied Earth Observations and Remote Sensing* 5 (3): 446–453.

[29] Bendory, T., S. Dekel, and A. Feuer. 2015. 'Super-Resolution on the Sphere Using Convex Optimization'. *IEEE Transactions on Signal Processing* 63 (9): 2253–2262.

[30] Bern'e, Olivier, A. Helens, P. Pilleri, and Christine Joblin. 2010. 'Non-negative Matrix Factorization Pansharpening of Hyperspectral Data: An Application to Midinfrared Astronomy'. In *Proceedings of 2nd Workshop on Hyperspectral Image and Signal Processing: Evolution in Remote Sensing (WHISPERS)*, 1–4. IEEE.

[31] Bevilacqua, M., A. Roumy, C Guillemot, and Alberi M.-L Morel. 2014. 'Single-Image Super-Resolution via Linear Mapping of Interpolated Self-Examples'. *IEEE Transactions on Image Processing* 23 (12): 5334–5347.

[32] Bhatt, J. S., M. V. Joshi, and M. S. Raval. 2014. 'A Data-Driven Stochastic Approach for Unmixing Hyperspectral Imagery'. *IEEE Journal of Selected Topics in Applied Earth Observations and Remote Sensing* 7 (6): 1936–46.

[33] Bioucas-Dias, J.M., A. Plaza, N. Dobigeon, M. Parente, Q. Du, P. Gader, and J. Chanussot. 2012. 'Hyperspectral Unmixing Overview: Geometrical, Statistical, and Sparse Regression-Based Approaches'. *IEEE Journal of Selected Topics in Applied Earth Observations and Remote Sensing* 5 (2): 354–379.

[34] Blanc, Philippe, T. Blu, T. Ranchin, L. Wald, and R. Aloisi. 1998. 'Using Iterated Rational Filter Banks Within the ARSIS Concept for Producing 10 m Landsat Multispectral Images'. *International Journal of Remote Sensing* 19 (2): 2331–2343.

[35] Blum, Rick S., and Zheng Liu. 2005. *Multi-Sensor Image Fusion and Its Applications*. Florida, USA: CRC Press.

[36] Bradley, A. P. 2003. 'Shift-invariance in the Discrete Wavelet Transform'. In *Proceedings of the 8th Digital Image Computing: Techniques and Applications*, 29–38.

[37] Bruckstein, Alfred M., David L. Donoho, and Michael Elad. 2009. 'From Sparse Solutions of Systems of Equations to Sparse Modeling of Signals and Images'. *SIAM Review* 51 (1): 34–81.

[38] Burt, P. J., and E. H. Adelson. 1983. 'The Laplacian Pyramid as a Compact Image Code. *IEEE Transactions on Communications* 31 (4): 532–540.

[39] Candes, Emmanuel. J., and David L. Donoho 1999. 'Curvelets: A Surprisingly Effective Nonadaptive Representation for Objects with Edges'. In *Curve and Surface Fitting: Saint-Malo Proceedings*, edited by A. Cohen, C. Rabut, and L. L. Schumaker. Nashville, TN: Vanderbilt Universities Press.

[40] Candes, Emmanuel, and Justin Romberg. 2005. *l1-magic: Recovery of Sparse Signal via Convex Programming*. 1–19.

[41] Capel, D., and A. Zisserman. 2000. 'Super-Resolution Enhancement of Text Image Sequences'. In *Proceedings of the 15th International Conference on Pattern Recognition (ICPR '00)*, 600–605.

[42] Capel, D., and A. Zisserman. 2001. 'Super-resolution from Multiple Views Using Learnt Image Models. In *Proceedings of the IEEE International Conference on Computer Vision and Pattern Recognition*, 627–634.

[43] Carper, W. J., T. M. Lillesand, and R. W. Kiefer. 1990. 'The Use of Intensity-Hue Saturation Transform for Merging Spot Panchromatic and Multispectral Image Data'. *Photogrammetric Engineering and Remote Sensing* 56 (4): 459–467.

[44] Chan, T. M., J. P. Zhang, J. Pu, and H. Huang. 2009. 'Neighbor Embedding Based Super-Resolution Algorithm through Edge Detection and Feature Selection'. *Pattern Recognition Letters* 30 (5), 494–502.

[45] Chang, C. 1999. 'Spectral Information Divergence for Hyperspectral Image Analysis. In *Proceedings of the International Geoscience and Remote Sensing Symposium*, 1, 509–511.

[46] Chang, Huibin, Xiaoqun Zhang, Xue-Cheng Tai, and Danping Yang. 2014. 'Domain Decomposition Methods for Nonlocal Total Variation Image Restoration'. *Journal of Scientific Computing* 60: 79–100.

[47] Chaudhuri, Subhasis, and Ketan Kotwal. 2013. *Hyperspectral Image Fusion*. Springer.

[48] Chavez, P. S. 1986. 'Digital Merging of Landsat TM and Digitized NHAP Data 1: 24,000 Scale Image Mapping'. *Photogrammetric Engineering and Remote Sensing* 52 (10): 1637–1647.

[49] Chavez, P. S. Jr., S. C. Sides, and J. A. Anderson 1991. 'Comparison of Three DiffErent Methods to Merge Multiresolution and Multispectral Data: Landsat TM and SPOT Panchromatic'. *Photogrammetric Engineering and Remote Sensing* 57 (3): 295–303.

[50] Chavez, P.S., and A. Y. Kwarteng. 1989. 'Extracting Spectral Contrast in Landsat Thematic Mapper Image Data Using Selective Principal Component Analysis'. *Photogrammetric Engineering and Remote Sensing* 55, 339–348.

[51] Chen, Scott Shaobing, David L. Donoho, and Michael A. Saunders. 1998. 'Atomic Decomposition by Basis Pursuit'. *SIAM Journal on Scientific Computing* 20 (1): 33–61.

[52] Chen, Zhao, Hanye Pu, Bin Wang, and Geng-Ming Jiang. 2014. 'Fusion of Hyperspectral and Multispectral Images: A Novel Framework Based on Generalization of Pan-Sharpening Methods'. *IEEE Geoscience and Remote Sensing Letters* 11 (8): 1418–1422.

[53] Cheng, Ming, Cheng Wang, and Jonathan Li. 2014. 'Sparse Representation Based Pan-sharpening Using Trained Dictionary'. *IEEE Geoscience and Remote Sensing Letters* 11 (1): 293–297.

[54] Chibani, Y., and A. Houacine. 2002. 'The Joint Use of IHS Transform and Redundant Wavelet Decomposition for Fusing Multispectral and Panchromatic Images'. *International Journal of Remote Sensing* 23: 3821–3833.

[55] Choi, J., K. Yu, and Y. Kim. 2011. 'A New Adaptive Component-Substitution Based Satellite Image Fusion by Using Partial Replacement'. *IEEE Transactions on Geosciences and Remote Sensing* 49 (1): 295–309.

[56] Choi, M. 2006. 'A New Intensity-Hue-Saturation Fusion Approach to Image Fusion with a Trade-off Parameter'. *IEEE Transactions on Geosciences and Remote Sensing* 44 (6): 1672–1682.

[57] Choi, M., R. Y. Kim, , M. R. Nam, and H. O. Kim. 2005. 'Fusion of Multispectral and Panchromatic Satellite Images using the Curvelet Transform'. *IEEE Transactions on Geosciences and Remote Sensing* 2 (2): 136–140.

[58] Combettes, Patrick L., and Jean-Christophe Pesquet. 2004. 'Image Restoration Subject to a Total Variation Constraint'. *IEEE Transactions on Image Processing* 13 (9): 1213–1222.

[59] Da Cunha, A. L., Jianping Zhou, and Minh N. Do. 2006. 'The Nonsubsampled Contourlet Transform: Theory, Design, and Applications'. *IEEE Transactions on Image Processing* 15 (10): 3089–3101.

[60] Do, Minh N., and M. Vetterli. 2003. 'Framing Pyramids'. *IEEE Transactions on Signal Processing* 51 (9): 2329–2342.

[61] Do, Minh N., and M. Vetterli. 2005. 'The Contourlet Transform: An Efficient Directional Multiresolution Image Representation'. *IEEE Transactions on Image Processing* 14 (12): 2091–2106.

[62] Dong, C., C. C. Loy, , K. He, and X. Tang. 2016. 'Image Super-Resolution Using Deep Convolutional Networks'. *IEEE Transactions on Pattern Analysis and Machine Intelligence* 38 (2): 295–307.

[63] Dong, W., L. Zhang, and G. Shi. 2011. 'Centralized Sparse Representation for Image Restoration'. In *Proceedings of the IEEE International Conference on Computer Vision* (ICCV), 1259–1266.

[64] Dou,W., Y. Chen, X. Li, and D. Z. Sui. 2007. 'A General Framework for Component Substitution Image Fusion: An Implementation Using the Fast Image Fusion Method'. *Computers and Geosciences* 33 (2): 219–228.

[65] Du, Q., O. Gungor, and J. Shan. 2005. 'Performance Evaluation for Pan-sharpening Techniques'. In *Proceedings of the International Geoscience and Remote Sensing Symposium* 6: 4264–4266.

[66] Du, Q., N. Younan, R. King, and V. Shah. 2007. 'On the Performance Evaluation of Pan-Sharpening Techniques'. *IEEE Geoscience and Remote Sensing Letters* 4 (4): 518–522.

[67] Duran, Joan, Antoni Buades, Bartomeu Coll, and Catalina Sbert. 2014a. 'A Nonlocal Variational Model for Pan-sharpening Image Fusion'. *SIAM Journal of Imaging Sciences* 7 (2): 761–796.

[68] Duran, Joan, Antoni Buades, Bartomeu Coll, and Catalina Sbert. 2014b. 'Implementation of Nonlocal Pan-sharpening Image Fusion'. *Image Processing Online* 4: 1–15.

[69] Dutilleux, P. 1989. 'An Implementation of the Algorithme a Trous to Compute the Wavelet Transform'. In: *Wavelets: Time Frequency Methods and Phase Space* edited by J. M. Combes, A. Grossman, Ph Tchamitchian, 298–304. Berlin: Springer.

[70] Ehlers, M. 1991. 'Multisensor Image Fusion Techniques in Remote Sensing'. *ISPRS Journal of Photogrammetry and Remote Sensing* 46: 19–30.

[71] Eshtehardi, A., H. Ebadi, M. J. Valadan, and A. Mohammadzadeh. 2007. 'Image Fusion of Landsat ETM+ and SPOT Satellite Images Using IHS, Brovey and PCA'. *ISPRS Journal of Photogrammetry and Remote Sensing.*

[72] Fang, Faming, Fang Li, Chaomin Shen, and Guixu Zhang. 2013. 'A Variational Approach for Pan-sharpening'. *IEEE Transactions on Image Processing* 22 (7): 2822–2834.

[73] Fang, Jun, Jing Li, Yanning Shen, Hongbin Li, and Shaoqian Li. 2014. 'Super-Resolution Compressed Sensing: An Iterative Reweighted Algorithm for Joint Parameter Learning and Sparse Signal Recovery'. *IEEE Signal Processing Letters* 21 (6): 761–765.

[74] Farsiu, S., M. D. Robinson, M. Elad, and P. Milanfar. 2004. 'Fast and Robust Multiframe Super Resolution'. *IEEE Transactions on Image Processing* 13 (10): 1327–1344.

[75] Farsiu, S., M. Elad, and P. Milanfar. 2006. 'Multi-frame Demosaicing and Superresolution of Color Images'. *IEEE Transactions on Image Processing* 15 (1): 141–159.

[76] Fasbender, D., J. Radoux, and P. Bogaert. 2008. 'Bayesian Data Fusion for Adaptable Image Pan-sharpening'. *IEEE Transactions on Geosciences and Remote Sensing* 46 (6): 1847–1857.

[77] Fernandes, F. C., R. L. van Spaendonck, and C. S. Burrus. 2003. 'A New Framework for Complex Wavelet Transforms'. *IEEE Transactions on Signal Processing* 51 (7): 1825–1837.

[78] Fernandes, F. C., R. L. van Spaendonck, and C. S. Burrus. 2005. 'Multidimensional, Mapping-Based Complex Wavelet Transforms'. *IEEE Transactions on Image Processing* 14 (1): 110–124.

[79] Figueiredo, M'ario A.T., and Robert D. Nowak. 2003. 'An EM Algorithm for Wavelet-Based Image Restoration. *IEEE Transactions on Image Processing* 12 (8): 906–916.

[80] Freeman, W. T., T. R, Jones, and E. C. Pasztor. 2002. 'Example-based Superresolution'. *IEEE Computer Graphics* and *Applications* 22 (2): 56–65.

[81] Gajjar, P. P., and M. V. Joshi. 2010. 'New Learning Based Super-Resolution: Use of DWT and IGMRF Prior'. *IEEE Transactions on Image Processing* 19 (5): 1201–1213.

[82] Galatsanos, N. P., and A. K. Katsaggelos. 1992. 'Methods for Choosing the Regularization Parameter and Estimating the Noise Variance in Image Restoration and their Relation'. *IEEE Transactions on Image Processing* 1 (3): 322–336.

[83] Garguet-Duport, B., J. Girel, J. M. Chasseny, and G. Pautou. 1996. 'The Use of Multiresolution Analysis and Wavelet Transform for Merging SPOT Panchromatic and Multispectral Image Data'. *Photogrammetric Engineering and Remote Sensing* 62 (9): 1057–1066.

[84] Garzelli, A., and F. Nencini. 2005. 'Interband Structure Modeling for Pan-sharpening of Very High-Resolution Multispectral Images'. *Information Fusion* 6: 213–224.

[85] Garzelli, A., and F. Nencini. 2006. 'Fusion of Panchromatic and Multispectral Images by Genetic Algorithms'. In *Proceedings of the International Geoscience and Remote Sensing Symposium*, 3810–3813.

[86] Geman, S., and D. Geman. 1984. 'Stochastic Relaxation, Gibbs Distribution and the Bayesian Restoration of Images'. *IEEE Transactions* on *Pattern Analysis* and *Machine Intelligence* 6(Nov.): 721–741.

[87] Gilboa, G., and S. Osher. 2008. 'Nonlocal Operators with Applications to Image Processing'. *Multiscale Modeling and Simulation* 7: 1005–1028.

[88] Gillespie, A. R., A. B. Kahle, and R. E. Walker. 1987. 'Color Enhancement of Highly Correlated Images II. Channel Ratio and Chromaticity Transformation Technique'. *Photogrammetric Engineering and Remote Sensing* 22 (3): 343–365.

[89] Glasner, D., S. Bagon, and M. Irani. 2009. 'Super-Resolution from a Single Image'. In *Proceedings of the IEEE International Conference on Computer Vision*, 349–356.

[90] Gomez, Richard B, Amin Jazaeri, and Menas Kafatos. 2001. 'Wavelet-based Hyperspectral and Multispectral Image Fusion'. In *Geo-spatial Image and Data Exploitation II, SPIE Proceedings* 4383: 36–42.

[91] González- Audicana, Maria, José Luis Saleta, Raquel Garcia Catalán, , and Rafael Garcia. 2004. 'Fusion of Multispectral and Panchromatic Images Using Improved IHS and PCA Mergers based on Wavelet decomposition'. *IEEE Transactions on Geosciences and Remote Sensing* 42 (6): 1291–1299.

[92] Gonzalez, R. C., and R. E. Woods. 1992. *Digital Image Processing*. Mass., USA: Addison-Wesley.

[93] Gonzalez-Audicana, Maria, Xavier Otazu, Octavi Fors, and A. Seco. 2005. 'Comparison between Mallat's and the 'a Trous' Discrete Wavelet Transform Based Algorithms for the Fusion of Fusion Multispectral and Panchromatic Images'. *International Journal of Remote Sensing* 3 (3): 595–614.

[94] Gonzalez-Audicana, Maria, Xavier Otazu, O. Fors, and J. A. Alvarex-Mozos. 2006. A Low Computational-Cost Method to Fuse IKONOS Images Using the Spectral

Response Function of its Sensors'. *IEEE Transactions on Geosciences and Remote Sensing* 44 (6): 1683–1691.

[95] Goto, T., S. Suzuki, S. Hirano, M. Sakurai, and T. Q. Nguyen. 2011 'Fast and High Quality Learning-Based Super-Resolution Utilizing TV Regularization Method'. In *Proceedings of the 18th IEEE International Conference on Image Processing*, September 2011, 1185–1188.

[96] Gou, S., S. Liu, Y. Wu, and L. Jiao. 2016. 'Image Super-Resolution Based on the Pairwise Dictionary Selected Learning and Improved Bilateral Regularisation'. *IET Image Processing* 10 (2): 101–112.

[97] Green, Robert O., Michael L. Eastwood, Charles M. Sarture, Thomas G. Chrien, Mikael Aronsson, Bruce J Chippendale, Jessica A. Faust, Betina E. Pavri, Christopher J. Chovit, Manuel Solis, Martin R. Olah, and Orlesa Williams. 1998. 'Imaging Spectroscopy and the Airborne Visible/Infrared Imaging Spectrometer (AVIRIS)'. *Remote Sensing of Environment* 65 (3): 227–248.

[98] Grohnfeldt, Claas, and Xiao Xiang Zhu. 2015. 'Towards a Combined Sparse Representation and Unmixing Based Hybrid Hyperspectral Resolution Enhancement Method'. In *Proceedings of the International Geoscience and Remote Sensing Symposium (IGARSS)*, 2015, 2872–2875, IEEE International.

[99] Grohnfeldt, Claas, Xiao Xiang Zhu, and Richard Bamler. 2013. 'Jointly Sparse Fusion of Hyperspectral and Multispectral Imagery'. In *Proceedings of the International Geoscience and Remote Sensing Symposium (IGARSS)*, 2013, 4090–4093, IEEE International.

[100] Grohnfeldt, Claas, Xiao Xiang Zhu, and Richard Bamler. 2014. 'The J Sparse FI-HM Hyperspectral Resolution Enhancement Method Now Fully Automated. In *Proceedings of the 6th Workshop on Hyperspectral Image and Signal Processing: Evolution in Remote Sensing (WHISPERS)*, 2014, 1–4, IEEE.

[101] Gross, Harry N, and John R. Schott. 1998. 'Application of Spectral Mixture Analysis and Image Fusion Techniques for Image Sharpening'. *Remote Sensing of Environment* 63 (2): 85–94.

[102] Guichard, F., and F. Malgouyres. 1998. 'Total Variation Based Interpolation'. In *Proceedings of Eusipco'98*, 1741–4, North Holland: Elsevier.

[103] Ha, Wonsook, Prasanna H. Gowda, and Terry A. Howell. 2013. 'A Review of Potential Image Fusion Methods for Remote Sensing-Based Irrigation Management: Part II'. *Irrigation Science* 31 (4): 851–869.

[104] Hansen, P. C. 1992. 'Analysis of Discrete Ill-Posed Problems by Means of the L-curve'. *SIAM Review* 34 (4); 561–580.

[105] Hardie, R. C., M. T. Eismann, and G. L. Wilson. 2004. 'MAP Estimation for Hyperspectral Image Resolution Enhancement Using an Auxiliary Sensor'. *IEEE Transactions on Image Processing* 13 (9): 1174–1184.

[106] Harikumar, V., P. P. Gajjar, M. V. Joshi, and M. S. Raval. 2014. 'Multiresolution Image Fusion: Use of Compressive Sensing and Graph Cuts'. *IEEE Journal of Selected Topics in Applied Earth Observations and Remote Sensing* 7 (5): 1771–1780.

[107] Haydn, R., G. W. Dalke, J. Henkel, and J. E. Bare. 1982. 'Application of the IHS Color Transform to the Processing of Multisensor Data and Image Enhancement'. *Proceedings of the International Symposium on Remote sensing of Arid and Semi-arid Lands*, 599–607.

[108] He, K., J. Sun, and X. Tang. 2013. 'Guided Image Filtering'. *IEEE Transactions* on *Pattern Analysis* and *Machine Intelligence* 35 (6): 1397–1409.

[109] He, Xiyan, Laurent Condat, Jocelyn Chanussot, and Junshi Xia. 2012. 'Pan-sharpening Using Total Variation Regularization'. In *Proceedings of the International Geoscience and Remote Sensing Symposium* 166–169.

[110] He, Xiyan, Laurent Condat, Jos M. Bioucas-Dias, Jocelyn Chanussot, and Junshi Xia. 2014. 'A New Pan-sharpening Method Based on Spatial and Spectral Sparsity Priors'. In *Proceedings of the International Geoscience and Remote Sensing Symposium* 23 (9): 4160–4174.

[111] Hong, G., and Y. Zhang. 2003. 'High Resolution Image Fusion Based on Wavelet and IHS Transformations'. In *Proceedings of the IEEE/ISPRS Joint Workshop on Remote Sensing and Data Fusion over Urban Areas*, Berlin, 99–104.

[112] Hu, J., and S. Li, S. 2011. 'Fusion of Panchromatic and Multispectral Images Using Multiscale Dual Bilateral Filter'. In: *Proceedings of the IEEE International Conference on Image Processing*, 1489–1492.

[113] Huang,W., L. Xiao, Z. Wei, H. Liu, and S. Tang. 2015. 'A New Pan-Sharpening Method with Deep Neural Networks'. *IEEE Geoscience and Remote Sensing Letters* 12 (5): 1037–1041.

[114] Ioannidou, S., and V. Karathanassi. 2007. 'Investigation of the Dual-Tree Complex and Shift-Invariant Discrete Wavelet Transforms on Quickbird Image Fusion. *Geoscience and Remote Sensing Letters* 4 (1): 166–170.

[115] Iqbal, Mahboob, Lie Chen, Xian-Zhong Wen and Chun-Sheng Li. 2012. 'Remote Sensing Image Fusion Using Best Bases Sparse Representation'. In *Proceedings of the International Geoscience and Remote Sensing Symposium,* 5430–5433.

[116] Jiang, C., H. Zhang, H. Shen, and L. Zhang. 2012. 'A Practical Compressed Sensing Based Pan Sharpening Method'. *IEEE Transactions on Geoscience Letters* 9 (4): 629–633.

[117] Jiji, C. V., and S. Chaudhuri. 2006. 'Single-Frame Image Super-resolution through Contourlet Learning'. *EURASIP Journal of Applied Signal Processing* 1–11.

[118] Jiji, C. V., M. V. Joshi, and S. Chaudhuri. 2004. 'Single Frame Image Superresolution Using Learned Wavelet Coefficients'. *International Journal of Imaging Systems and Technology* 14 (3): 105–112.

[119] Jing, Hong, and Liudi Liu. 1997. 'Color Space Conversion Methods' Applications to the Image Fusion'. *Optical Technology* 44–48.

[120] Joseph, George 2005. *Fundamental of Remote Sensing*. 2nd Ed. Hyderabad: Universities Press.

[121] Joshi, M. V., and A. Jalobeanu. 2010. 'MAP Estimation for Multiresolution Fusion in Remotely Sensed Images Using an IGMRF Prior Model'. *IEEE Transactions on Geosciences and Remote Sensing* 48 (3): 1245–1255.

[122] Joshi, M. V., L. Bruzzonne, and S. Chaudhuri. 2006. 'A Model Based Approach to Multiresolution Fusion in Remotely Sensed Images'. *IEEE Transactions on Geosciences and Remote Sensing* 44 (9): 2549–2562.

[123] Kamarainen, Joni-Kristian, Ville Kyrki, and Heikki Klviinen. 2006. 'Invariance Properties of Gabor Filter-Based Features: Overview and Applications'. *IEEE Transactions on Image Processing* 15 (5): 1088–1099.

[124] Kang, Xudong, Shutao Li, and Jon Atli Benediktsson. 2014. 'Pansharpening with Matting Model'. *IEEE Transactions on Geosciences and Remote Sensing* 52 (8): 5088–5099.

[125] Katsikis, V. N., and D. Pappars. 2008. 'Fast Computing of the Moore Penrose Inverse Matrix'. *Electronic Journal of Linear Algebra* 17(Nov.): 637–650.

[126] Kawakami, Rei, Yasuyuki Matsushita, John Wright, Moshe Ben-Ezra, Yu-Wing Tai, and Katsushi Ikeuchi. 2011. 'High-resolution Hyperspectral Imaging via Matrix Factorization'. In *Proceedings of the Conference on Computer Vision and Pattern Recognition (CVPR)*, 2011, 2329–2336, IEEE.

[127] Khan, Muhammad Murtaza, Jocelyn Chanussot, Laurent Condat, and Annick Montanvert. 2008. 'Indusion: Fusion of Multispectral and Panchromatic Images Using the Induction Scaling Technique'. *IEEE Journal of Selected Topics in Applied Earth Observations and Remote Sensing* 5 (1): 98–102.

[128] Kim, Changhyun, Kyuha Choi, and Jong Beom Ra. 2013. 'Example-Based Super-Resolution via Structure Analysis of Patches'. *IEEE Signal Processing Letters* 20 (4): 407–410.

[129] Kim, K. I., and Y. Kwon. 2008. 'Example-based Learning for Single-Image Superresolution'. In *Proceedings of the 30th Annual Symposium on Deutsche Arbeitsgemeinschaft f'ur Mustererkennung*, 456–465.

[130] Kim, Y., C. Lee, D. Han, and Y. Kim. 2011. 'Improved Additive-Wavelet Image Fusion'. *IEEE Geoscience and Remote Sensing Letters* 8 (2): 263–267.

[131] King, R. L., and J. W. Wang. 2001. 'A Wavelet Based Algorithm for Pan Sharpening Landsat 7 Imagery'. In *Proceedings of the International Geoscience and Remote Sensing Symposium*, 849–851.

[132] Kronland-Martinet, R., J. Morlet, and A. Grossman. 1987. 'Analysis of Sound Patterns through Wavelet Transforms'. *IEEE Transactions* on *Pattern Analysis* and *Machine Intelligence* 1 (2): 273–301.

[133] Kumar, A. S. Kiran, and Roy A. Chowdhury. 2005. 'Hyper-Spectral Imager in Visible and Near-Infrared Band for Lunar Compositional Mapping'. *Journal of Earth System Science* 114 (6): 721–724.

[134] Kumar, N., and A. Sethi. 2016. 'Fast Learning-Based Single Image Super-Resolution' (Accepted for publication). *IEEE Transactions on Multimedia*, 99.

[135] Kumar, S., and M. Hebert. 2003. 'Discriminative Random Fields: A Discriminative Framework for Contextual Interaction in Classification'. In *Proceedings of the Ninth IEEE International Conference on Computer Vision*, 1150–1159.

[136] Laben, C. A., and B. V. Brower. 2000. 'Process for Enhancing the Spatial Resolution of Multispectral Imagery Using Pan-Sharpening'. U.S. Patent 6011875, 219–228.

[137] Lanaras, Charis, Emmanuel Baltsavias, and Konrad Schindler. 2015. 'Hyperspectral Super-Resolution by Coupled Spectral Unmixing'. In *Proceedings of the IEEE International Conference on Computer Vision*, 3586–3594.

[138] Landgrebe, D. 2002. 'Hyperspectral Image Data Analysis'. *IEEE Signal Processing Magazine* 19 (1): 17–28.

[139] Laporterie-D'ejean, Florence, Hélène de Boissezon, Guy Flouzat, and Marie-José Lef'evre-Fonollosa. 2005. 'Thematic and Statistical Evaluations of Five Panchromatic/Multispectral Fusion Methods on Simulated PLEIADES-HR Images'. *Information Fusion* 6 (3): 193–212.

[140] Lee, J., and C. Lee. 2010. 'Fast and Efficient Panchromatic Sharpening. *IEEE Transactions on Geosciences and Remote Sensing* 48 (1): 155–163.

[141] Levesque, J., and K. Staenz. 2004 (Sept). 'A Method for Monitoring Mine Tailings Revegetation Using Hyperspectral Remote Sensing'. In Proceedings of the *IEEE International Geoscience and Remote Sensing Symposium*, vol. 1, September 2004, 578.

[142] Li, D., and S. Simske. 2010. 'Example Based Single-frame Image Superresolution by Support Vector Regression'. *Journal of Pattern Recognition Research* 5 (1): 104–18.

[143] Li, S., and B. Yang. 2011. 'A New Pansharpening Method Using a Compressed Sensing Technique. *IEEE Transactions on Geosciences and Remote Sensing* 49 (2): 738–746.

[144] Li, S., J. T. Kwok, and Y. Wang. 2002. 'Using the Discrete Wavelet Frame Transform to Merge Landsat TM and SPOT Panchromatic Images'. *Information Fusion* 3 (1): 17–23.

[145] Li, S. Z. 1995a. *Markov Random Field Modeling in Computer Vision*. Tokyo: Springer-Verlag.

[146] Li, Shutao, Xudong Kang, and Jianwen Hu. 2013a. 'Image Fusion with Guided Filtering'. *IEEE Transactions on Image Processing* 22 (7): 2864–2875.

[147] Li, Shutao, Haitao Yin, and Leyuan Fang. 2013b. 'Remote Sensing Image Fusion via Sparse Representations Over Learned Dictionaries'. *IEEE Transactions on Geosciences and Remote Sensing* 51 (9): 4779–4789.

[148] Li, Yuying, and Fadil Santosa. 1996. 'A Computational Algorithm for Minimizing Total Variation in Image Restoration'. *IEEE Transactions on Image Processing* 5 (6): 987–995.

[149] Li, Z., and H. Leung. 2009. 'Fusion of Multispectral and Panchromatic Images Using a Restoration-Based Method'. *IEEE Transactions on Geosciences and Remote Sensing* 47 (5): 1482–1491.

[150] Liang, Dong, Haifeng Wang, Yuchou Chang, and Leslie Ying. 2011. 'Sensitivity Encoding Econstruction with Nonlocal Total Variation Regularization'. *Magnetic Resonance in Medicine* 65: 1384–1392.

[151] Licciardi, G. A., A. Villa, M. M. Khan, and J. Chanussot. 2012. 'Image Fusion and Spectral Unmixing of Hyperspectral Images for Spatial Improvement of Classification Maps'. In *Proceedings of the IEEE International Geoscience and Remote Sensing Symposium*, July 2012, 7290–7293.

[152] Lillesand, T., and R. Kiefer. 1994. *Remote Sensing and Image Interpretation*. Third ed., John Wiley and Sons.

[153] Lillo-Saavedra, M., and C. Gonzalo. 2006. 'Spectral or Spatial Quality for Fused Satellite Imagery? A Trade-Off Solution Using the Wavelet A Trous Algorithm'. *International Journal of Remote Sensing* 27 (7): 1453–1464.

[154] Liu, J. 2000. 'Smoothing Filter-Based Intensity Modulation: A Spectral Preserve Image Fusion Technique for Improving Spatial Details'. *International Journal of Remote Sensing* 21 (18): 3461–3472.

[155] Loncan, Laetitia, Luis B. de Almeida, José M. Bioucas-Dias, Xavier Briottet, Jocelyn Chanussot, Nicolas Dobigeon, Sophie, Fabre, Wenzhi, Liao, Giorgio A. Licciardi, Miguel Simoes, et al. 2015. 'Hyperspectral Pansharpening: A Review'. *IEEE Geoscience and Remote Sensing Magazine* 3 (3): 27–46.

[156] Lou, Y., X. Zhang, S. Osher, and A. Bertozzi. 2010. 'Image Recovery Via Nonlocal Operators'. *Journal of Scientific Computing* 42: 185–197.

[157] Luo, B., M. M. Khan, T. Bienvenu, J. Chanussot, and L. Zhang, L. 2013. 'Decision-Based Fusion for Pansharpening of Remote Sensing Images'. *IEEE Geoscience and Remote Sensing Letters* 10 (1): 19–23.

[158] Mahyari, A. G., and M.Yazdi. 2010. 'Fusion of Panchromatic and Multispectral Images Using Temporal Fourier Transform'. *IET Image Processing* 4 (4): 255–260.

[159] Mahyari, A. G., and M. Yazdi. 2011. 'Panchromatic and Multispectral image Fusion Based on Maximization of Both Spectral and Spatial Similarities'. *IEEE Transactions on Geosciences and Remote Sensing* 49 (6): 1976–1985.

[160] Malgouyres, F., and F. Guichard. 2001. 'Edge Directional Preserving Image Zooming: A Mathematical and Numerical Analysis'. *SIAM Journal on Numerical Analysis* 39 (1): 1–37.

[161] Mallat, S., and Guoshen Yu. 2010. 'Super-Resolution with Sparse Mixing Estimators'. *IEEE Transactions on Image Processing* 19 (11): 2889–2900.

[162] Mallat, S. G., and Zhang, Zhifeng. 1993. 'Matching Pursuits with Time-Frequency Dictionaries'. *IEEE Transactions on Signal Processing* 41 (12): 3397–3415.

[163] Masi, Giuseppe, Davide Cozzolino, Luisa Verdoliva, and Giuseppe Scarpa. 2016. 'Pansharpening by Convolutional Neural Networks'. *Remote Sensing* 8 (7): 594.

[164] Mitchell, H. B. 2010. *Image Fusion: Theories, Techniques and Applications.* Springer.

[165] Moeller, M., T. Wittman, A., Bertozzi, and M. Burger. 2009. 'A Variational Approach for Sharpening High Dimensional Images'. Ph.D. dissertation, Inst. Computational & Applied Math.,WestfalischeWilhelms Universitat Munster, Munster, Germany.

[166] Mohammadzadeh, Ali, Ahad Tavakoli, and Mohammad J. Valadan Zoej. 2006. 'Road Extraction Based on Fuzzy Logic and Mathematical Morphology from Pansharpened Ikonos Images'. *The Photogrammetric Record* 21 (113): 44–60.

[167] Mookambiga, A, and V. Gomathi. 2016. 'Comprehensive Review on Fusion Techniques for Spatial Information Enhancement in Hyperspectral Imagery'. *Multidimensional Systems and Signal Processing* 27 (4): 863–889.

[168] Morozov, V. A. 1984. *Methods for Solving Incorrectly Posed Problems.* New York: Springer-Verlag.

[169] Nadernejad, E., S. Sharifzadeh, and H. Hassanpour. 2008. 'Edge Detection Techniques: Evaluations and Comparisons'. *Applied Mathematical Sciences* 2 (31): 1507–1520.

[170] Nencini, Filippo, Andrea Garzelli, Stefano Baronti, and Lucaino Alparone. 2007. 'Remote Sensing Image Fusion Using the Curvelet Transform. *Information Fusion* 8 (2): 143–156.

[171] Ng, M. K., H. Shen, E. Y. Lam, and L. Zhang. 2007. 'A Total Variation Regularization Based Super-Resolution Reconstruction Algorithm for Digital Video'. *EURASIP Journal on Advances in Signal Processing*, 2007: 745–785.

[172] Nguyen, T. T., and S. Oraintara. 2008a. 'The Shiftable Complex Directional Pyramid-Part I: Theoretical Aspects'. *IEEE Transactions on Image Processing* 56 (10): 4651–4660.

[173] Nguyen, T. T., and S. Oraintara. 2008b. 'The Shiftable Complex Directional Pyramid-Part II: Implementation and Applications'. *IEEE Transactions on Image Processing* 56 (10): 4661–4672.

[174] Nunez, J., X. Otazu, O. Fors, A. Prades, V. Pala, and R. Arbiol. 1999. 'Multiresolution Based Image Fusion with Additive Wavelet Decomposition'. *IEEE Transactions on Geosciences and Remote Sensing* 37 (3): 1204–1211.

[175] Ogawa, T., and M. Haseyama. 2011. 'Adaptive Single Image Superresolution Approach Using Support Vector Data Description'. *EURASIP Journal of Advanced Signal Processing* 2011 (1): 1–13.

[176] Oliveira, J. P., J. M. Bioucas-Dias, and M. A. T. Figueiredo. 2009. 'Adaptive Total Variation Image Deblurring: A Majorization-Minimization Approach'. *Signal Processing* 89 (9): 1683–1693.

[177] Omer, O. A. 2010. 'Learning-Based Document Image Super-Resolution with Directional Total Variation'. *International Journal of Open Problems in Computer Science and Mathematics* 3 (4): 592–616.

[178] Otazu, X., M. Gonzalez-Audicana, O. Fors, and J. Nunez. 2005. 'Introduction of Sensor Spectral Response into Image Fusion Methods. Application to Wavelet Based Methods'. *IEEE Transactions on Geosciences and Remote Sensing* 43 (10): 2376–2385.

[179] Ouwerkerk, J. D. Van. 2006. 'Image Super-Resolution Survey'. *Image and Vision Computing* 1039–1052.

[180] Palsson, F., J. Sveinsson, and M. Ulfarsson. 2014. 'A New Pansharpening Algorithm Based on Total Variation'. *IEEE Geoscience and Remote Sensing Letters* 11 (1): 318–322.

[181] Palubinskas, Gintautas. 2016. 'Model-Based View at Multi-Resolution Image Fusion Methods and Quality Assessment Measures'. *International Journal of Image and Data Fusion* 7 (3): 203–218.

[182] Pati, Y. C., R. Rezaiifar, and P. S. Krishnaprasad. 1993. 'Orthogonal Matching Pursuit: Recursive Function Approximation with Applications to Wavelet

Decomposition'. *Proceedings of the Twenty-Seventh Asilomar Conference on Signals, Systems and Computers*, 1993, 40–44.

[183] Pearlman, J., C. Segal, L. Liao, S. Carmana, M. Folkman, B. Browne, L. Ong, and S. Ungar. 1998. 'The Hymap Airborne Hyperspectral Sensor: The System, Calibration and Performance'.

[184] Peleg, T., and M. Elad. 2014. 'A Statistical Prediction Model Based on Sparse Representations for Single Image Super-Resolution'. *IEEE Transactions on Image Processing* 23 (6): 2569–2582.

[185] Pellemans, A. H. J. M., R. W. L. Jorddans, and R. Allewiijin. 1993. 'Merging Multispectral and Panchromatic SPOT Images with Respect to the Radiometric Properties of the Sensor'. *Photogrammetric Engineering and Remote Sensing* 59 (1): 81–87.

[186] Phoong, S. M., C. W. Kim, P. P. Vaidyanathan, and R. Ansari. 1993. 'A New Class of Two-Channel Biorthogonal Filter Banks and Wavelet Bases'. *IEEE Transactions on Signal Processing*, 43 (3): 649–665.

[187] Pohl, Christine, and John. L. van Genderen. 1998. 'Multi-sensor Image Fusion in Remote Sensing: Concepts, Methods and Applications. *International Journal of Remote Sensing* 19 (5): 823–854.

[188] Pohl, Christine, and John. L. van Genderen. 2016. *Remote Sensing Image Fusion: A Practical Guide*. CRC Press.

[189] Polatkan, G., M. Zhou, L. Carin, D. Blei, and I. Daubechies. 2015. 'A Bayesian Nonparametric Approach to Image Super-Resolution'. *IEEE Transactions on Pattern Analysis andMachine Intelligence* 37 (2): 346–358.

[190] Portilla, J., and E. P. Simoncelli. 2000. 'A Parametric Texture Model Based on Joint Statistics of Complex Wavelet Coefficients'. *International Journal of Computer Vision* 40 (1): 49–70.

[191] Zhang, Q., L.Wang, H. Li, and Z. Ma. 2011. 'Similarity-Based Multimodality Image Fusion with Shiftable Complex Directional Pyramid'. *Pattern Recognition Letters* 32 (13): 1544–1553.

[192] Rahmani, S., M. Strait, D. Merkurjev, M. Moeller, and T. Wittman. 2010. 'An Adaptive IHS Pan-sharpening Method'. *IEEE Geoscience and Remote Sensing Letters* 7 (4): 746–750.

[193] Rajagopalan, A. N., and S. Chaudhuri. 1999. 'An MRF Based Approach to Simultaneous Recovery of Depth and Restoration from Defocussed Images'. *IEEE Transactions on Pattern Analysis and Machine Intelligence* 21 (7): 577–589.

[194] Rajan, D., and S. Chaudhuri. 2002. 'Generation of Super-resolution Images from Blurred Observations Using an MRF Model'. *Journal of Mathematical Imaging and Vision* 16: 5–15.

[195] Rajan, D., and S. Chaudhuri. 2003. 'Simultaneous Estimation of Super-Resolved Scene and Depth Map from Low Resolution Defocused Observations'. *IEEE Transactions on Pattern Analysis and Machine Intelligence* 25 (9): 1102–1117.

[196] Ranchin, T., and L. Wald. 2000. 'Fusion of High Spatial and Spectral Resolution Images: The ARSIS Concept and its Implementation. *Photogrammetric Engineering and Remote Sensing* 66 (1): 49–61.

[197] Ranchin, Thierry., B. Aiazzi, L. Alparone, S. Baronti, and L.Wald, L. 2003. 'Image Fusion: The ARSIS Concept and some Successful Implementation Schemes'. *ISPRS Journal of Photogrammetry and Remote Sensing* 58 (1–2): 4–18.

[198] Ranchin, Thierry, L. Wald, and M. Mangolini. 1994. 'Efficient Data Fusion Using Wavelet Transforms: The Case of SPOT Satellite Images'. In *Proceedings of the International Symposium on Optics, Imaging Instruments, and Mathematical Imaging: Wavelet Applications in Signal and Image Processing*, 2034, 171–178.

[199] Rickard, Lee J., Robert W. Basedow, Edward F. Zalewski, Peter R. Silverglate, and Mark Landers. 1993. 'HYDICE: An Airborne System for Hyperspectral Imaging'. In *SPIE Proceedings of the Conference on Imaging Spectrometry of the Terrestrial Environment*, September 1993, doi: 10.1117/12.157055.

[200] Robinson, Gary D, Harry N. Gross, and John R. Schott. 2000. 'Evaluation of Two Applications of Spectral Mixing Models to Image Fusion'. *Remote Sensing of Environment* 71 (3): 272–281.

[201] Rudin, L., S. Osher, and E. Fatemi. 1992. 'Nonlinear Total Variation Based Noise Removal Algorithms'. *Physica D* 60 (1–4): 259–268.

[202] S. Paris, P. Kornprobst, J. Tumblin. 2009. 'Bilateral Filtering: Theory and Applications'. *Foundations and Trends in Computer Graphics and Vision* 4 (1): 1–73.

[203] Saeedi, J., and K. Faez. 2011. 'A New Pan-Sharpening Method Using Multiobjective Particle Swarm Optimization and the Shiftable Contourlet Transform.' *ISPRS Journal of Photogrammetry and Remote Sensing* 66 (3): 365–381.

[204] Schetselaar, E. M. 1998. 'Fusion by the IHS Transform Should We Use Cylindrical of Spherical Coordinates?' *International Journal of Remote Sensing* 19 (4): 759–765.

[205] Schowenderdt, R. A. 1997. *Remote Sensing: Models and Methods for Image Processing.* 2nd ed. Orlando, FL: Academic.

[206] Schultz, R. R., and R. L. Stevenson. 1994. 'A Bayesian Approach to Image Expansion for Improved Definition'. *IEEE Transactions on Image Processing* 3 (3): 233–242.

[207] Schultz, R. R., and R. L. Stevenson. 1996. 'Extraction of High-Resolution Frames from Video Sequences'. *ISPRS Journal of Photogrammetry and Remote Sensing* 5 (6): 996–1011.

[208] Selesnick, I. W., R. G. Baraniuk, and N. G. Kingsbury. 2005. 'The Dual-Tree Complex Wavelet Transform'. *IEEE Signal Processing Magazine* 22 (6): 123–151.

[209] Selva, Massimo, Bruno Aiazzi, Francesco Butera, Leandro Chiarantini, and Stefano Baronti. 2015. 'Hyper-sharpening: A First Approach on SIM-GA Data'. *IEEE Journal of Selected Topics in Applied Earth Observations and Remote Sensing* 8 (6): 3008–3024.

[210] Shah, V. P., N. H. Younan, and R. L. King. 2008. 'An Efficient Pan-Sharpening Method via a Combined Adaptive PCA Approach and Contourlets'. *IEEE Transactions on Geosciences and Remote Sensing* 46 (5): 1323–1335.

[211] Shaw, G., and D. Manolakis. 2002. 'Signal Processing for Hyperspectral Image Exploitation'. *IEEE Signal Processing Magazine* 19 (1): 12–16.

[212] Shettigara, V. K. 1992. 'A Generalised Component Substitution Technique for Spatial Enhancement of Multispectral Images Using a Higher Resolution Data Set. *Photogrammetric Engineering and Remote Sensing* 58 (5): 561–567.

[213] Shi, H., B. Tian, and Y. Wang. 2010. 'Fusion of Multispectral and Panchromatic Satellite Images Using Principal Component Analysis and Nonsubsampled Contourlet Transform'. In *Proceedings of the Seventh International Conference on Fuzzy Systems and Knowledge Discovery* (FSKD), 2313–2315.

[214] Shi, W., C. Zhu, Y.Tian, and J. Nichol. 2005. 'Wavelet-based Image Fusion and Assessment'. *International Journal of Applied Earth Observation and Geoinformation* 6 (3–4): 241–251.

[215] Shi, W. Z., C. Q. Zhu, C. Y. Zhu, and M. X.Yang. 2003. 'Multi-bandwavelet for Fusing SPOT Panchromatic and Multi-Spectral Images. *Photogrammetric Engineering and Remote Sensing* 69 (5): 513–520.

[216] Shi, Yan, Xiaoyuan Yang, and Yuhua Guo. 2014. 'Translation Invariant Directional Framelet Transform Combined with Gabor Filters for Image Denoising'. *IEEE Transactions on Image Processing,* 23 (1): 44–55.

[217] Shin, M. C., D. B. Godlgof, K. W. Bowyer, and S. Nikiforou, S. 2001. 'Comparison of Edge Detection Algorithms Using a Structure from Motion Task'. *IEEE Transactions on Systems, Man, and Cybernatics, Part B* 31 (4): 589–601.

[218] Simões, Miguel, José Bioucas-Dias, Luis B. Almeida, and Jocelyn Chanussot. 2015. 'A Convex Formulation for Hyperspectral Image Superresolution via Subspace-Based Regularization'. *IEEE Transactions on Geoscience and Remote Sensing* 53 (6): 3373–3388.

[219] Simoncelli, E. P., and W. T. Freeman. 1995. 'The Steerable Pyramid: A Flexible Architecture for Multi-Scale Derivative Computation'. In *Proceedings of the International Conference on Image Processing* (ICIP), 3 (3): 3444–3447.

[220] Souza, Carlos, Laurel Firestone, Luciano Moreira Silva, and Dar Roberts. 2003. 'Mapping Forest Degradation in the Eastern Amazon from SPOT 4 through Spectral Mixture Models'. *Remote Sensing of Environment* 87 (4): 494–506.

[221] Stathaki, Tania. 2008. *Image Fusion: Algorithms and Applications*. Academic Press.

[222] Stephenson, T. A., and T. Chen. 2006. 'Adaptive Markov Random Fields for Example-Based Super-Resolution of Faces'. *EURASIP Journal of Applied Signal Processing* doi 2006: 031062.

[223] Sun, J., N. Zheng, H. Tao, and H. Shum. 2003. 'Image Hallucination with Primal Sketch Priors'. In *Proceedings of the IEEE International Conference on Computer Vision and Pattern Recognition, II*, 729–736.

[224] Sun, Yicheng, Guohua Gu, Xiubao Sui, Yuan Liu, and Chengzhang Yang. 2015. 'Single Image Super-Resolution Using Compressive Sensing with a Redundant Dictionary'. *IEEE Photonics Journal* 7 (2): 1–11.

[225] Tang, Y., P. Yan, Y. Yuan, and X. Li. 2011. 'Single-Image Super-Resolution via Local Learning'. *International Journal of Machine Learning and Cybernetics* 2 (1): 15–23.

[226] Thomas, C., T. Ranchin, L. Wald, and J. Chanussot. 2008. 'Synthesis of Multispectral Images to High Spatial Resolution: A Critical Review of Fusion Methods Based On Remote Sensing Physics. *IEEE Transactions on Geosciences and Remote Sensing* 46 (5): 1301–1312.

[227] Tom, V. T. 1987. 'System for and Method of Enhancing Images Using a Multiband Information'. US Patent 4683496.

[228] Tsai, R. Y., and T. S. Huang. 1984. 'Multiframe Image Restoration and Registration'. *Advanced Computer Vision and Image Processing* 317–339.

[229] Tseng, D. C., Y. L. Chen, and S. C. Liu. 2001. 'Wavelet-based Multispectral Image Fusion'. In *Proceedings of the International Geoscience and Remote Sensing Symposium* 1956–1958.

[230] Tu, T. M., S. C. Su, H. C. Shyu, and P. S. Huang. 2001. 'A New Look at IHS-like Image Fusion Methods'. *Information Fusion* 2 (3): 177–186.

[231] Tu, T. M., P. S. Huang, C. L. Hung, and C. P. Chang. 2004. 'A Fast Intensityhue-Saturation Fusion Techniques with Spectral Adjustment for IKONOS Imagery'. *IEEE Geoscience and Remote Sensing Letters* 1 (4): 309–312.

[232] Tu, T. M., C.L. Hsu, P. Y. Tu, and C. H. Lee. 2012. 'An Adjustable Pansharpening Approach for Ikonos/Quickbird/Geoeye-1/Worldview-2 Imagery'. *IEEE Journal of Selected Topics in Applied Earth Observations and Remote Sensing* 5 (1): 125–134.

[233] Tu, T.M., W. C. Cheng, C. P. Chang, P. S. Huang, and J.-C. Chang. 2007. 'Best Trade-off for High-Resolution Image Fusion to Preserve Spatial Details and Minimize Color Distortion'. *IEEE Transactions on Geosciences and Remote Sensing* 4 (4): 302–306.

[234] Ungar, S. G., J. S. Pearlman, J. A. Mendenhall, and D. Reuter. 2003. 'Overview of the Earth Observing One (EO-1) Mission'. *IEEE Transactions on Geoscience and Remote Sensing* 41 (6): 1149–1159.

[235] Upla, K. P., P. P. Gajjar, M. V. Joshi, A. Banerjee, and V. Singh. 2011. 'A Fast Approach for Edge Preserving Super-Resolution. In *Proceedings of the IEEE International Conference on Multimedia and Expo* (ICME), 1–6.

[236] Vaidyanathan, P. P. 1992. *Multirate Systems and Filter Banks*. Englewood Cliffs, NJ: Prentice-Hall.

[237] Vetterli, M., and C. Herley. 1993. 'Wavelets and Filter Banks: Theory and Design'. *IEEE Transactions on Signal Processing* 40 (9): 2207–2232.

[238] Vijayaraj, V., C. G. O. Hara, and N. H. Younan. 2004. 'Quality Analysis of Pansharpened Images'. In *Proceedings of the International Geoscience and Remote Sensing Symposium* 1, 85–88.

[239] Vivone, G., L. Alparone, J. Chanussot, M. Dalla Mura, A. Garzelli, G. Licciardi, R. Restaino, and L.Wald. 2014. 'A Critical Comparison of Pansharpening Algorithms.' In *Proceedings of the International Geoscience and Remote Sensing Symposium*

[240] Vivone, G., L. Alparone, J. Chanussot, M. Dalla Mura, A. Garzelli, G. Licciardi, R. Restaino, and L. Wald. 2015. 'A Critical Comparison Among Pansharpening Algorithms'. *IEEE Transactions on Geoscience and Remote Sensing* 53 (5): 2565–2586.

[241] Vrabel, J. 1996. 'Multispectral Imagery Band Sharpening Study'. *Photogrammetric Engineering and Remote Sensing* 62 (9): 1075–1083.

[242] Wald, L. 1999. 'Some Terms of Reference in Data Fusion'. *IEEE Transactions on Geosciences and Remote Sensing* 37 (3): 1190–1193.

[243] Wald, L. 2000. 'Quality of High Resolution Synthesized Images: Is There a Simple Criterion?' In *Proceedings of the International Conference on Fusion of Earth Data* 46–61.

[244] Wald, L. 2002. *Data Fusion: Definitions and Architectures. Fusion of Images of Different Spatial Resolutions*. Paris, France: Les Presses de lcole des Mines, 197.

[245] Wald, L., T. Ranchin, and M. Mangolini. 1997. 'Fusion of Satellite Images of Different Spatial Resolutions: Assessing the Quality of Resulting Images'. *Photogrammetric Engineering and Remote Sensing* 63 (6): 691–699.

[246] Wang, J., S. Zhu, and Y. Gong. 2009. 'Resolution-Invariant Image Representation for Content-Based Zooming'. In *Proceedings of the International Conference on Multimedia and Expo* (ICME), 918–921.

[247] Wang, J., S. Zhu, and Y. Gong. 2010. 'Resolution Enhancement Based on Learning the Sparse Association of Image Patches'. *Pattern Recognition Letters* 31 (1): 1–10.

[248] Wang, Z., and A. C. Bovik. 2002. 'A Universal Image Quality Index'. *IEEE Transactions on Signal Processing Letters* 9 (3), 81–84.

[249] Wang, Z., and A. C. Bovik. 2009. 'Mean Squared Error: Love it or Leave it?' IEEE *Signal Processing Magazine* 98–117.

[250] Wang, Z., D. Ziou, C. Armenakis, D. Li, and Q. Li. 2005. 'A Comparative Analysis of Image Fusion Methods. *IEEE Transactions on Geosciences and Remote Sensing* 43 (6): 81–84.

[251] Wei, Qi, Nicolas Dobigeon, and Jean-Yves Tourneret. 2015a. 'Bayesian Fusion of Multi-Band Images'. *IEEE Journal of Selected Topics in Signal Processing* 9 (6): 1117–1127.

[252] Wei, Qi, Nicolas Dobigeon, and Jean-Yves Tourneret. 2015b. 'Fast Fusion of Multi-Band Images Based on Solving a Sylvester Equation'. *IEEE Transactions on Image Processing* 24 (11): 4109–4121.

[253] Wei, Qi, José Bioucas-Dias, Nicolas Dobigeon, and Jean-Yves Tourneret. 2015c. Hyperspectral and Multispectral Image Fusion Based on a Sparse Representation'. *IEEE Transactions on Geoscience and Remote Sensing* 53 (7): 3658–3668.

[254] Weldon, Thomas P., William E. Higgins, and Dennis F. Dunn. 1996. 'Efficient Gabor Filter Design for Texture Segmentation'. *Pattern Recognition* 29 (12): 2005–2015.

[255] Wen, You-Wei, and Raymond H. Chan. 2012. 'Parameter Selection for Total- Variation-Based Image Restoration Using Discrepancy Principle'. *IEEE Transactions on Image Processing* 21 (4): 1770–1781.

[256] Wilson, T. A., S. K. Rogers, and M. Kabrisky. 1997. 'Perceptual Based Image Fusion for Hyperspectral Data'. *Photogrammetric Engineering and Remote Sensing* 35: 1007–1017.

[257] Wu, W., Z. Liu, and X. He. 2011. 'Learning-Based Super Resolution Using Kernel Partial Least Squares'. *Image and Vision Computing* 29 (6): 394–406.

[258] Wycoff, Eliot, Tsung-Han Chan, Kui, Jia, Wing-Kin Ma, and Yi Ma. 2013. 'A Non-Negative Sparse Promoting Algorithm for High Resolution Hyperspectral Imaging'. In *Proceedings of the IEEE International Conferenc on Acoustics, Speech and Signal Processing* (ICASSP), 2013, 1409–13, IEEE.

[259] Xu, M., H. Chen, and P. K. Vershney. 2011. 'An Image Fusion Approach Based on Markov Random Fields'. *IEEE Transactions on Geosciences and Remote Sensing* 49 (12): 5116–5127.

[260] Yang, C., J. Huang, and M. Yang. 2011. 'Exploiting Self-similarities for Single Frame Super-Resolution'. In *Proceedings of ACCV 2010, Lecture Notes in Computer Science*, 6494, 497–510.

[261] Yang, J., J. Wright, T. S. Huang, and Y. Ma. 2010. 'Image Super-Resolution via Sparse Representation'. *IEEE Transactions on Image Processing,* 19 (11): 2861–2873.

[262] Yang, Min-Chun, and Y.-C. F. Wang. 2013. 'A Self-Learning Approach to Single Image Super-Resolution'. *IEEE Transactions on Multimedia* 15 (3): 498–508.

[263] Yang, Zhili, and Jacob, Mathews. 2013. 'Nonlocal Regularization of Inverse Problems: A Unified Variational Framework'. *IEEE Transactions on Image Processing* 22 (8): 3192–3203.

[264] Yesou, H., Y. Besnus, and Y. Rolet. 1993. 'Extraction of Spectral Information from Landsat TM Data and Merger with SPOT Panchromatic Imagery – A Contribution to the Study of Geological Structures'. *ISPRS Journal of Photogrammetry and Remote Sensing* 48 (5): 23–36.

[265] Yocky, D. A. 1995. 'Image Merging and Data Fusion by Means of the Discrete Two Dimensional Wavelet Transform'. *Journal of the Optical Society of America: A* 12 (8): 1834–1841.

[266] Yocky, D. A. 1996. 'Multi Resolution Wavelet Decomposition Image Merger of Landsat Thematic Mapper and SPOT Panchromatic Data. *Photogrammetric Engineering and Remote Sensing* 62 (9): 1067–1074.

[267] Yokoya, Naoto, Takehisa Yairi, and Akira Iwasaki. 2012. 'Coupled Nonnegative Matrix Factorization Unmixing for Hyperspectral And Multispectral Data Fusion'. *IEEE Transactions on Geoscience and Remote Sensing* 50 (2): 528–537.

[268] Yokoya, Naoto, Claas Grohnfeldt, and Jocelyn Chanussot. 2017. 'Hyperspectral and Multispectral Data Fusion: A Comparative Review of the Recent Literature'. *IEEE Geoscience and Remote Sensing Magazine* 5 (2): 29–56.

[269] Yuhas, R. H., A. F. H. Goetz, and J. W. Boardman. 1992. 'Discrimination among Semi-Arid Landscape Endmembers Using the Spectral Angle Mapper (SAM) Algorithm. In *Summaries of the 4th JPL Airborne Earth Science Workshop*, 147–149.

[270] Zeng, WL, and X. B. Lu. 2013. 'A Robust Variational Approach to Super-Resolution with Nonlocal TV Regularisation Term'. *The Imaging Science Journal* 61 (2): 268–278.

[271] Zhang, Jixian. 2010. 'Multi-source Remote Sensing Data Fusion: Status and Trends'. *International Journal of Image Data Fusion* 1 (1): 5–24.

[272] Zhang, Liangpei., Lei Zhang, X. Mou, and D. Zhang. 2011a. 'FSIM: A Feature Similarity Index for Image Quality Assessment'. *IEEE Transactionson. Image Processing* 20 (8): 2378–2386.

[273] Zhang, Liangpei, Huanfeng Shen, Wei Gong, and Hongyan Zhang. 2012. 'Adjustable Model-Based Fusion Method for Multispectral and Panchromatic Images'. *IEEE Transactions on Systems, Man, and Cybernatics B* 42 (6): 1693–1704.

[274] Zhang, Yifan. 2011. 'Spatial Resolution Enhancement for Hyperspectral Image Based on Wavelet Bayesian Fusion'. *Proceedings of the 4th International Congress on Image and Signal Processing* (CISP), vol. 3, 1671–1675, IEEE.

[275] Zhang, Yifan, Steve De Backer, and Paul Scheunders. 2008. 'Bayesian Fusion of Multispectral and Hyperspectral Image in Wavelet Domain.' In *Proceedings of the IEEE International Geoscience and Remote Sensing Symposium*, vol. 5, V-69-V-72, IEEE.

[276] Zhang, Yifan, Steve De Backer, and Paul Scheunders. 2009. 'Noise-resistant Wavelet-Based Bayesian Fusion of Multispectral and Hyperspectral Images'. *IEEE Transactions on Geoscience and Remote Sensing* 47 (11): 3834–3843.

[277] Zhang, Yifan, Shaohui Mei, and Mingyi He. 2011b. 'Bayesian Fusion of Hyperspectral and Multispectral Images Using Gaussian Scale Mixture Prior'. *Proceedings of the Geoscience and Remote Sensing Symposium* (IGARSS), 2011, 2531–2534, IEEE International.

[278] Zhang, Yun. 2004. 'Understanding Image Fusion'. *Photogrammetric Engineering and Remote Sensing* 70 (6): 657–661.

[279] Zhong, Jinying, Bin Yang, Guoyu Huang, Fei Zhong, and Zhongze Chen. 2016. 'Remote Sensing Image Fusion with Convolutional Neural Network'. *Sensing and Imaging* 17 (1): 10.

[280] Zhou, J., D. L. Civco, and J. A. Silander. 1998. 'A Wavelet Transform Method to Merge Landsate TM and SPOT Panchromatic Data'. *International Journal of Remote Sensing* 19 (3): 743–757.

[281] Zhou, Zhiqiang, Silong Peng, Bo Wang, Zhihui Hao, and Shaolin Chen. 2012. 'An Optimized Approach for Pansharpening Very High Resolution Multispectral Images'. *IEEE Transactions of Geoscience Letters* 9 (4): 735–739.

[282] Zhu, S.C., Y. Wu, and D. Mumford. 1998. 'Filters, Random Fields and Maximum Entropy (FRAME): Toward a Unified Theory for Texture Modeling'. *International Journal of Computer Vision*, 27 (2): 107–126.

[283] Zhu, X. X., and R. Bamler. 2013. 'A Sparse Image Fusion Algorithm with Application to Pansharpening'. *IEEE Transactions on Geosciences and Remote Sensing* 51 (5): 2827–2836.

[284] Zhu, Xiao Xiang, Class Grohnfeldt, and Richard Bamler. 2016. 'Exploiting Joint Sparsity For Pansharpening: The J-Sparse FI Algorithm'. *IEEE Transactions on Geoscience and Remote Sensing* 54 (5): 2664–2681.

[285] Zhu, Zhiliang, Fangda Guo, Hai Yu, and Chen Chen. 2014. 'Fast Single Image Super-Resolution via Self-Example Learning and Sparse Representation'. *IEEE Transactions on Multimedia* 16 (8): 2178–2190.

[286] Zhukov, Boris, Dieter Oertel, Franz Lanzl, and Gotz Reinhackel. 1999. 'Unmixing-based Multisensor Multi Resolution Image Fusion'. *IEEE Transactions on Geoscience and Remote Sensing* 37 (3): 1212–1226.